THE INDEPENDENT PARALEGAL'S HANDBOOK

THIRD EDITION

by Attorney Ralph Warner

NOLO PRESS · BERKELEY

Your Responsibility When Using A Self-Help Law Book

We've done our best to give you useful and accurate information in this book. But laws and procedures change frequently and are subject to differing interpretations. If you want legal advice backed by a guarantee, see a lawyer. If you use this book, it's your responsibility to make sure that the facts and general advice contained in it are applicable to your situation.

Keeping Up to Date

To keep its books up to date, Nolo Press issues new printings and new editions periodically. New printings reflect minor legal changes and technical corrections. New editions contain major legal changes, major text additions or major reorganizations. To find out if a later printing or edition of any Nolo book is available, call Nolo Press at 510-549-1976 or check the catalog in the *Nolo News*, our quarterly newspaper.

To stay current, follow the "Update" service in the *Nolo News*. You can get the paper free by sending us the registration card in the back of the book. In another effort to help you use Nolo's latest materials, we offer a 25% discount off the purchase of any new Nolo book if you turn in any earlier printing or edition. (See the "Recycle Offer" in the back of this book.)

This book was last revised in: **September 1994**

Third Edition

First Printing: September 1994
Cover Design: Toni Ihara
Book Design: Terri Hearsh
Illustrations: Mari Stein
Proofreading & Index: Susan Cornell

Warner, Ralph E.
    The independent paralegal's handbook / Ralph Warner ; edited by Karen Chambers ; illustrated by Mari Stein. — 3rd ed.
        p. cm.
    ISBN 0-87337-268-9:
    1. Legal assistants-—United States—Handbooks, manuals, etc.
I. Title.
KF320.L4W37   1994
340' . 023'73--dc20
                                    94-27913
                                    CIP

Printed on paper with recycled content
Printed in the USA

Acknowledgments

Of the many wonderful people who helped me with this new edition, two special friends come first—Stephen Elias, Nolo Press Associate Publisher, and Catherine Jermany, long-time leader for the independent paralegal movement. Over the last fifteen years, I have talked about the independent paralegal movement with Steve and Catherine so many times, I have long since lost track of where my ideas stop and theirs start. Fortunately, as with any of life's exciting collaborations, it makes no difference to any of us, as long as we collectively deepen our understanding of this truly fascinating subject.

My special thanks to Karen Chambers, who helped greatly with legal research and rewriting for Chapter 2.

I am also appreciative of the help I received from Rosemary Furman, Toni Ihara, Lois Isenberg, Jolene Jacobs, Bob Mission, Robin Smith, Glynda Mathewson, Bob Anderson, Virginia Simons and Sharon Goetting. These people truly pioneered the independent paralegal movement, and their willingness to share their experiences and insights with me give this book a depth it would otherwise lack.

Thank you to Rose Palmer, a brave and enthusiastic woman who heads a nonprofit organization that provides legal and advocacy assistance to women on issues of child support, custody, visitation and domestic violence. Rose helped me better understand how nonlawyers can successfully bring legal information and services to large groups of people bypassed by lawyers.

Over many years, I have received much valuable counsel from my very good friends at HALT—Americans for Legal Reform. Former Executive Director, Glen Nishimura, helped by consistently reminding me that government regulation often protects incompetent, price-gouging providers, not consumers. And Debbie Chalfie, HALT's former Legislative Director, has given me so many great ideas on how to break down the lawyer's monopoly that I've long since lost count. I'm happy to say that this tradition of HALT helpfulness continues to the present day in the person of Bill Fry, HALT's current Executive Director, an inspired leader in the movement to make our legal system more democratic and affordable.

I am also indebted to Afroditi Price, President of the California Association of Freelance Paralegals, Inc., for many good suggestions on improving the chapter on freelance paralegals.

Finally, I would like to thank a number of other friends who extended a helping hand along the way, including Tony Mancuso, Kay Ostberg, Michael Phillips, Salli Rasberry and, most especially, Susan Cornell and Stephanie Harolde, both of whom contributed many helpful editorial suggestions.

Table of Contents

Introduction

1 • The Historical Background

2 • The Law

3 • How To Do Your Job And Stay Out of Jail

Appendix • Interviews

Introduction

Here is a book for people who want to work in our legal system but do not wish to work for a lawyer or to become one. Revised in this third edition, it is designed as a resource for those who wish to help consumers prepare their own paperwork in uncontested actions such as bankruptcy, divorce, small business incorporations, landlord-tenant, or probate. I refer to these people as "independent paralegals" (IPs), although they are also commonly called "legal technicians" and "legal typists." Unfortunately, many lawyers use none of these terms, instead referring to nonlawyers who help consumers prepare legal paperwork as "criminals."

Of course, these days most Americans aren't particularly horrified by the criminal offense of practicing law without a license. In fact, compared to a real crime, like burglary or arson, unauthorized practice is a bit of a joke. Before you laugh too hard, however, remember that independent paralegals still face a number of lawyer-designed laws, court decisions, and rules of court whose sole purpose is to suppress their activities. And remember, too, that should an IP be accused of the crime of practicing law without a license, the people who will prosecute and judge her will all be lawyers.

Have you stopped laughing? If you haven't, consider Rosemary Furman, a pioneering Florida independent paralegal, who was sentenced to four months in jail (even though she was never charged with a crime and was denied the right to trial by jury) in 1984 by a trial judge who said, "Only her imprisonment will provide the sting to preserve the integrity of the court." And don't assume that what happened to Furman was an isolated instance. In 1989, a Louisiana independent paralegal, Jerome Papania, was arrested by seven officers and charged with unauthorized practice for helping consumers type bankruptcy forms. In 1990, Mershan Shaddy, an independent paralegal in San Diego, California was sentenced to jail for providing customers information about divorce law. And as this book went to press in the spring of 1991, another IP, Dennis Ridderbush, was jailed for 20 days for typing bankruptcy forms in Wisconsin.

Enter this guidebook. It's purpose is to help independent paralegals carry on their business competently and make a decent living while they steer clear of organized lawyerdom's monopolistic rules defining who can practice law and stay out of jail. Unfortunately, when it comes to this last goal (the crucial part about not getting locked up), I can make no guarantees. Although I will teach you a method to prepare legal paperwork that has been widely judged not to constitute unauthorized practice, anyone who begins a career as an independent paralegal must accept the fact that it is possible to deliver excellent, honest services at a reasonable price and still end up being harassed by lawyers.

Enough negatives. Despite the obstacles created by the legal profession, the independent paralegal movement is growing rapidly all across America. The average American, faced with almost daily news stories about the glut of lawyers (close to one million at last count), at the same time that he finds even routine legal services prohibitively expensive, is increasingly supportive of high-quality, low-cost paralegal alternatives. For example, in states such as Arizona and California more than 60% of divorces and 30% of bankruptcies are now done without lawyers. The rapid growth in popularity of self-help law books, legal services delivered by telephone and fax, and self-help law computer programs are other manifestations of what amounts to a major change in how ordinary Americans gain access to the legal system. Indeed, it's probably fair to say that the only group still shocked by the growth of the nonlawyer legal form preparation business is lawyers.

And even many of them are not as shocked as they used to be. For example, at a speech before the American Bar Association in December of 1993, Attorney General Janet Reno has advocated allowing nonlawyers to provide a range of basic legal services directly to the public, a position she has since often repeated. Reno said, in part:

> *Increasing access to the justice system is the right thing to do, it is the fair thing to do, and it is the smart thing to do.... We should consider new and innovative forms of legal assistance.... There can be nonlawyers who can make a difference.*

As a co-founder of both Nolo Press, the publisher of close to 100 self-help law products, and the Wave Project, one of the first self-help divorce typing businesses, I have been involved in the independent paralegal movement for well over 20 years. This doesn't mean I have all the answers about how to survive and prosper as an independent paralegal. It does mean that I have a number of suggestions which should ease the task of the nonlawyer determined to deliver competent services in the hostile shadow of the American legal profession. By way of example, this book covers:

- What types of legal paperwork an independent paralegal can safely and profitably prepare;
- How to get the necessary training to work as an independent paralegal;
- What to call your business;
- How to market your services in a cost-effective way;
- How to let customers know you are not a lawyer;
- How to work with lawyers when necessary;
- How to minimize the chance of harassment by the bar;
- What to do if you are threatened by the bar;
- How much to charge;
- How to think about working with computers.

In addition, this book contains interviews with a number of prominent people in the independent paralegal field. Many of these are IPs who have been successfully delivering services to the public for many years. Others are involved in IP training, the development of self-help law materials used by IPs, or the effort to get states to adopt legislation to legalize the occupation. In many ways, these interviews, which you will find in the Appendix, are the most important part of the book and I urge you to take the time to read them carefully.

Many of the suggestions in this book are aimed at helping you to deal with problems you are sure to face as part of starting any new business. These range from choosing a name and finding a good location, to getting a business license and buying necessary equipment. Sometimes it is necessary to borrow money to begin. Certainly, once your doors are open, it is important to quickly generate a positive cash flow. None of this is easy, especially when you remind yourself that embarking on a career as an independent paralegal involves not only putting yourself through normal "new business trauma," but simultaneously coping with the hostility of the legal profession.

This raises the question of why anyone would want to become an independent paralegal. Or, to ask the question more directly, "Why do you even consider working in a field where persecution, or at least official harassment, is a distinct possibility, and criminal conviction, including even a jail sentence, is not out of the question?"

One obvious answer is that running an independent paralegal business is potentially profitable. Lawyers' fees are so outrageous that independent paralegals can significantly undercut them (often by as much as 70%) and still make an excellent living. Indeed, a few farsighted business commentators predict that independent paralegal businesses will be one of the major success stories of the next decade.

But the prospect of making good money doesn't begin to explain why so many pioneer paralegals have been willing to assume the risk inherent in challenging organized lawyerdom. In talking to dozens, some of whom have been in business for almost 20 years, I sense that, for most, the determination to persevere is drawn from the same sort of stubborn conviction that motivated Massachusetts colonists to toss chests of tea into the Boston Harbor in 1767. Like their colonial forefathers, angered by King George III's nasty monopoly on tea, these men and women stand up to organized lawyerdom's even nastier monopoly over the delivery of legal services, because they believe it is wrong and that Americans have an inalienable right to affordable access to their own legal system.

A powerful presentation of why IPs are so badly needed is presented in a fascinating study by the legal reform organization HALT, entitled "Fixing the Lawyer Monopoly—The Right of Citizens to Employ Independent Paralegals When Handling Their Legal Affairs."[1] Here is a brief excerpt:

> *Our country has more lawyers than any in the world, but the average person cannot get legal help. Citizens in the United States have more trouble resolving their legal problems than peoples of any other free nation in the world. The reason is that American lawyers have been granted a monopoly on "legal services" and have defined it so broadly that it includes services they cannot provide and do not even recognize as needed....*
>
> *Relying on "lawyers only" to meet the public's legal needs has proved untenable. Without access to legal services as it has been defined by lawyers, many people lack access to justice. But access to legal services need not be interpreted as access to lawyers. HALT argues that everyone should*

---

[1] The entire report is available to HALT members for $10.00. I highly recommend it. For information on joining HALT, see Ch. 15, Section F.

have a range of choices—among lawyers, legal clinics, legal services and independent paralegals—depending on their means and the complexity of the case. People have the right to handle their legal affairs on their own—to do self-help and go into court pro se. They should also be able to employ a low-cost, expert independent paralegal to supply forms, give information, do their typing and point them in the right direction. For complex matters they can retain a lawyer or, if eligible, get free legal services.

While obviously I don't minimize the problems inherent in embarking on a career as an independent paralegal, I believe that with a lot of determination and a little luck, you can establish a profitable business and provide a valuable service helping nonlawyers with their own legal paperwork. This should become easier in the future, as public support for deregulation of the legal profession is almost sure to grow.

A Few Words About Terminology

Because lawyers in private practice, legislatures, bar associations, prosecutor's offices, and judge's robes have all been trained to defend their monopoly to deliver legal services, I often refer to them here with the shorthand term "organized lawyerdom," except when it's important to distinguish among them.

Also, as noted, for convenience I refer to nonlawyers who help other nonlawyers deal with the legal system as "independent paralegals" (IPs) even though some people in the field describe themselves in other ways—as a "legal technician," "form preparer," "legal typing service," "legal information specialist," "divorce counselor" or "public paralegal."

When describing the people who hire independent paralegals, I use the word "customer," rather than "client." I do this both because I believe it is wise for paralegals to distinguish themselves from lawyers as much as possible and because I personally don't like the word client, which has Latin roots in the terms "to hear" and "to obey." "Customer," on the other hand, conjures up the image of a powerful person, someone who expects good and conscientious service and who won't patronize a business again if she isn't satisfied.

And then there is the pesky personal pronoun. My solution to the problem of how to handle gender is to use "he" and "she" more or less alternately throughout the book. While this solution isn't perfect, it makes more sense to me than only using "he" or adopting other cumbersome schemes such as writing "he and she," "he/she" or "s(he)" every time an abstract person must be identified.

Finally, a few words about Nolo Press, and Americans for Legal Reform—HALT. Throughout this text, you will find many references to Nolo's self-help law materials and HALT's political organizing efforts. You may even begin to wonder why I plug these groups so much. The simple answer is that the activities of Nolo and HALT are at the heart of so many aspects of the independent paralegal movement that the references are unavoidable. Just the same, by way of full disclosure, I want to make it clear that I have a financial interest in Nolo and that I have worked closely for many years with a number of staffers at HALT and am proud to be a member of that nonprofit organization, which is dedicated to making America's legal system more accessible, affordable and democratic.

CHAPTER

1

The Historical Background

A person who decides on a career as an independent paralegal almost by definition must engage in a struggle with organized lawyerdom, a powerful adversary. Before you do this, you should learn some history—that is, understand the historical forces that have led to the current confrontation between independent paralegals and organized lawyerdom. Second, while you should respect these lessons, you should not allow them to control your strategy or tactics. Does this sound paradoxical? It isn't. Because we live in an age of unprecedented change, the lessons of history, while important, should be only one element in your strategy to keep your business from being suppressed by organized lawyerdom.

Reading history and not being ruled by it is never easy. Unfortunately, the natural human response is to draw such inflexible lessons from past events that history is repeated. Thus, it is a cliché that the best-trained generals tend to refight the last war, learned economists make predictions based on yesterday's recession, and baseball managers repeatedly rely too much on aging players who hit last year's home runs.

Independent paralegals, however, do have one dubious advantage over generals and coaches, who are trying to extrapolate past successes into future victories: IPs don't have many past victories to cloud their vision. Indeed, an independent paralegal who slavishly applies history's lessons is likely to conclude that a career as an independent paralegal is hopeless. Why? Because the IP will learn that in the nineteenth and early twentieth centuries, organized lawyerdom, relying on superior financial, organizational and political resources, effectively crushed America's once vibrant self-help law tradition. Does this mean that the current independent paralegal movement will also be suppressed by a vastly more powerful legal profession? Not at all. For reasons I develop in this chapter, I think that if paralegals as a group are willing both to learn from past mistakes and adopt new strategies, they can win the legal right to exist.

A. An American Tradition: "Every Man His Own Lawyer"

Let's look back four-and-one-half centuries. What can we say about the practice of law in colonial America? Very little, because in the early days of the American experience neither a lawyer elite nor a lawyer-dominated dispute resolution system existed in most colonies. Especially in Puritan New England, the Quaker communities in Pennsylvania, and the Dutch settlements in New York, there was a strong religious and egalitarian spirit hostile to the very notion of lawyers. Colonists solved their disputes within the community, which in those early days was heavily influenced by the church. Church elders were expected to guide disputing members of their congregations to a "just" result. The ultimate punishment for deviant behavior was exile from both church and community. For example, Anne Hutchinson, a woman who challenged several orthodox views in the Massachusetts Bay Colony, was tried by the church for heresy and exiled to the wilderness; she eventually ended up in Rhode Island.

When a particular dispute threatened to prove intractable, formal mediation techniques, similar to those newly popular today, were often used to help the disputants arrive at their own compromise. In 1635, a Boston town meeting ordered that no congregation member could litigate before trying arbitration, and Reverend John Cotton, the leading Puritan minister of the time, stated that to sue a fellow church member was a "defect in brotherly love." In 1641, the "Body of Liberties" adopted by the Massachusetts Bay Colony prohibited all freemen from being represented by a paid attorney:

Every man that findeth himselfe unfit to plead his own cause in any court shall have libertie to employ any man against whom the court doth not except, to help him, Provided he give him noe fee or reward for his pains.

In the second half of the seventeenth century, England increasingly asserted its political authority over the colonies, with the result that the common law tradition—complete with courts, trial by jury, and inevitably, lawyers—began to take hold. As you might guess, once established, it didn't take these first American lawyers long to try to suppress competition. Indeed, in Virginia, as early as 1642, legislation prohibited pleading a case without license from the court. Apparently, however, the egalitarian, every-man-his-own-spokesman tradition was strong even in relatively affluent Virginia; lawyers who charged for their services were banned from Virginia courts in 1645. They were allowed back in 1647, licensed in 1656, again prohibited from receiving compensation in 1657 and finally again allowed to practice with pay, if licensed, in 1680. Similar legislative ambivalence toward lawyers was evident in other colonies.[1]

One hundred years later, by the middle 1700s, lawyers were in evidence in all colonial commercial centers. Their prominence reflected the fact that although respect for religion still ran strong in America, ecclesiastical control of nearly all aspects of colonial life had receded before new waves of colonists more interested in secular than heavenly success.

In 1750s' America, there were as yet no law schools as we know them today. Young lawyers served an apprenticeship with an established practitioner and when they had learned enough legal ropes were questioned by a local judge (who had very likely received much the same sort of catch-as-catch-can training) and admitted to practice. When it came to legal knowledge, the gap between an attorney and the average educated citizen, never great in the cities, was almost non-existent in rural America. Even James Mason and Thomas Jefferson, authors of many of the important documents leading up to American independence, thought of themselves as farmers who had happened to study some law.

Many notable patriots of the Revolutionary War, including John Adams, Alexander Hamilton, Aaron Burr, and Patrick Henry, had legal training. Indeed, depending on how you define the term, about 40% of those who signed the Declaration of Independence were lawyers. Despite the promi-

---

[1] I am indebted to Charles Warren, *A History of the American Bar* (Boston, Little Brown) and Roscoe Pound, *The Lawyer From Antiquity to Modern Times* (West Publishing Co., 1953), for much of this historical background.

nence of these lawyer-patriots, the American Revolution marked the beginning of a long period of declining prestige for the legal profession. Much of the reason for this is traceable to the fact that the majority of the established bar sided with King George III rather than George Washington, and when the war was lost, left the colonies for England or Canada. As Thomas Jefferson remarked in a letter to James Madison, "Our lawyers are all Tories."

It should also be noted that a number of patriots with legal training, such as Jefferson and Madison, were radical ideologists, interested in legal theory as it contributed to the creation of a new social order, but not enamored with the traditional practice of law. Many patriot-lawyers saw the English legal system, with its formal rules of pleading and courts of equity, as fundamentally undemocratic, and opposed its wholesale adoption after independence.[2] In this context, the creation of a written constitution guaranteeing citizens certain fundamental rights can be seen as a reaction against the English common law system, which consisted of a collection of laws and court decisions that could be changed, willy-nilly, by Parliament and King.

Despite the fact that there were plenty of lawyers in late eighteenth century America, there is strong evidence that most citizens did not rely on them as a primary source of legal knowledge. Eldon Revare James, in *A List of Legal Treatises Printed in the British Colonies and the American States Before 1801*, found that:

> *In the hundred years between the publication in 1687 of William Penn's gleanings from Lord Coke and the issuance of the American editions of Buller's Nisi Pruis and Gilbert's Evidence in 1788, not a single book that could be called a treatise intended for the use of professional lawyers was published in the British Colonies and American States. All of the books within this period which by any strength of definition might be regarded as legal treatises were for the use of laymen.*

One of the most popular of these law books directed at the nonlawyer was entitled *Every Man His Own Lawyer,* which was in its ninth edition by

---

[2] Much the same thing happened during Franklin Roosevelt's New Deal and again in the years of social and political ferment in the late 1960s, when a minority of radical lawyers broke with the legal establishment to argue that the legal system, itself, had become repressive.

1784. Published in London, but widely distributed in the colonies, this was a comprehensive guide to both civil and criminal law, divided into seven sections covering the following diverse topics:

I. Of Actions and Remedies, Writs, Process, Arrest and Bail.

II. Of Courts, Attorneys and Solicitors therein, Juries, Witnesses, Trials, Executions, etc.

III. Of Estates and Property in Lands and Goods, and how acquired; Ancestors, Heirs, Executors and Administrators.

IV. Of the Laws relating to Marriage, Bastardy, Infants, Idiots, Lunaticks.

V. Of the Liberty of the Subject, *Magna Charta,* and *Habeas Corpus* Act and other statutes.

VI. Of the King and his Prerogative, the Queen and Prince, Peers, Judge, Sheriffs, Coroners, Justices of Peace, Constables, etc.

Use of this book was sufficiently widespread that it appears in a historical vignette featuring the second President of the United States, John Adams. It seems that before the Revolution, Adams, then a Boston lawyer and farmer, campaigned against "pettifoggers" (a derogatory term for independent paralegals and even some marginal lawyers) and led lawyer efforts to suppress the practice of law by "untrained" persons. Adams, like so many members of the profession today, worried about the loss of fees when he remarked that "looking about me in the country I found the practice of law grasped into the hands of deputy sheriffs, pettifoggers and even constables who filled all the writs upon bonds, promissory notes and accounts, received the fees established for lawyers and stirred up many unnecessary suits."

Apparently to prove the extent of the problem presented by the proliferation of nonlawyer practitioners, Adams relates this story about a pettifogger and tavern keeper named Kibby: "In Kibby's barroom, in a little shelf within the bar, I spied two books. I asked what they were. He said, '*Every Man His Own Lawyer* and *Gilbert on Evidence.*' Upon this, I asked some questions of the people there and they told me that Kibby was a sort of lawyer among them; that he pleaded some of their cases before justices, arbitrators, etc."[3]

As the new nation took shape, lawyers, with a number of conspicuous exceptions, tended to be poorly trained if they were trained at all. Indeed, ex-

---

[3] See Roscoe Pound, *The Lawyer From Antiquity to Modern Times* (West Publishing, 1953).

cept in Eastern commercial centers such as Boston, where at times an apprentice lawyer was required to work in a law office for as long as seven years before gaining admission to the bar, an American lawyer was little more than a man who could read and write and who owned a fireproof box. Still, in the last years of the eighteenth century and first decade of the nineteenth, urban lawyers were able to hold onto many of the prerogatives of their profession, thanks to laws in a number of states that established professional licensure requirements. This hard-won prominence was not to last, however. Along with a number of other "establishment" groups, from bankers to Freemasons, the legal profession did not fare well as America moved west. According to Daniel Lewolt, writing in *Americans for Legal Reform*, Vol. 5, No. 1 (Fall 1984):

> *The final blows were administered to legal professionals during the Andrew Jackson years. Frontiersmen, whose muddy boots had been allowed to trample White House rugs during Jackson's inaugural celebration, believed that justice should be popular and egalitarian and that experience was the best teacher. After 1830, even the requirement of reading [law] with a lawyer as a condition of practicing law was eliminated, and virtually anyone could practice law.*

Lewolt's view is supported by Leonard Tabachnik, who finds in *Professions for the People* (Schenkman Publishing, 1976) that:

> *The belief that professionalism advances science and protects the public from quackery was completely rejected by state legislators during the Age of Jackson: ...By 1840, only 11 of 30 states maintained regulations for admission to the Bar.*

With the legal profession in retreat during these years, how did people settle disputes? The average citizen settled many on his own, without formal legal help, relying on one of several lay legal guides, such as Thomas Wooler's *Every Man His Own Attorney*, published in 1845.[4] In an interesting parallel to modern self-help law books, Wooler wrote in his introduction:

---

[4] I am indebted to a fascinating article by Mort Reber, entitled "A Return to Self-Reliance," which appeared in the *People's Law Review* (Nolo Press, 1980), for much of this information.

When attorneys are employed, they must be paid; and their charges are not always regulated whether by their abilities or their services to a client, but by their own desire to make as much as they can. This evil can only be remedied by making their clients well informed on common subjects, and able to see what course they are taking in matters of more intricacy.

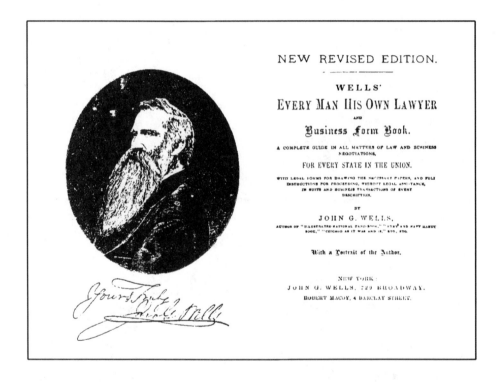

In addition, John Wells' *Every Man His Own Lawyer* (a different book than the one of the same title behind Kibby's bar that so annoyed John Adams and the members of the other, more powerful, bar), was sold as "a complete guide in all matters of law and business negotiations for every State of the Union, containing legal forms and full instructions for proceeding, without legal assistance, in suits and business transactions of every description." Apparently the popularity of this book was widespread. The author writes in the introduction to the 1879 edition:

The original edition of this work was prepared and presented to the public many years ago and was received with great favor, attaining a larger scale [hundreds of thousands according to Wells] it is believed, than any work published within its time." [5]

One might imagine that during the middle years of the nineteenth century, when almost any American could practice law and there was widespread interest in and support for self-help alternatives to lawyers, the intellectual quality of work done by the legal profession was low and individual lawyers were members of an endangered species. Just the opposite was true. As noted by Barlow Christensen in his article, "The Unauthorized Practice of Law: Do Good Fences Really Make Good Neighbors—Or Even Good Sense?" in the American Bar Foundation Research Journal (1980, No. 2):

The history of the profession during this period is paradoxical. On the one hand, this time is generally acknowledged to have been the great formative era in American law, during which were produced the great institutional cases that formed the foundation for the legal system as it exists today. It was also an era of great lawyers—Luther Martin, William Pinkney, William Wirt, Jeremiah Mason, Daniel Webster, Rufus Choate.[6] In addition, it was an era of great judges, including James Kent, John Marshall and Joseph Storey. On the other hand, however, it was, as well, an era of decentralization and deprofessionalization of the profession, a return to the virtually unregulated profession of the colonial period.

B. The Lawyers Take Over

By now, you are probably asking, "So what happened?" How did lawyers develop their stranglehold over almost every aspect of making, administering and carrying out our laws? The full answer to this question is complex, a subject worthy of a book of its own. Here I can only suggest some of the histori-

---

[5] *Ed. Note:* Although you can't always trust authors when it comes to assessing the popularity of their work, I have been able to find Wells' book in a number of collections of nineteenth century books, giving some credence to his claims.

[6] For some reason Christensen leaves out Abraham Lincoln and Stephen Douglas.

cal forces that combined to produce the political climate conducive to letting lawyers assert a virtual monopoly over our legal system. These include:

- **Non-English Speaking Immigrants:** In the late nineteenth and early twentieth centuries, huge numbers of non-English speakers immigrated to the United States. These new Americans had a stiff language barrier to overcome. In addition, they had not been brought up in the comparatively democratic, always argumentative, every person on his feet having his say, tradition of the English Protestant church and, to a lesser extent, English common law. In short, this influx of humanity created a huge group that was, at least initially, at a considerable disadvantage when dealing with the American legal system. In an age when unsuspecting new immigrants really were sold shares in the Brooklyn Bridge, many people were taken advantage of by all sorts of quick buck artists, including the legal variety. As a result, confidence that the average citizen could competently handle her own legal affairs began to erode, and calls for better professional standards began to be heard.

- **Rapid Urbanization:** The decline of communities where people knew each other also had a negative effect on legal self-reliance. The New England town meeting style of local government, so much a part of rural small town America in the eighteenth and nineteenth centuries, didn't work in the urban America of the twentieth century. Similarly, the power of many nineteenth century spiritual and immigrant communities dedicated to solving disputes without the intervention of lawyers began to wane.[7] After the Civil War, New York, Chicago and a dozen more big, anonymous cities that had been growing for decades came to dominate the states in which they were located, and, through their newly-huge banks, insurance companies and stock exchanges, the commercial and

---

[7] In the nineteenth century, all sorts of groups, including Shakers, Seventh Day Baptists, Swedenborgians, the Socialist followers of Owen and Fourier, Orthodox Jews, and literally hundreds of others, established communities that handled disputes without lawyers. Rather typically, John Noyes, the founder of the Oneida community, considered litigation "as the private equivalent of war," and it was said that the members of the Amana community in Iowa "live[d] in such perpetual peace that no lawyer is found in their midst." For more on the story of how a number of American communities tried to do without lawyers entirely, see Jerold Auerbach, *Justice Without Law: Resolving Disputes Without Lawyers,* Oxford University Press (1983).

political life of the nation. In the large cities, family and church ties had little power to bind people and help them settle their disputes outside of court. Increasingly, disputes now had to be dealt with in the public arena of the civil and criminal courts—the traditional spider webs of the professional bar—complete with their arcane language, obfuscatory procedures and long delays.

- **New Technology and Business Concentration:** Unprecedented development of new technologies in almost every industry, particularly energy, transport and telecommunications, changed the relationship of Americans to their employers, spurred the growth of big labor unions to protect workers' rights and required more and better trained lawyers to invent, administer (and all too often manipulate) the business and legal infrastructure that held it all together. For example, within the relatively few years between the end of the Civil War and the beginning of the first World War, modest factories clustered mostly in areas with access to water and power gave way to institutions such as Standard Oil, the Ford Motor Company, General Electric, railroads that spanned half a continent, and yes, even the Coca Cola Company. In this brave new corporate world, disputes that would have been settled face to face in simpler times were now routinely turned over to big city law firms.

- **The Closing of the Frontier:** In the last decade of the nineteenth century, America ran out of free farm and range land. No longer could the average person realistically hope to pack up the wagon, gather the kids, hitch up old Dobbin and head west to homestead a free 160 acres. This is important because the American tradition of always moving west had helped prevent establishment groups, including lawyers, from dominating American political and legal institutions. No sooner did one city gain economic clout and its professionals start building themselves mansions on the hill, than the center of gravity of the entire country lurched west. When America ran out of open land, lawyers and other establishment figures, including bankers, insurance agents, physicians, and brokers, had a chance to catch up with western migration for the first time in almost 300 years. Before long, they were able to control the political and economic life of the new states, just as they already did in the old, and the winds of legal change which had usually blown from the west were substantially stilled.

- **Consumer Reform:** The early consumer movement, which fought for reasonable standards of product safety, honest and accountable business practices and opposed price-fixing and other monopolistic practices, paradoxically played an important role in the increase in organized lawyerdom's power. The reformers (often called "muckrakers"), inspired by authors like Upton Sinclair (*The Jungle*) and Lincoln Steffens (*The Shame of the Cities*), broke with the common law tradition of *caveat emptor* ("let the buyer beware") to argue that in an industrial society dominated by large scale capitalism, the government must intervene in the commercial life of the nation to see that the ordinary citizen has a reasonable opportunity to avoid cynical exploitation by big business. This consumer crusade resulted in much of the progressive legislation adopted during the presidencies of Theodore Roosevelt and Woodrow Wilson, and laid the foundation for later reforms that have resulted in all sorts of good things, from purer food to safer workplaces. But it often produced negative results as it related to traditional professional groups such as lawyers and doctors. These "professionals" used the consumer reform movement to sell the nation on the rationale of "professional responsibility" and to justify organizing themselves into publicly-sanctioned monopolies. For example, when it came to training new lawyers, the legal profession now emphasized formal schooling over the traditional apprenticeship method, and pushed required written examinations as an alternative to being admitted to practice on the recommendation of a practitioner or judge.

All of these changes quickly worked to the pecuniary benefit of American lawyers. Already by the turn of the century, lawyers had gained substantially in wealth, power and community standing. Among the presidents elected between 1890 and 1932, Cleveland, Harrison, McKinley, Taft, Coolidge, Harding[8], and Franklin Roosevelt were members of the bar, and Supreme Court justices Oliver Wendell Holmes and Louis Brandeis were among the most respected men in America. Even Teddy Roosevelt spent a year at Columbia law school before concluding that the practice of law was too boring.

---

[8] Warren Harding was as unsuccessful as a lawyer as he was as president, quitting the profession early on to go into the newspaper business.

The Great Goddess Gobbledygook and Her Devotees

It was particularly remarkable how quickly lawyers were able to use the new educational and certification requirements to eliminate nonlawyer competition. As late as 1890, less than half of the states and territories had meaningful educational requirements for lawyers. But by 1915, only 13 states and one of the remaining territories allowed admission to law practice without attending law school. By 1940, all states effectively required professional study to be a lawyer.[9] Perhaps because it was so easy for organized lawyerdom to sell the American public on the image of an educated professional bar dedicated to high standards of integrity and service, lawyers had little incentive to actually back up this image with substantive consumer protection. For example, once new lawyers passed a general knowledge examination that had little to do with the day-to-day work of a practicing lawyer, there were absolutely no requirements for continuing skills testing or education. And legal consumers who were cheated or overcharged by the professional incompetence of individual lawyers, were then, as now, provided with little meaningful recourse.

---

[9] Willard Hurst, *The Growth of American Law: The Law Makers* (Little Brown & Co., 1950).

It wasn't until the depression of the 1930s that lawyers really had to defend their newly-minted monopoly. Bad economic times hit the legal profession particularly hard, striking as they did at the roots of its new power base as the protector of corporate America. Suddenly, from skyscraper to street corner, there were too many lawyers chasing too few clients—at least those who could pay their bills. The result might have been a legal profession that made a concerted effort to try to make good cheap legal help available to millions of newly poor Americans. In fact, despite lip service to helping widows and orphans, organized lawyerdom did just the opposite, banding together as never before to fix prices by use of a number of anti-competitive devices. These included, most prominently, bar association-mandated minimum fees, "treaties" with other professions, including bankers, accountants and real estate brokers, designed to respect each other's service monopolies, and a concerted campaign to eliminate all nonlawyer competition.

Just as the Depression caused a lot of people to consider handling their own legal work, or to seek help from more reasonably-priced nonlawyer practitioners, the bar adopted a surprisingly militant campaign to rid the nation of the last vestiges of the self-help law movement that had survived from the nineteenth century.[10] If you doubt the accuracy of this assertion, consider that the first American Bar Association committee ever to deal specifically with unauthorized practice was formed in 1930, and by 1938, over 400 state and local bar associations had formed similar committees.

The great increase in interest in unauthorized practice by bar associations led naturally to an increase in the number of nonlawyers who were prosecuted. As noted by Deborah Rhode in her fascinating 1981 study of unauthorized practice published in the *Stanford Law Review*,[11] a 1937 survey

---

[10]The American Bar Association also lead a 50-state effort to close down unaccredited mostly night law schools which, in the previous several decades, had produced the majority of American lawyers. The idea was frankly to limit the supply of new lawyers in an effort to push up legal fees. For the fascinating story of the suppression of America's unaccredited law schools, see Richard Abel's *American Lawyers* (Oxford University Press, 1989).

[11]Rhode, "Policing the Professional Monopoly: A Constitutional and Empirical Analysis of Unauthorized Practice Prohibitions," *34 Stan. L. Rev.* 1 (1981).

of reported unauthorized practice cases devoted 94 pages to all pre-1930 decisions and 619 pages to unauthorized practice suits decided between 1930 and 1937. Much of the reason for this increase in enforcement was the passage of new unauthorized practice statutes with tougher penalties. Most of this new legislation was orchestrated by the newly-organized local and state bar unauthorized practice committees, all of which claimed their activities were designed not to feather the nest of the legal profession but to protect the public from unqualified and incompetent law practitioners. Interestingly, Deborah Rhode's in-depth study finds almost no evidence that the public ever asked for, or needs, this "protection."

When good economic times returned after the Second World War, the legal profession suddenly found that there weren't enough lawyers to go around. This isn't surprising when you realize that relatively few lawyers were trained during the Depression. This shortage of lawyers, coinciding as it did with the unprecedented expansion and prosperity of the American middle class, resulted in an economic golden age for lawyers. Or, put simply, in the 1950s it was a snap to make big bucks in the law business. And just in case any nonlawyers were tempted to try to participate in this bonanza, the tough unauthorized practice statutes passed in the 1930s were still on the books to keep out interlopers.

In fairness, it should be noted that during the Eisenhower years, the average American's new-found admiration for "professionalization" also contributed to the maintenance of organized lawyerdom's monopoly. In the prosperous 1950s, it seemed as if everyone wanted their kids to be lawyers, doctors or orthodontists (as popular as law school was, learning to straighten middle class children's teeth was surely the growth profession of the decade). Against this background, it wasn't hard for the legal profession to convince most people that "a person who represents himself has a fool for a client."

C. The Modern Movement Away From Lawyers

Paradoxically, just as the legal profession reached the zenith of its power in the early 1960s, the first hints of its present vulnerability were becoming apparent. In its effort to clamp down on potential competitors, organized lawyerdom acted as if it, and it alone, was equipped to serve the legal needs of the broad American public. Although many lawyers believed it (and despite two generation's accumulation of evidence to the contrary, a few still do), this was far from true. Lawyers had gained status and wealth serving corporate America, the growing bureaucracy of federal and state governments, and, to a lesser extent, individuals in upper income brackets. Except for a few profitable (to lawyers), but very limited, legal areas, such as personal injury litigation and probate, the legal profession barely dealt with the average American of 1965.

That the majority of middle-class Americans were underserved by the legal profession (and that blue-collar and ethnic Americans weren't served at all) became embarrassingly obvious in the late-1960s. This widespread recognition was triggered in part by the Johnson administration's sponsorship of federally-funded legal services for the poor (legal aid), the first ever coordinated delivery of legal help nationwide. Everyone who worked in a legal services office in those years (and increasingly reporters who covered the war on poverty) was struck by an incredible fact—despite the bargain basement ambience of the largely ghetto-based offices, each had to employ a number of people who did nothing but turn away middle-class Americans not poor enough to qualify for legal aid, but not affluent enough to retain a lawyer under the traditional fee for services model. In short, when middle class Americans lined up on the streets of Watts, Bedford-Stuyvesant, and the South Side of Chicago (places they had gone previously only after rolling up the windows and locking the doors of their Pontiacs) to wait in line to talk to a lawyer, the fiction that American lawyers served the average American was revealed to be just that.

But it wasn't only the discovery that lawyers had priced their services out of the financial reach of most Americans that resulted in the profession's great fall in the public regard. Widespread latent dissatisfaction with the legal profession also surfaced during the investigation of the Watergate break-in in 1973. Many, if not most, of the people accused of illegal conduct—including Dean, Erlichmann, Colson, Chapin, Segretti, Mitchell, and Nixon himself, were lawyers. Instead of admitting they were wrong, these men first told a series of whopping lies and then, even after they were forced to admit their culpability, tried to wriggle off the hook on one or another legal technicality. In short, almost every American with a TV set learned that being a lawyer had little to do with the bar association's image of a profession dedicated to the pursuit of truth and justice. Woody Guthrie, it seemed, had been right all along when he sang about a profession which did its robbing not with a six-gun but a fountain pen.

After Watergate, most Americans understood that a majority of lawyers were out to make a pile of money fast, and if ignoring the rules they were supposed to respect helped them achieve their goal quicker, so be it. And when it came right down to it, why should this be shocking? Wasn't this trend of "life in the fast lane," "damn the rights of others," "winning is everything" approach equally fashionable among stockbrokers, doctors, football coaches, morticians, bankers, car salespeople and others? Yes, but since these other groups hadn't tried so hard to put their occupation on a pedestal, they were less vulnerable to attack.

Not only did the public, as a whole, lose respect for the legal profession, some individuals with legal questions and problems began to look for ways to solve them without lawyers. One consequence was that America began to rediscover its strong historical tradition of legal self help. By the middle 1970s, Norman Dacey's *How To Avoid Probate* and Ed Sherman's *How To Do Your Own Divorce in California* were best sellers. In California, Nolo Press had been established, and had published over 20 successful self-help law books. And of particular interest to readers of this book, non-lawyer (independent paralegal) typing services began to offer legal form preparation services directly to the public.

Specifically, in California, the Wave Project, which was staffed by dropped-out teachers, social workers, legal secretaries and business people, began advertising that it would type forms for people who wanted to do their own divorces for a fee of $50-$75. And in Florida, Rosemary Furman, a former court clerk disgusted with the money-grubbing hypocrisy she found in the courthouse, did much the same thing (see the interview with Rosemary Furman in the Appendix for details). The Wave Project, which was begun by Ed Sherman and myself in 1972, operated about 20 independent paralegal legal form preparation offices throughout California. Many of these businesses still exist. Several are run by their original owners, although they have dropped the Wave Project name in favor of the more prosaic California Divorce Center.

Soon after the Wave Project began to list its services in the classified sections of newspapers, organized lawyerdom took notice. As you can probably imagine, the bar's reaction wasn't to applaud. Organized lawyerdom attacked the Wave Project in two principal ways. The first involved local bar associations or judges complaining to county district attorneys that the non-lawyer proprietors of the Wave Project offices were guilty of the crime of practicing law without a license. As a result, almost every Wave Project office was confronted by a hostile deputy district attorney challenging its right to exist. In a number of counties, the district attorney's office went so far as to send an investigator with a hidden recording device into the office and try to trick the independent paralegal operator into giving what they defined as "legal advice." (See Jolene Jacobs' interview in the Appendix.) Assuming the IP did say something a deputy D.A. thought amounted to the practice of law, the visit would normally be followed by a citation letter (occasionally an immediate arrest was made) ordering the IP to present herself at the D.A.'s office at a certain date and time. The D.A. would then usually inform the independent paralegal that she could be prosecuted for the crime of practicing law without a license unless she shut down her business. (See Chapter 2 for details of how this happens.)

Most independent paralegals refused to close down. Several, including Bob Mission (see interview in the Appendix), were arrested and formally charged with unauthorized practice. A number of IPs who were cited but not prosecuted eventually ended up working out a compromise with the district attorney under which they promised to restrict the content of advertisements or otherwise limit the scope of their businesses in exchange for being allowed to continue operating. Of the formal prosecutions, some were dropped on the basis of the sort of settlement just mentioned, several resulted in victory for the independent paralegal, and a number, perhaps the majority, ended when the independent paralegal became so exhausted and/or scared that he agreed to close up shop.

The second way organized lawyerdom attacked the Wave Project focused on several of the people who founded or coordinated it. For example, Ed Sherman, whose book *How To Do Your Own Divorce in California* launched the self-help law movement on the west coast, was dragged through a two-year battle during which the bar association tried to seize his license to practice law based on his Wave Project activities. (The actual charges included advertising legal services and aiding and abetting the unlicensed practice of law.) Phyllis Eliasberg, who took over coordination of the Wave Project from Ed Sherman and myself in 1974, faced similar charges.

Sherman's license was eventually ordered suspended, but oddly, at the last moment the California Bar backtracked and the suspension never took effect. Part of the reason for this was undoubtedly the U.S. Supreme Court's decision in *Bates v. State Bar of Arizona,* 433 U.S. 350 (1977), which made attorney advertising legal. Probably of as much importance, however, was the fact that organized lawyerdom was shocked by the bad publicity they were receiving as a result of prosecuting Sherman and Eliasberg. By deciding to stop this harassment, the California Bar showed more savvy than did the Florida Bar, which persisted in prosecuting Rosemary Furman for UPL, even after this resulted in CBS's "60 Minutes" featuring her as a national folk heroine for typing $50 divorces.

By the early 1980s, about one-hundred independent paralegals existed in Florida, California and several other western states. In addition to divorce, those pioneers began preparing legal forms for other problems, including bankruptcy, step-parent adoption, and change of name. Later in the 1980s, as more form preparation services were added, many IPs began to prosper. So much so that by the mid-1990s, California alone had as many as two thousand IPs, and in a number of other states, including Florida, Arizona and Oregon, IP practice was common, as evidenced by the fact that in Arizona and California the majority of divorces were completed with neither spouse being represented by a lawyer[12].

As the IP movement gained momentum, legislation affecting this new business was introduced in a number of states. Some bills were designed to make it clear that the delivery of basic legal form preparation services by non-lawyers is legal. In other states, including California, bills were proposed to formally study what, if any, state regulation of this new industry was needed. Although, as of this writing in Summer 1994, no broad-based legislation affecting IPs has been passed, this is likely to change soon.

 See Chapter 15 for a brief history of recent events in California and Florida.

---

[12]These figures are based on two sources. For Arizona, a report entitled "Self-Representation in Divorce Cases," compiled by Sales, Beck & Haan (American Bar Association). For California, an article entitled "Pro Per Behavior" in the magazine *California Lawyer*, May 1994.

The Law

This chapter is concerned with the laws, court rules, and powers claimed by bar associations that, taken together, define the unauthorized practice of law. Mastering this information is crucial to your success as an independent paralegal because the unauthorized practice laws are organized lawyerdom's principal way to attack nonlawyers who challenge its monopoly power to deliver legal services. As we go through this chapter, it's important to keep in mind the general truth that it's one thing to know what any law says and quite another to understand what the words mean in the real world. Especially in the context of regulations governing the unauthorized practice of law, which are incredibly vague, it is necessary to understand the nuances of both community and law enforcement attitudes in your city and state.

In Chapter 3, I discuss in detail what an independent paralegal can do to avoid charges of unauthorized practice of law. Basically, as an IP, you should do three things: tell the world you are not a lawyer, give your customers the information they need to make their own decisions and limit yourself to legal form preparation.

A. Introduction to the Concept of Unauthorized Practice of Law (UPL)

What exactly is the practice of law and how can you avoid doing it? Unfortunately, the term "practice of law" is nowhere clearly and unambiguously defined. Courts in many states prescribe who can deliver legal services under their inherent power to regulate law practice. Unfortunately, the reasoning in their decisions tends to be circular: only lawyers can practice law. Statutes that make unauthorized practice a crime in the majority of states are no more helpful, defining the practice of law as "what lawyers do" or "what lawyers are trained to do," terms which are impossible to interpret by any meaningful objective standard.

But all hope is not lost. Although you probably can't get much help from definitions of the practice of law, you may be able to get some guidance from finding out what is not considered to be the practice of law. Probably the best place to look is at the court decisions of your own state, the rules that regulate your state's bar, and any pronouncements on the subject issued by your state's supreme court.[1] For example, in the aftermath of the Rosemary Furman affair, the Florida Supreme Court amended the Rules Regulating the Florida bar to read:

> *It shall not constitute the unlicensed practice of law for nonlawyers to engage in limited oral communications to assist individuals in the completion of legal forms approved by the Supreme Court of Florida. Oral communications by nonlawyers are restricted to those communications reasonably necessary to elicit factual information to complete the form(s) and inform the individual how to file such form(s)."*

Since then, the Florida Supreme Court has gone on to approve hundreds of pages of legal forms, thus opening wide the window for Florida independent paralegals to help consumers prepare these forms, free of worry that they will be charged with UPL.[2]

Let's take a look at some recent case decisions that will give you a sense of the approaches different state courts have taken in deciding what constitutes UPL. In *The People v. Landlords Professional Services*,[3] a California case involving an eviction service that helped people prepare and file unlawful detainer actions, the court, applying a statute that made UPL a crime, found that the service was engaged in the unauthorized practice of law because:

1. The advertisement suggested that the eviction service did more than simply provide clerical assistance. The ad implied that the service actually accomplished evictions.

---

[1] You will find tips for doing legal research throughout this chapter. For a thorough guide, see Elias, *Legal Research: How to Find and Understand the Law* (Nolo Press). Nolo also publishes a 2-1/2 hour videotape, entitled *Legal Research Made Easy: A Roadmap Through the Law Library Maze*, by Bob Berring.

[2] In another example, a Nevada court said that stenographic and scrivener services that provided their customers with simple and straightforward kits so that the customers could make self-informed decisions would not be considered UPL. *State Bar of Nevada v. Johnson* (No. CV89-5814, Nev. 2nd Dist. Ct., April 12, 1990).

[3] 215 Cal.App.3d 1599 (4th Dist.,1989).

2. "Call and talk to us" on the ad and "counselor" on the business card were general invitations for discussion and suggested that the service sells expertise.

3. The service provided specific information and advice directed to the client's personal problems and concerns.

The court found that the service provided by the IP business would not amount to the "practice of law" as long as the service was "merely clerical," because:

- It is not UPL to make forms available for clients' use.
- It is not UPL to fill in forms and file and serve them at the specific direction of the client.
- It is not UPL to give a client a detailed manual containing specific advice.
- It is not UPL as long as the service doesn't personally advise the client with regard to her particular case.

An opinion written by the Washington Supreme Court illustrates just how unpredictable application of UPL regulations to any specific situation can be.[4] Here the court invoked its own inherent power to regulate the practice of law to find that the preparation of certain real estate forms necessary to buy and sell houses, which had, in the past, always been prepared by lawyers, could now be completed by nonlawyers. In allowing nonlawyer involvement in real estate transactions, the court relied on the public's interest in freedom of choice, convenience and the lower costs provided by nonlawyers. In doing so, the court specifically ruled that:

> *There are sound and practical reasons why some activities that fall within the broad definition of the "practice of law" should not be unauthorized simply because they are done by laypersons.*

B. Criminal Penalties for Unauthorized Practice

More than two-thirds of the states have criminal statutes that make unauthorized practice a misdemeanor, which typically means that fines are limited to about $1,000, and jail time to one year or less in a county correctional facility. For example, in California, the UPL statute reads like this:

---

[4] *Cultum v. Heritage House Realtors, Inc.*, 103 Wash. 2d 623 (1985).

Any person advertising or holding himself or herself out as practicing or entitled to practice or otherwise practicing law who is not an active member of the State bar is guilty of a misdemeanor."

In states where UPL is a crime, public prosecutors play a key role in UPL enforcement. It's a deputy district or state attorney who first decides if a particular independent paralegal is committing unauthorized practice and should either be prosecuted or pursued in a civil action. (See Section D, be-low, for more on enforcement of UPL laws.)

Note: Arizona is an Exception. Arizona is currently the only state where there is no UPL law, and where courts rarely assert their inherent pow-ers to regulate the practice of law (see Section C, below) to actively restrict the activities of IPs.

HOW TO LOOK UP YOUR STATE'S UPL STATUTE

Obviously, it's important to find out how courts have defined the unauthorized prac-tice of law in your state. Go to a large public library or, better yet, a law library (often found at county court houses or publicly-funded law schools). Find the book contain-ing your state's laws (often referred to as statute books or code books). If possible, use the "annotated" version of your legal code, which contains not only the laws themselves but also useful information about relevant court cases, articles and other secondary sources that discuss each law. Locate the volume entitled General Index and look up the Unauthorized Practice of Law, which will refer you to the appropriate code and section.

Once you have found and read the law in the hardbound volume, check the same statute number in the inserted "pocket part" (just inside the back cover). This will contain any changes passed by your state's legislature from the time the hard-bound book was published up to about six months to one year ago. If your legisla-ture has met since then, ask a law librarian to show you how to check to see if there have been even more current changes.

C. Judicial Penalties for Unauthorized Practice—the Inherent Powers Doctrine

Courts in most states assert the power to define and regulate the practice of law. In legal parlance, this is often referred to as the "inherent powers doctrine."[5] Judges claim this power originally comes from their inherent authority to regulate what happens in their own courts, and by extension the practice of law generally. (See "How Powerful are a Court's Inherent Powers," in this chapter.) This inherent powers doctrine is then elevated to constitutional dimensions by the "separation of powers" clause, which grants each branch of government (executive, legislative and judicial) the right to regulate its own affairs. For example, if a state legislature passes a law or regulation that affects lawyers or the practice of law, the state supreme court can find it unconstitutional because it invades the exclusive province of the judiciary. In practice, they often don't, as long as the law strictly limits what nonlawyers can do. However, courts are far more likely to overrule legislation when they believe

---

[5] For a more in-depth discussion, see Wolfram "Lawyer Turf and Lawyer Regulation— The Role of the Inherent-Powers Doctrine", *University of Arkansas at Little Rock Law Journal,* Volume 12, Number 1 (1989-90).

it goes too far in allowing nonlawyers to perform legal tasks. In the following sections, we will review some court decisions that will give you an idea of how the inherent powers doctrine is applied and how it might be relevant to you as an IP.

HOW POWERFUL ARE A COURT'S INHERENT POWERS?

The concept of inherent powers goes back hundreds of years to a time when most legal matters were brought before courts. Judges, who were assumed to have broad "inherent" powers over their own courtrooms, also asserted power over the people who regularly appeared before them (lawyers) and how these people conducted their business (the practice of law). Today the legal system bears little resemblance to that of the 18th century. For one thing, the majority of legal matters never get near a court. Nevertheless, lawyers and judges, eager to protect their historical monopoly, stretch the doctrine of inherent judicial power far beyond its historical meaning to justify judicial regulation of every aspect of our legal system, including even the activities of independent paralegal form preparers. In the long run, this attempt to inflate the inherent powers doctrine out of all reasonable recognition will probably fail; in the short run, it could be dangerous to your livelihood.

1. Court Regulation of Independent Paralegals Who Appear Before State Administrative Hearings

Administrative agencies are created by statute and basically exist to facilitate some legislative purpose, such as administering health, labor or retirement programs. Many of these agencies have mechanisms to hear and resolve disputes that somewhat resemble a court of law. For example, a person who is denied Social Security disability benefits has the right to an administrative hearing.

Because, as we have seen, many state courts assert inherent powers to regulate the entire legal system, nonlawyers who represent people before state (and sometimes even federal) agencies may be charged with unauthorized practice. This can be true even though the state legislature or the agency itself allows nonlawyers to appear before it. And if this isn't confusing enough, consider that in some states, judges choose not to use their inherent power to block nonlawyers representing people before agencies (they go along with this so-called unauthorized practice of law) while others just say no. With this in mind, let's look at a few cases.

In a decision by the Florida Supreme Court, the court found that the preparation of documents and presentation of non-contested juvenile dependency cases by lay counselors was unauthorized practice.[6] The court said if advice involved important rights and required knowledge of law greater than that of the average citizen, it constituted unauthorized practice. Apparently applying this rule, the Florida Supreme Court has also stated that preparing a living trust constitutes unauthorized practice.[7] But in a more positive move, the Florida Supreme Court has also recently used the inherent powers doctrine to approve the preparation of many divorce and landlord-tenant forms by IPs. (See Chapter 15, Section B.)

In Rhode Island, the supreme court considered two statutes that allowed nonlawyers to represent people in informal hearings within the Department of Worker's Compensation.[8] The purpose of these nonlawyer "employee assistants" was to give help and advice to employees under the Workers' Compensation Act. The court concluded that although the activities subject to the statutes could be considered the practice of law, they were okay because any definition of the practice of law must be responsive to the public interest. The court explicitly states that the legislature may aid the court's inherent power to define the practice of law and determine who may practice, but the legislature must abide by the court's standard. The court points out that it has not interfered with a number of legislative acts which, in effect, carved out exceptions to the practice of law because they constituted a response to a public need.

---

[6] *Florida Bar Re: Advisory Opinion HRS Nonlawyer Counselor,* 547 So.2d 909 (1989).

[7] *The Florida Bar Re: Advisory Opinion—Nonlawyer Preparation of Living Trusts,* Case No. 78,358. However, in this opinion, the Florida Court allowed nonlawyers to gather necessary information to prepare a living trust. This may allow IPs to continue to do form typing for customers who have obtained their own forms and instructions and simply want the IP to assemble them.

[8] *Unauthorized Practice of Law Committee v. State of Rhode Island, Department of Workers' Compensation,* 543 A.2d 662 (1988).

In short, while theoretically the Rhode Island legislature's power to regulate state administrative proceedings is second to the courts, in practice, the court will not upset the legislature's decision if it agrees with the public policy being advanced. This approach, which leaves the final decision up to the courts, is the prevailing approach in the United States,[9] according to legal commentator Gregory T. Stevens.[10]

Because of the differences between what a state law or agency regulation says and what actually happens, it is not always easy to know whether an independent paralegal can appear before a particular agency on behalf of a claimant or not. Probably the best approach is to simply call any agency you are interested in and ask.

2. Federal Administrative Agency Hearings

The federal system gives exclusive regulatory control of federal agencies to Congress. The Administrative Procedure Act authorizes federal agencies to allow nonlawyers to practice before them without regard to whether the activities would be unauthorized practice in the state where the agency proceeding occurs. One example of where this occurs involves the Social Security system, where nonlawyers are permitted to represent people appealing from the denial of a disability claim. This does not mean that all federal agencies allow nonlawyers to do this, only that each agency has the power to allow nonlawyer representation if it so chooses. According to one U.S. Supreme Court decision, states cannot restrict the right of any person to perform a function that falls within the scope of federal authority.[11] However, to guarantee the right of nonlawyers to appear, the agency in question must explicitly allow nonlawyer representation. If it fails to do so, states can prohibit UPL in a federal agency proceeding.

For example, in Florida, the state bar's committee on the unauthorized practice of law wanted the court to find that certain nonlawyer involvement in

---

[9]"The Proper Scope of Nonlawyer Representation in State Administrative Proceedings: A State Specific Balancing Approach," *43 Vand. L. Rev.* 245 (January 1990).

[10]For example, see *UPL Comm. v. Employers Unity, Inc.* 716 P.2d 460 (Colo. 1986); *UPL Comm. v. State Dept. of Workers Comp.*, 543 A.2d 662 (RI 1988).

[11]*Sperry v. U.S.*, 373 U.S. 379 (1963).

preparing pension plans was unauthorized practice.[12] In this instance, federal statutes and regulations authorized nonlawyers to practice before federal agencies. The Florida Supreme Court ruled that because the federal agency granted such authority, the states could not use their own definition of UPL to limit it, and thus, the court did not find unauthorized practice in this instance.

a.   Bankruptcy Court—Who Regulates Unauthorized Practice?

There is no clear federal law or regulation dealing with whether or not non-lawyers can appear before a federal bankruptcy court or prepare paperwork for consumers who wish to represent themselves. In the absence of a federal law on the subject, state unauthorized practice laws and rules of court apply. This means a state prosecutor or court can go after independent paralegals who provide customers with legal advice in the bankruptcy field.

What about the inherent power of federal bankruptcy court judges to regulate unauthorized practice in their own courts? This doctrine is alive and well, and many federal bankruptcy judges assert it. Does this mean state UPL authorities are likely to voluntarily defer to the local federal bankruptcy judge to regulate UPL in its jurisdiction? Yes, and as a practical matter, they often do. Most bankruptcy enforcement is carried out by United States Bankruptcy judges.[13]

More information about bankruptcy. In Chapter 3, I discuss how an independent paralegal can run a bankruptcy typing service in a way that largely avoids the risk of being found guilty of the unauthorized practice of law. I discuss the regulation of fees charged by independent paralegals for preparing bankruptcy forms in Chapter 9.

---

[12] *The Florida Bar Re: Advisory Opinion—Nonlawyer Preparation of Pension Plans,* No. 74, 479 (1990).

[13] Two recent Bankruptcy Court decisions, both finding an IP guilty of UPL, are *In re Webster et al v. Larson,* 120 Bankr. 111 (1990) and *In re Bachman* (Case No. 88-04588—Southern District of Florida).

D. Enforcement of Unauthorized Practice Rules

Is there a way to predict whether a UPL action is likely in a particular area? Not with any accuracy. This is because most UPL proceedings, civil and criminal, are triggered by an individual lawyer, bar association or judge, often because the IP is perceived to be infringing on what many lawyers believe is their exclusive domain. In some states, bar associations are authorized to bring court UPL actions directly against IPs. Often, the bar seeks an injunction to prohibit all or some activities of the paralegal service. Because of the uncertain definition of "practicing law," some courts will provide guidelines that the IP is directed to follow, and as long as the IP agrees to do this, he or she will usually be able to remain in business. Bar associations may also refer cases to the state or local prosecutor to demand that UPL charges be filed against a particular IP. A prosecutor or court may also initiate UPL proceedings on their own.

What happens if you do run afoul of the enforcement division of your state supreme court, or a bar association committee that threatens to turn you in to a court or to the local prosecutor? Deborah Rhode, in her *Stanford Law Review* study,[14] finds that normally no formal action is taken. Typically, what happens is this:

1. The bar association or court contacts the independent paralegal—often by letter, but sometimes personally—and asks her to cease what it considers the offending conduct.

2. If the IP doesn't comply, the bar may subpoena her to appear before a bar association hearing, at which point she is likely to be formally told to stop preparing forms for nonlawyers. This sort of intimidation causes many people to close down.

But what happens if the independent paralegal politely but firmly insists on her constitutional right to continue helping nonlawyers do their own legal paperwork? Depending on the make-up of the particular bar committee or the

---

[14]Rhode, "Policing the Professional Monopoly: A Constitutional and Empirical Analysis of Unauthorized Practice Prohibitions," *34 Stanford Law Rev.* 1 (1981). Although this study is dated, it is the only one of its kind that is currently available. See also Rhode, "The Delivery of Legal Services by Nonlawyers," *Georgetown Journal of Legal Ethics,* Vol. 4:209 (1990).

attitude of the state supreme court, and on the law of the particular state, the bar association or court may:

1. Do nothing.

2. Initiate its own civil court proceeding to try to put the independent paralegal out of business. As touched on earlier, this generally takes the form of an action in a trial court to enjoin the IP from engaging in whatever activity organized lawyerdom alleges constitutes the unauthorized practice of law. If a resulting injunction is violated, the IP is typically held in contempt of court and jailed or fined, or both. (This is basically what happened to Rosemary Furman in Florida.)

3. In the approximately 36 states where UPL is a crime, the matter may potentially be referred to a criminal prosecutor. Prosecutors, who are normally overloaded with higher profile criminal cases, such as those involving drugs and violence, will generally only prosecute a UPL case when they think they have a good chance of winning. Practically, this means that they most often go after nonlawyers who either incompetently practice law or fraudulently misrepresent their skills or status, as when an unlicensed person claims to be a lawyer. In either of these situations, the prosecutor can legitimately claim that he is putting out of business someone who is a danger to the public.

To see how a typical UPL complaint might be handled, let's take a fairly typical example. Suppose a prosecutor is told by a bar associate that Mary Smith, a nonlawyer, prepared divorce forms for Leroy Jackson. First, the prosecutor knows that acting as a public stenographer is not a crime. At the very least, the prosecutor understands that to prove a criminal case she will have to establish that Smith transferred some legal expertise to Jackson (remember that states differ somewhat as to amount and types of legal information that must be transferred to constitute UPL). Assuming the prosecutor believes that Smith did transfer enough legal expertise or advice to Jackson to constitute UPL, the prosecutor will next likely look to see if Smith's advice was inaccurate or resulted in any harm. Assuming this was not the case (Jackson was pleased with Smith's service, which resulted in his getting a divorce at low cost), the prosecutor will be faced with trying to convict a person who is providing a good service at a reasonable price. If Smith requests a jury trial, as she is almost sure to do, this sort of case can often be difficult for the prosecutor to win unless Smith was clearly holding herself out or acting like a lawyer.

Faced with this sort of situation, many prosecutors are likely to decide to wait until they have a stronger case, one where an independent paralegal misrepresented her credentials or services, or where her legal advice resulted in customer harm. Smith will probably not be prosecuted and her file will become inactive. Sometimes, however, the prosecutor may try to work a case up a bit, especially if the complaint has come from lawyers or judges who have political clout. If the prosecutor does decide to pursue Smith further, the next step will probably be to anonymously contact her typing service and request legal information. Often this means an investigator posing as a customer, and almost certainly carrying a concealed tape recorder, will ask Smith a number of broad questions designed to get her to give what the District Attorney's office considers to be legal advice.

As we discuss in Chapter 3, the best way for an independent paralegal who fears this sort of investigation to protect herself is to consistently avoid answering broad customer questions about substantive law. To stay out of legal hot water, the independent paralegal wants to present herself as a typing service and no more.[15]

Assuming a prosecutor decides to continue working up a UPL case against Smith, the next step, short of actually prosecuting, is usually to request a meeting. Normally, it happens something like this. Smith receives a letter (often called a "citation" or "cite" letter in the trade) asking her to show up at the prosecutor's office on a certain date to meet with deputy district attorney so-and-so to discuss the allegation that she has engaged in illegal activities—to wit, practicing law without a license. The first thing Smith or any other IP should know about this sort of letter is that it is often part of a campaign to

---

[15]I discuss a number of techniques to avoid giving what organized lawyerdom considers to be legal advice throughout this book. The best approach is to refer the customer to another information source, such as a self-help law book or audio tape. An obvious problem in this area, however, is that some lawyers define unauthorized practice so broadly that it includes almost any interaction between an independent paralegal and the public where money changes hands but doesn't end up in a lawyer's pockets. As I discuss later in this chapter, many, if not most, of organized lawyerdom's efforts to characterize law practice so expansively have been rejected by courts.

intimidate the IP into giving up her business, not the first step in a formal prosecution. A prosecutor who has already decided to prosecute an IP will probably not bother to write a cite letter.

The second thing Smith should understand about the citation letter process is that even though she is not required to show up, it's wise to do so. When a district attorney is unsure of her legal ground (which is often the case if she sends a cite letter), she looks for a reason to either pursue a formal action or forget the matter. Smith's failure to show up may well be reason enough for her to decide to get tough. Of course, Smith is entitled, but not required, to have a lawyer present at any conference with law enforcement personnel.

At the meeting, a deputy district attorney may try to scare Smith into voluntarily abandoning her business. In the past, many independent paralegals have done just that, concluding that even though they haven't done anything illegal, they don't have the resources to "fight city hall." Assuming Smith was operating a quality business and following the advice contained in this book on how to empower her customers without engaging in UPL, there is no reason for her to be intimidated into quitting. And surely, she will be comforted to know that most people who have refused to close down haven't, in fact, been prosecuted. (See Virginia Simons' and Jolene Jacobs' interviews in the Appendix.)

What's Smith's best strategy at this point? First, she should try to get the prosecutor to talk about the issues she believes justify a prosecution. In this context, Smith should try to get the deputy prosecutor to agree that it's legal for nonlawyers to use self-help law books to carry out legal tasks. Next, Smith should try to get her to concede that the act of typing forms for lay people doesn't constitute the practice of law. Finally, Smith should see if the prosecutor will agree that typing forms following a customer's instructions gleaned from a self-help law book does not constitute unauthorized practice. Since this is now the legal view of many state courts (see Section E, below), it shouldn't be difficult, especially if Smith does some legal research and comes to the meeting armed with her state's court decisions.

Assuming Smith can get a prosecutor to concede that typing legal forms following the instructions of nonlawyers is not in and of itself illegal, she has laid the groundwork for a compromise that will allow her to continue her business without further hassle. Why do I say this? Because once the prosecutor concedes that her core form typing activity is not illegal, her next step should be to cooperate with the prosecutor so that it's clear her future activities will be limited to this type of operation. In short, unless the prosecutor's requests are so outrageous that they will amount to Smith going out of business, she will be wise to try to find some common ground on which to compromise, even if she feels she is giving up important legal rights. The reason for this is that a compromise recognizes Smith's right to exist. It gets the prosecutor off her back and allows her crucial time to make the sort of alliances in the community that will make it difficult to prosecute her in the future. Later, once Smith feels she is sufficiently established and has the allies (e.g., media people, prominent citizens, and maybe even judges and lawyers) necessary to fight back, she can always challenge what she feels are organized lawyerdom's illegal restrictions on her business.

As part of a settlement, Smith might agree to change her classified ads from "Divorce—$200" to "Self-Help Divorce Typing—$200." Or maybe, in an extreme situation, not to advertise in the local paper at all. (As I point out in Chapter 10, there are many other good ways to market your services.) Further, Smith might agree that all her customers will be given or sold a copy of a relevant self-help law book so each has the legal information necessary to make his own informed decisions.

But suppose no compromise with the prosecutor is possible and Smith is told flat out that if she doesn't close up shop in ten days, she will be charged with the crime of practicing law without a license. Based on the rarity of recent prosecutions in this area and my own conversations with a number of people faced with this sort of ultimatum, there is still a fairly good chance that she won't be prosecuted. Of course, I can't give her any such guarantee. But, if she feels that her business has been conducted with integrity and competence, and especially if she has some support from the media or the local legal community, she will probably want to keep operating at the same time that she makes the types of changes in her ads and operating policies discussed above to make her business as bulletproof as possible.

Finally, even if UPL charges are filed, Smith should know that this doesn't mean that either a trial or conviction will result. In many instances, she will again be given a chance to close her business in exchange for having the prosecution dropped at a pre-trial conference or meeting. Why? Because, as I have emphasized repeatedly, organized lawyerdom is anxious not to create any more national anti-lawyer martyrs, as it did with Rosemary Furman in Florida. (See interview in the Appendix.) Unless Smith is plainly guilty of consumer fraud, lawyers will usually be almost as anxious to keep her out of the courtroom as she is to stay out.

If you have purchased errors and omission insurance, there is a good chance your insurance carrier will pay for your legal defense against unauthorized practice changes. See Chapter 12, Section E for more on errors and omissions insurance for independent paralegals.

HOW TO LOCATE UPL COURT CASES

HALT—Americans for Legal Reform—publishes a list of UPL cases entitled "UPL-Case and Opinion Summaries." With over 250 listings on an IBM (and compatible) floppy disk, this is the single best source of UPL information. It costs $35 to HALT members (see Ch. 15F for HALT membership information).

To find cases in your state not on the HALT disk, there are a number of ways to proceed. The first place to check is the case notes, which you will find with the your state's UPL statute in the annotated code. (See "How to Look Up Your UPL Statutes," earlier in this chapter.) Once you locate at least one relevant case and read it, you will almost surely be referred to other UPL cases. Also, with the case citation you have, use Shepard's Case Citations to get citations to all other cases that mention that case.

Another way to check for UPL cases is to check a case digest for your state. (All populous states have them.) A digest is a collection of case summaries that are organized by subject matter and indexed. To use a digest for your state, check the subject-matter index under "unauthorized practice of law."

A third way to identify cases in your state is to read all the cases mentioned in the text and footnotes of this chapter. Typically, these will refer to (cite) UPL cases from other states, one of which may be yours.

Also, law review articles on UPL cite a number of cases. The important articles are:

- Rhode, "Policing the Professional Monopoly: A Constitutional and Empirical Analysis of Unauthorized Practice Prohibitions," 34 *Stanford Law Rev.* 1 (1981).
- Michelman, "Guiding the Invisible Hand: The Consumer Protection Function of Unauthorized Practice Regulation," *Pepperdine L. Rev.,* Vol. 12, No. 1 (1984).
- Wolfram, "Lawyer Turf and Lawyer Regulation—The Role of the Inherent-Powers Doctrine," *University of Arkansas at Little Rock Law Journal*, Volume 12, Number 1 (1989-90).
- Rhode, "The Delivery of Legal Services by Nonlawyers," *Georgetown Journal of Legal Ethics*, Vol 4: 209 (1990).

Finally, check the *Index of Legal Periodicals* under the heading "Unauthorized Practice." This publication lists all law review and law journal articles in the unauthorized practice area. You may well find a current one that discusses the case law of your state. Once you know the case name and citation, you are ready to actually look up the case. Cases are compiled in volumes called "case reports," "reports" or "reporters." Ask you librarian where these reports are located and how to find the case you're looking for.

Legal Research Note: Nolo's *Legal Research: How To Find and Understand the Law* (Elias) and its video, *Legal Research Made Easy: A Roadmap through the Law Library Maze,* thoroughly explain how to accomplish all the tasks mentioned here.

E. A Review of Unauthorized Practice Litigation of the Past Twenty-Five Years

Before you can use the legal system to fight back, it's wise to learn what others in a similar situation have accomplished. To this end, let's go back a couple of decades and briefly outline how the unauthorized practice battle has unfolded. Note that while 25 years ago most judicial decisions involved the sale of self-help law books and kits, as we get closer to the present, this type of activity is much less subject to official question, and courts and prosecutors have become more concerned with IPs providing legal advice.

1967 The New York Court of Appeals (the highest N.Y. court) overturns the conviction of Norman Dacey, the nonlawyer author of *How to Avoid Probate* (Crown Books), holding that the publication and sale of a book about how a lay person can accomplish legal procedures did not constitute unauthorized practice. *N.Y. County Lawyers' Association v. Dacey*, 234 N.E.2d 459 (1967).

1973 The Florida Supreme Court holds that the inclusion of printed instructions along with legal forms constitutes the unlawful practice of law, but that the sale of naked forms by nonlawyers without instructions is okay. *Florida Bar v. American Legal and Business Forms*, Inc., 274 So.2d 225 (1973).

1975 Advertisement, publication and sale of legal forms and instructions was upheld as long as there was no personal contact between purchaser and seller. *Oregon State Bar v. Gilchrist*, 538 P.2d 913 (1975).

1976 The Michigan Supreme Court arrives at the same conclusion as Gilchrist, but several justices write extraordinary separate opinions. One of these cogently argues that offering personal help in filling out divorce forms, in addition to selling them, should not constitute unauthorized practice. *State Bar v. Cramer*, 399 Mich. 116 (1976).

1976 Colorado allows the preparation of divorce forms by an independent paralegal if the functions carried out are only those of a scrivener. In other words, if the form preparer sticks absolutely to the role of a public stenographer and takes down the customer's words verbatim, she is not guilty of practicing law without a license. While this case is worded conservatively, it basically allows independent paralegals to operate above ground in Colorado. *Colorado Bar Assn. v. Miles*, 557 P.2d 1202 (1976).

1978 A California Superior Court arrives at substantially the same conclusion, allowing scrivener services, as did the Colorado court in the Miles case. *State Bar v. Benson,* EA-C 16879 (Superior Court Los Angeles County, 1978).

1978 The Florida Supreme Court reverses its 1973 ruling discussed above and allows the sale of legal forms along with written instructions and personal contact between buyer and seller, provided the seller only copies information supplied by customers. *Florida Bar v. Brumbaugh,* 355 So.2d 1186 (1978).

1978 Missouri, Kansas and New York courts refuse to allow personal contact between an independent paralegal and customers, although both say sale of forms and explanatory materials is okay. In *McGiffert v. State ex rel. Stowe,* 366 So.2d 680 (1978), an Alabama court holds that advertising services to obtain divorce "without attorney's fee" by a nonlicensed person is unauthorized practice.

1984 The Arizona state legislature repeals its statute that prohibits UPL. Although there is still a court rule prohibiting UPL, there has essentially been no UPL enforcement since 1984 and independent paralegals and publishers of self-help legal form books and kits have captured much of the business of preparing legal forms for divorce and other basic legal services.

1984 California disbands its state unauthorized practice office and leaves enforcement of unauthorized practice laws to local district attorneys. Except in cases of fraud or misrepresentation, this means that in the years ahead, little enforcement of unauthorized practice will take place in California outside of a few counties where the bar is able to influence the district attorney to initiate criminal prosecutions.

1984 Independent paralegal Rosemary Furman is held in contempt of court and sentenced to jail for violating an injunction ordering her not to engage in unauthorized practice, which among other things consisted of giving nonlawyers procedural advice and typing forms. Furman's request for a jury trial is denied. *Florida Bar v. Furman,* 451 So.2d 808 (1984). Giving up on Florida's outrageously pro-lawyer procedures, she takes her campaign against lawyers' monopolistic practices to a national audience via television, personal appearances, etc. (See Furman interview in the Appendix.) The Florida governor eventually commutes Furman's sentence on condition that she cease running her typing service.

1985 The State Bar of Wisconsin stops handling both attorney discipline and unauthorized practice cases because it fears that to continue to do so would place it in jeopardy of being sued for violating anti-trust laws.

1985 A number of states begin to follow the lead of California and enact simplified procedures for divorce, child support collections, will preparation, and other tasks, specifically designed to eliminate the need for lawyers. This trend towards state-sponsored self-help legal remedies gives increased validity to the argument of independent paralegals that many routine legal services can be safely accomplished without lawyer help.

1985 The Washington State Supreme Court concludes that the drafting of contracts to buy and sell real estate by brokers does not constitute the
unauthorized practice of law. The public, the court reasons, is better
served by the freedom to choose from a range of providers, even if this
means nonlawyers perform functions traditionally reserved by the legal
profession. *Cultum v. Heritage House Realtors, Inc.,* 694 P.2d, 630
(1985).

1986 The American Bar Association's Commission on Professionalism recom-
mends the limited licensing of paralegals to provide such services as
real estate closings, simple wills, etc. Although there is little active follow-up, the fact that the ABA no longer seems interested in crusading
against nonlawyer form preparers is important.

1987 Recognizing the huge, unmet need for moderately-priced immigration
counseling, California authorizes non-lawyer immigration consultants to
operate as long as they disclose in writing that they are not lawyers. Cal.
Business & Professions Code § 27420.

1987 The Florida Supreme Court states that it is not UPL for IPs to engage in
limited oral communications to help individuals complete court-
approved legal forms.

1988 The California Public Protection Committee, appointed in 1986 by the
state bar to investigate public harm from nonlawyer legal services and
to determine if regulation of the nonlawyer providers would be appropriate, concluded that the state UPL laws should be repealed and that
"legal technicians" (IPs) should be allowed to perform certain legal services provided that the IPs register and inform clients that they are not
lawyers.

1990 In 1989, the California State Bar, acknowledging that a vast number of
Californians do not have reasonable access to the legal process, authorized the Commission on Legal Technicians to determine guidelines for
the practice and regulation of IPs. This commission issued a report in
1990, recommending that qualified (meaning regulated) IPs should be
allowed to engage in the limited practice of law in the areas of bankruptcy, family, and landlord and tenant law. The State Bar, apparently
not liking what the report says, buries it.

1990 In a Nevada Case, the court states that it is not UPL for a legal scrivener
service to offer forms and procedures that induce self-reliance by the
customer. However, if the customer relies on the express or implied ex-

pertise of the IP form preparation service, it is unlawful practice. *State Bar of Nevada v. Johnson et al.,* No. CV89-5814 (Nev. 2nd Dist. Ct., April 12, 1990).

1990 A Wisconsin bankruptcy court, invoking its own inherent power to determine what constitutes UPL, states that unauthorized actions include providing counseling, advice and recommendations with respect to any provision of the Bankruptcy Code. In this case, although the IP claimed to do nothing more than sell forms and provide a typing service, the court found that the IP exercised legal judgment in counseling the customer, among other things, as to which property exemptions should be chosen. In Re: *John M. Webster v. Rodney A. Larson,* 120 Bankr. 111 (1990).

1991 The Florida Supreme Court (Rule 10-1.1(b)) approves a series of basic divorce and other legal forms specifically designed to be prepared by nonlawyers.

1992 Legislation to legalize IPs is defeated in Oregon, California and other states. Supporters vow to keep fighting.

1993 The American Bar Association, in a publication entitled "Self-Representation in Divorce Cases," finds that in Maricopa County, Arizona (the area of the ABA study), at least one party was not represented by a lawyer in 90% of divorce cases. And in over half, both parties represented themselves.

1993 In a speech to the American Bar Association, U.S. Attorney General Janet Reno endorses the idea of nonlawyers providing basic legal information and form preparation.

1994 The judiciary committees of both houses of the California Legisature pass a bill allowing IPs to register with the state as part of a two-year study looking into whether further regulation of the booming IP business in California is needed.

F. The Constitution and the Independent Paralegal[16]

This is not the place for a detailed scholarly treatise weighing all the constitutional theories that underlie the bar's efforts to proscribe the activities of nonlawyer competitors, including independent paralegals. The subject has already been ably covered by a number of law review articles. Again, one of the best of these is "Unauthorized Practice," by Deborah Rhode, in Volume 34:1 of the Stanford Law Review.[17] In addition, what is ultimately judged to be constitutional in this area is almost sure to be influenced more by changing societal views as to the right of the average person to gain affordable access to legal services than it will by the study of old cases.

---

[16]A number of legal commentators believe that direct enforcement actions by state and local bar associations also violate the Sherman Anti-Trust Act. We do not discuss this here because of the rapid move by most bar associations to back off from direct enforcement of unauthorized practice actions, instead referring these proceedings to state supreme courts or to the local prosecutor.

[17]Another excellent general article challenging the bar's assertion that it needs to regulate independent paralegals is Christensen, "The Unauthorized Practice of Law: Do Good Fences Really Make Good Neighbors—or Even Good Sense?," *American Bar Foundation Research Journal* (Spring 1980).

Just the same, it's wise for all independent paralegals to understand a little about how the constitution relates to organized lawyerdom's continuing drive to protect its monopoly power over the legal system. Let's start our discussion by asking a basic question. Where does the United States Constitution say that only lawyers can legally help the public prepare their own legal paperwork or, for that matter, accomplish other "legal" tasks?

The answer, of course, is that the Constitution doesn't mention the subject. Why, then, haven't organized lawyerdom's activities long since been held as an obvious restriction of the free speech right of independent paralegals, or an unwarranted intrusion on the right of the public to petition their government by representing themselves in court?[18]

Organized lawyerdom justifies its right to regulate independent paralegals under the rather vague umbrella of the Constitution's police power. Legislatures and courts, lawyers contend, have a legitimate interest in regulating the quality of legal services available to the public. This public interest rationale, it should be noted, has long been accepted as establishing a constitutional basis to regulate the First Amendment rights (freedom of speech, etc.) of all sorts of other groups, from teachers and bill collectors to operators of toxic waste dumps.

Specifically, when it comes to justifying their right to ban independent paralegals, lawyers claim that because independent paralegals are not subject to bar association rules of conduct, examinations for competence, educational standards and the protections guaranteed clients by the lawyer-client relationship (whatever they are), there is a substantial risk that IPs will provide the public with an unacceptably low quality of service.

This rationale falls apart for two principal reasons. First, there is little evidence that existing unregulated IPs pose a greater threat to the public than

---

[18]In this context, the United States Supreme Court has ruled that if prisoners are denied the right to legal help in preparing habeas corpus petitions, they must be afforded a reasonable alternative. *Johnson v. Avery,* 393 U.S. 483 (1969). Shouldn't ordinary citizens who can't afford the high prices charged by lawyers be allowed to take advantage of low cost alternatives to gain access to the legal forum their tax dollars support? For more on this access argument, see "On Letting the Laity Litigate: The Petition Clause and Unauthorized Practice Rules," *Univ. of Penn. Law Review,* Vol. 132 (1984).

do lawyers, as they are now regulated (loosely at best) by bar associations. Second, the fact that paralegals are not subject to regulation is an argument for regulation, not absolute prohibition of their entire business.

In addition, it is fair to ask whether the rules lawyers operate under are adequate to guarantee the public a competent level of service. After all, the rationale behind banning nonlawyers falls apart pretty quickly if lawyers themselves can't demonstrate competence. So the question becomes: Can they?

Given that lawyers do not learn basic form preparation skills in law school, are not tested on these skills on the multistate bar exam, and serve no apprenticeship to practicing lawyers, the answer is clearly no. There is absolutely no evidence that lawyers can competently handle legal form preparation services. Indeed, with close to 100,000 formal consumer complaints being filed against lawyers each year, it is reasonable to conclude that lawyers should be better trained and tested.

By contrast, attempts by bar investigators in several states to unearth complaints against IPs have been notably unsuccessful. Indeed, at several public hearings by the California Bar's Public Protection Committee, and the Commission on Legal Technicians, far more members of the public showed up to complain about lack of lawyer competence than testified against IPs. In its report of April 1988, the Public Protection Committee found that "there are a number of highly qualified and dedicated legal technicians [IPs] who deliver valuable assistance for fair consideration."

Similarly, a number of years ago, when title companies began to fill out real estate documents, the Colorado Supreme Court found "no convincing evidence that the massive changeover in the performance of this service from attorneys to title companies has been accompanied by any great loss, detriment or inconvenience to the public. The uncontroverted evidence was that lawyers for this simple operation considerably slowed the loan closings and cost the persons involved a great deal of money."[19]

Barlow Christensen, in his study of unauthorized practice published in the American Bar Foundation's Research Journal (Spring 1980) concludes:

Suppression of the practice of law by nonlawyers has been proclaimed to be in the public interest, a necessary protection against incompetence,

---

[19]*Conway-Bogue Realty Investment Co. v. Denver Bar Association,* 312 P.2d 998 (1957).

divided loyalties, and other evils. But this interest of the public is one that has been defined, articulated, promulgated, and enforced not by the public but by the legal profession. And nowhere, in all of the literature or in any of the court decisions, is there evidence of a public voice with respect to this supposed public interest.

Even if we assume that the independent paralegal movement does present a threat to American consumers because an occasional paralegal might provide poor service, is this a sufficient constitutional justification for the prohibition against all independent paralegal activity currently advocated by organized lawyerdom? Probably not. More reasonably, it supports regulating paralegals with legitimate and fair rules that really do protect the public, not the legal profession.

How to regulate IPs in the public interest. In Chapter 15, I discuss the HALT-sponsored Legal Technicians Bill, which provides a regulatory scheme for independent paralegals.

There are three reasons why current unauthorized practice regulations are unconstitutional and should have been adjudged to be so long ago. The first has to do with the vague and self-serving nature of the basic statutory definition of the unauthorized practice of law. As noted earlier in this chapter, most states define the practice of law as either being something lawyers customarily do, or something it takes a lawyer's knowledge to do, or something it takes more than ordinary intelligence and knowledge to do, or something you have to get a license to do, or all four. These definitions are so hopelessly circular, vague and ambiguous that they fail to fairly inform either the IP or the general public as to what conduct is prohibited.[20]

A second and even more powerful reason why most restrictions on IP activities are unconstitutional involves their violation of the U.S. Constitution's

---

[20]To illustrate, consider that in some states (let's call them "Type A" states), real estate brokers have traditionally prepared property deeds, while in others ("Type B" states) this task has customarily been accomplished by lawyers. Does this mean Type B states can constitutionally charge a real estate broker who prepares a deed with unauthorized practice because lawyers normally do this work, but State A states can't, because lawyers haven't traditionally handled it?

First Amendment guarantee of freedom of speech. This argument has been most prominently advanced by Stephen Elias, an author and leader of the self-help law movement, in a book entitled *Fed Up With the Legal System: What's Wrong and How to Fix It* (Nolo Press). Elias writes:

> *Information—especially information about how to approach and use the organs of our government—is the lifeblood of a democracy. The more freely such information flows, the better the democracy works. Blockages tend to unfairly concentrate power in the hands of the privileged.*
>
> *Today we face a legal access crisis precisely because information about how to approach and use our courts moves sluggishly if at all. It is dammed up by a class of professionals known as lawyers. In all states except Arizona, lawyers have used their power to enact statutes restricting to lawyers the right to provide legal information designed to solve an individual's legal needs. And in all but a few states, the laws go on to provide that a nonlawyer who gives legal advice has committed a crime punishable by imprisonment.*
>
> *Almost no other type of speech has ever been similarly forbidden in advance to the public. The reason is clear. Prohibitions on disseminating information are almost always ruled to be unconstitutional violations of the First Amendment, which forbids any law that abridges the freedom of speech. This is especially true when it comes to speech about how to deal with public bodies such as Congress, state legislatures, and administrative agencies. There is no good reason to treat the courts differently than any other organ of government.*
>
> *Courts have allowed only a handful of narrow exceptions to this near-absolute rule prohibiting advance restrictions to free speech. Obscenity, incitement to violence and false speech (libel, slander, fraud) are examples of the kinds of speech that the government may legally abridge. The government also may restrict commercial speech, such as advertising, if the restriction directly serves substantial state interests and the restriction is in reasonable proportion to the interests served.*
>
> *If speech does not fall within these types of exceptions, it is fully protected under the First Amendment. It may be restricted only if the government has a compelling interest for doing so and the restriction is as narrowly tailored as possible to satisfy the compelling interest.*

*The U.S. Supreme Court has ruled that legal advice is fully protected speech rather than commercial speech, even though the legal advice is given for a fee. (*Board of Trustees, State University of New York v. Fox, *492 U.S. 469 (1989).) That means that the government must have a compelling interest in stopping nonlawyers from giving legal advice. It's a tough standard to meet.*

Consumer protection is the reason usually advanced by the legal profession to justify handing it the exclusive right to give legal advice. According to this view, poor legal advice can cause such serious harm that a license should be required of those who provide it. Numerous studies of this issue, however, have shown that this fear is unwarranted. No study has produced concrete evidence that legal advice from nonlawyers causes more harm than that sold it by licensed lawyers.

When you think about it, denying consumers who can't afford a lawyer the right to purchase legal advice from more affordable sources is a ridiculous way to protect them. The argument put forth by lawyers' groups seems to be that it is better for most consumers to have no legal advice than for some to receive advice that may be wrong. Interestingly, this argument is raised by lawyers, almost never by consumers, and lawyers persist in making it even though there have been very few complaints about existing nonlawyer legal form preparation businesses. It's as if accountants and tax lawyers could put H&R Block and other tax preparers out of business because they didn't approve of their training or level of advice.

Thus there seems to be no compelling reason to deny nonlawyers the right to offer the public information about our laws and courts. But even if there were a compelling interest, the method of regulation—barring everyone but lawyers from giving legal advice—is much broader than it needs to be. For example, the term "legal advice" is never clearly defined in the laws that forbid nonlawyers from giving it. This means that when a complaint against a nonlawyer is made, a judge (also a lawyer, of course) has no reasonable standard to use when deciding whether or not legal advice was given. As a result, unauthorized practice laws make criminals out of anyone who utters words that might, even after the fact, be interpreted as legal advice by a court. This sort of blanket censorship of all unlicensed legal advice is surely as blatant a violation of the First Amendment as you'll ever find.

So the question becomes, is their an alternative approach to regulating who provides legal information to the public, that doesn't violate the First Amendment, but still provides a reasonable level of consumer protection. The answer is yes.

States can and should continue to regulate the legal profession even as they decriminalize legal advice by nonlawyers. People who wish to call themselves lawyers and represent others in court would still have to qualify for this privilege. However, people who choose not to go this route would not be prosecuted for giving legal advice.

This is a workable, sensible system; it is exactly the way most states now regulate the accounting profession. You may call yourself a Certified Public Accountant if you meet the state's qualifications; otherwise you are free to give tax preparation, bookkeeping or accounting advice as long as you don't use the CPA label. Consumers are free to choose a CPA, and pay a higher rate for the expertise the label carries with it, or consult someone without the CPA credential who probably charges less.

But what happens if a non-lawyer provides poor services or gives bad advice? If a customer loses money because of wrong legal advice given by a nonlawyer, the complaint could and should be addressed under the same consumer protection rules that are applied to other similar businesses. Dissatisfied customers could sue in small claims or regular court for damages, or ask local prosecutors—or a more specialized regulatory agency if one becomes appropriate—to shut down businesses that make a practice of dispensing shoddy legal advice. Incidentally, this is exactly what happens if you are wronged by a lawyer.

A third powerful reason why traditional unauthorized practice regulations are unconstitutional has to do with the manner in which bar associations prosecute people who they believe are guilty of the unauthorized practice of law. Even assuming that legislatures, and in some circumstances courts, are entitled to reasonably regulate how IPs fill out legal forms, organized lawyerdom must still meet a reasonable standard of fairness (due process) when it comes to enforcing its rules. This is not being done anywhere today.

As outlined above, actions against independent paralegals are commonly instituted not in a criminal proceeding in which the IP has the right to a jury trial, but by bar committees made up primarily or exclusively of lawyers or, more typically, by judicial officials acting on bar association complaints. This was the situation faced by Rosemary Furman in Florida. (See Rosemary Furman interview in Appendix.) In either instance, the complaint leading to bar or court action is almost always from a member of the legal profession angry at low-cost competition, not from a consumer with a legitimate beef. And in some situations, especially where bar associations try to order IPs out of business on their own initiative, everyone involved in the process of investigating and sanctioning the independent paralegal (a decision usually made in secret) is an attorney with a pecuniary interest in suppressing nonlawyer competition. In other professions, courts have not allowed such interested parties to have absolute regulatory power. For example, in *Gibson v. Berryhill*, 331 F.Supp. 122 (1971) aff'd, 411 U.S. 564 (1973), a federal court held that a board made up of optometrists in private practice wasn't sufficiently impartial to be allowed to prohibit another optometrist from working for a corporation.

Also, as noted earlier, in many instances, before official action to go after an IP is taken, a bar committee or court first threatens the independent paralegal in an "informal" proceeding. Thus, the independent paralegal often finds herself in the surreal situation of being called to account by a group of lawyers, told to stay off their turf, and threatened with a fine and jail, all as part of an extra-judicial proceeding in which the independent paralegal has no fair way to defend her conduct. It's worthy of note that in other areas of American life, including the regulation of books claimed to be pornographic, where First Amendment rights were being restricted by quasi-official, but essentially private, review boards, the U.S. Supreme Court has found a constitutional violation.[21]

If actions by lawyers to suppress non-lawyer competition are so obviously biased, why aren't there court decisions saying they are unconstitutional? Partly because lawyers' groups are adept at backing off in situations when a court case might produce a bad precedent, and partly because very few independent paralegals have had enough financial resources to fully litigate the issue. But mostly because judges, blinded by their claim of absolute power over the legal system based on the "inherent powers" doctrine (see Section C above), have so far applied a biased standard of what constitutes fair procedure. Indeed, the current legal standards and procedures applied to people who compete with lawyers are so unfair that, sooner or later, they are bound to be ruled in violation of both First Amendment guarantees of free speech and the U.S. Constitution's due process clause.

Let's shift gears now and assume for a moment that to be constitutional, regulation of paralegals must be strictly limited to rules necessary to protect American people from incompetent work done by untrained people and that these rules must be both fairly and impartially administered. What might such a regulation scheme look like?[22]

- Legal recognition of the fact that every citizen's right to self-representation and reasonable access to the courts necessarily includes the right to get competent help from reasonably-priced service providers.

- State unauthorized practice of law regulations should be strictly limited so that they do not prohibit the preparation of routine legal forms, and the giving of common sense procedural and factual advice needed to prepare such forms.

- For form preparation in more complicated legal areas where there is a higher possibility of consumer harm, registration and licensure of IPs may make limited sense. But all state-imposed requirements should have a clear logical relationship between the task to be performed and the requirements needed to perform it. For example, if an IP must pass a test as a condition of qualifying for a license, the test should be tightly based

---

[21]*Bantam Books Inc. v. Sullivan,* 372 U.S. 58 (1963).

[22]See Chapter 15 for a discussion of the HALT bill currently being considered in California and Oregon.

on the skill the IP needs to carry out the particular form preparation task. (An IP who applies for a license to help customers prepare probate papers should be tested on that skill and not on general legal knowledge or principles.)

- Administration of any regulatory system dealing with independent paralegals should not be left in the hands of bar associations, state supreme courts or other lawyers' groups who have a clear bias in favor of suppressing competition. Instead, any regulations should be administered by a consumer agency in the public interest. Adding a minority of lay people to existing bar association unauthorized practice committees or turning enforcement power over to the judiciary does not accomplish this goal.

How To Do Your Job And Stay Out of Jail

Given the inherently fuzzy boundaries of what constitutes the "unauthorized practice of law," how do you protect yourself? There are no foolproof ways to avoid attacks by organized lawyerdom, but you can greatly reduce your vulnerability if you consistently do three things:

1. Tell the world you are not a lawyer,
2. Provide your customers access to the basic legal information necessary to make their own decisions, and
3. Limit yourself to legal form preparation—don't give legal advice.

A. Tell the World You Are Not a Lawyer

Making it clear that you are not licensed to practice law is not only an honest way to run your business, it protects you from the charge that you have fraudulently misrepresented your services. In addition, a strong statement making it clear that you are an IP typing service or legal technician, not a lawyer, will establish one essential part of your defense should you ever be charged with unauthorized practice.

If organized lawyerdom, through a bar association, public prosecutor, state court, or a state regulatory body, such as the Department of Consumer Affairs or Bureau of Professional Standards, ever scrutinizes your business, the first thing it will look at is whether you make it absolutely clear you are not a lawyer. In this context, it's not enough that you don't use the word "lawyer" or "attorney" in your advertisements. The thing organized lawyerdom will look for is whether a potential customer reading your promotional material, or coming to your place of business, is clearly and unequivocally put on notice that you are not a lawyer, and that you do not provide legal expertise.[1]

When you think about it, making sure you are squeaky clean when it comes to informing the public that you help consumers prepare legal forms, but are not an attorney and do not give legal advice, is reasonable. Incidentally, this isn't a big hardship from a business point of view either, since the majority of your customers will seek you out precisely because you don't charge lawyer prices or have lawyer attitudes.

---

[1] In *State Bar of Nevada v. Johnson,* No. CV89-5814 (Nev. 2nd Dist. Ct., April 12, 1990), the judge repeatedly emphasizes the importance of legal typing services (IPs) making it clear to the public that they are not lawyers and do not practice law.

Think of it this way. If you consult a person who claims to be a CPA, or a chef "trained in Paris," or a "juggler" who used to work for the Ringling Brothers Circus, you expect that person to tell the truth about his background. If the "CPA" in fact turns out to be a tax preparer who has taken a few accounting courses, the "chef" worked for a week washing dishes at a fast food place in Paris, Illinois, and the "juggler's" job at Ringling Brothers involved following an elephant with a shovel, you are likely to feel ripped off, and justifiably so. This isn't to say that you might not choose a non-CPA tax preparer in the first place. You well might. But you're entitled to the information that lets you make the choice knowingly.

Here are some detailed suggestions as to how to tell the world you are not a lawyer:

Business Name: I present a detailed discussion of good and bad business names in Chapter 5. For now, the main point is to choose a name for your business that cannot possibly be read to imply that you are a lawyer. The best way to do this is to emphasize "self-help" in your title.

Promotional Materials: All brochures and flyers you distribute should clearly state that you are not a lawyer. This message should not be buried in the text, but set out, near the top, in at least 10-point boldface type. Something like this works well: "The ABC Self-Help Typing Service is not staffed by lawyers and does not give legal advice."

Logos and Stationery: Your stationery and, if you use one, your logo, should reinforce your message that you are a self-help typing service. Prominent use of the term "self-help" is an excellent way to do this. Thus, The Jefferson County Typing Service might add to its stationery a line such as this: "Quality Nonlawyer Form Preparation for Self-Help Divorce and Bankruptcy."

In choosing a logo, you'll particularly want to avoid using the scales of justice or similar symbols associated with lawyers. Instead, why not choose a graphic image that reinforces the idea of people helping themselves.

Advertisements and Circulars: If you use print, radio or TV ads (see Chapter 10, "Marketing Your Services"), you will probably not be able to afford to include a lengthy statement that you are not a lawyer and do not provide legal expertise. Fortunately, there are several cost-efficient ways to get your point across. One is to emphasize the self-help aspect of your service. For example, instead of titling an ad "Divorce" or "Bankruptcy," you might say "Divorce Yourself" or "Do Your Own Bankruptcy," incorporating the concept of self-help directly into your sales message. If your business name already embodies this concept, so much the better.

Here is a newspaper advertisement for an independent paralegal business that I feel does a poor job of notifying the public that no lawyers are involved:

The problem with this ad is that it nowhere informs the public that it is a nonlawyer typing service. Although it can be argued that the name "Legal Alternatives, Inc." informs the public that no lawyers are involved, this is far from obvious (there are lots of alternatives in the world, including alternative lawyers), and a prosecutor or bar association would probably contend that the prominent use of the word "legal" is likely to confuse the public.

Here is an excerpt from a flyer that does a much better job of informing the public that the paralegal business doesn't involve attorney services:

SELF-HELP DIVORCE CENTER

A sensible non-lawyer alternative since 1972

You Make The Decisions, We Do The Paperwork

- ■ We type forms for: Legal divorce, annulment and legal separation

- ■ Our fees are reasonable: our basic charge is $90-$180 (+ court filing fee)

- ■ Our typing service is efficient and reliable

If you have already decided on divorce and have a good grasp of the legal and practical rules and procedures you face, you do not necessarily need the services of an attorney. If you can make your own decisions about property, custody, support; and if your spouse does not hire an attorney to contest the divorce, you can sensibly get your own legal divorce without a lawyer.

Employees at the Self-Help Divorce Center are trained to record your decisions on the proper divorce forms. Taking it step-by-step, we type your divorce papers under your guidance and instruction and send them to you as you need them. We rely on the book *How To Do Your Own Divorce in California,* by Attorney Ed Sherman, and recommend that you carefully read it.

SELF-HELP DIVORCE CENTER

870 Main Street, Suite 10
Lexington, CA 94450

(In the Bradley Building across from Macys Park at Eighth and Main)

Monday-Friday   •   Evening and Saturday appointments available
904-5757   •   432-4485

Office Signs: It is essential that you prominently display a sign in your office making it clear who you are and what you do. A straightforward plaque mounted on your waiting room or office wall that says something like the following will do the job.

ACME TYPING:
A NONLAWYER FORM PREPARATION SERVICE

The Acme Typing Service is designed to help non-lawyers prepare their own paperwork to file their own bankruptcy, divorce, step-parent adoption, and other uncontested legal actions. You make all legal and practical decisions. Our role is to prepare the necessary paperwork under your direction. We are not lawyers and do not give legal advice. If you are unsure about any of the legal aspects of your case, please see a lawyer.

Why is it necessary to display a sign if your ads and flyers make it clear that you are not a lawyer? Because it is an extremely convenient way to document that you've made every effort to tell the public that you are not a lawyer and do not provide legal services. If you still aren't convinced, think of it this way: lawyers, who after all are past masters at elevating form over substance, truly believe in the power of disclaimers. Remember, they are the ones who get paid to write all those little warnings on the back of everything from parking lot tickets to new car purchase agreements by which customers must disclaim all sorts of rights and accept dozens of unpalatable responsibilities. Again, the point is simple—lawyers will have a difficult time claiming (and more important, a judge will have even more trouble concluding) that you are misleading the public if you constantly and obviously emphasize that you aren't a lawyer and that your customers must accept the responsibility that comes with doing their own legal work.

Signed Statements: While office signs, truth in advertising and promotional materials emphasizing that you are not a lawyer are important, they are not a substitute for your most important self-protection device. This is a written statement signed by all your customers clearly acknowledging three things:

1. You aren't a lawyer,
2. Your customers are representing themselves and have access to the legal materials necessary to make their own informed decisions, and
3. Your role is limited to preparing legal forms under your customers' direction.

Each statement should be signed in duplicate (or immediately photo-copied) during the initial customer interview, with one copy given to the customer and the other retained in your permanent file. If you deal with customers who aren't fluent in English, all statements, signs, information and disclaimers should also be available in Spanish, Chinese, Vietnamese, or other relevant languages or dialects. You may find it convenient to make this signed statement part of a more detailed information sheet, which establishes the price of your services and some details about how your business works. However you present it, it should read something like this:

IMPORTANT INFORMATION ABOUT THE ACME TYPING SERVICE

The Acme Typing Service is a secretarial service designed to assist people who want to do their own legal paperwork, for ___[divorces]__ , _____[incorporations]_____ , and _____[bankruptcies]_____. We are not lawyers and do not give legal advice. It is up to you to inform yourself as to the laws and procedures that affect your situation and to make your own legal decisions. To this end, we recommend the following publications: ___[enter names of best self-help manuals]___ .

The role of the Acme Typing Service is solely to prepare legal paperwork following your instructions.

I have read and accept the foregoing statement of Acme Typing Service policy.

I have a copy of *How To Do Your Own Divorce in California,* by Attorney Ed Sherman, and have read it carefully.

_____　　　_____
Date　　　　　　　　　　　　Signature

Nobody at Northside Secretarial Service has represented herself to be an Attorney. I have neither sought nor received legal advice. It is my intention to represent myself in Court and I have paid my fee for secretarial service ONLY.

_____   _____
Date   Signature

Get information in the customer's own handwriting: In Chapter 8, I discuss many of the techniques necessary to running a quality legal typing business. One of these is either to get all factual information in the customer's own handwriting or, if it's necessary to employ an oral interview technique, to have your customer check all the information you collect and sign a statement that it is correct.

Why is it best to have your customers provide information in their own handwriting? Because if you are ever charged with unauthorized practice, your best line of defense will be that you prepared legal forms under the direction of your customer. Being able to produce all key information in your customer's handwriting will make it far easier to document that your customer, not you, supplied the necessary information.

If you don't believe this can be important, consider these guidelines set out in U.S. Bankruptcy Judge A. Jay Cristol's opinion in the case of *In re Bachman* (# 881-04588, Southern District of Florida, 1990):

> *Typing services...may type bankruptcy forms for their clients, provided they only copy the written information furnished by clients...A problem arises when information is taken orally...it is suggested that typing services may take information from clients orally, provided that they record the conversations and preserve the tapes.*

B. Provide Your Customers Access to the Basic Legal Information Necessary to Make Their Own Decisions

Legal form preparers who run afoul of organized lawyerdom usually do so because they directly transfer legal expertise to their customers. Or put another way, they act like junior lawyers.[2] Fortunately, because of the wealth of good quality self-help legal information currently on the market, there is no need to do this. The IP's role should be to identify, gather and sell the legal material their customers will need to make their own informed decisions. If the IP limits himself to typing forms under his customers' directions, he should not be vulnerable to charges of UPL.

Several years ago, because of the lack of legal material directed to the nonlawyer, referring the customers to written information to answer questions was difficult. Today, however, as a result of the proliferation of self-help law articles, books, and computer software, as well as the simultaneous development of many simplified materials for lawyers that are reasonably accessible to nonlawyers, it is much easier. To follow this approach, your first job as an independent paralegal is to locate legal information that will answer the common substantive legal questions your customers ask. Once you do, it's best to keep this material in your office for your customers to look at or, if for some reason doing this is impossible, you will want to tell them where to get it.

---

[2] In Florida, by order of the Florida Supreme Court, a nonlawyer who clearly discloses that he or she isn't a lawyer may prepare court-approved divorce, child support, landlord-tenant and some other forms free of fear of UPL charges.

Sometimes even one or two good books will answer most questions in a particular field. For example *How to File for Bankruptcy,* by Elias, Leonard & Renauer (Nolo Press), is a detailed "how-to" guide for people who wish to file a Chapter 7 bankruptcy. It does not deal with every complication that can arise in a bankruptcy, but it does very thoroughly answer routine questions. Because it is such a good resource, it makes sense to require that every bankruptcy customer own it, even if you must supply the book yourself and add a few dollars to your typing fee to cover it.

But isn't the approach of referring customers to written materials so that they can get answers to questions more cumbersome than simply answering them in the first place? Sure, but especially in the parts of the country where organized lawyerdom is determined to suppress independent paralegals, it is also an essential strategy to your survival. In addition, you should understand that many of the self-help legal materials currently on the market are of good quality and will empower your customers to do better legal work. In other words, taking the little bit of extra trouble to help your customers use good self-help law materials as part of your business will not only provide you with a good measure of legal protection, it will enhance your customer satisfaction, and therefore your business.

As you take the time to help your customers educate themselves, consider that this approach can be markedly superior to that followed by most lawyers. Traditionally, lawyers have often preferred to tell their clients what to do, while simultaneously hoarding the basic legal information necessary to sensibly question the advice. For example, should a client ask how much spousal support is reasonable in a given situation, a typical lawyer will provide a dollar figure, with no explanation of the laws and practice that make that number (and often a whole range of alternative numbers) make sense. Even worse, the fact that the lawyer has a financial incentive to choose a dollar figure high enough to inflame the other spouse and result in extended litigation (and therefore a higher lawyer fee) will never be disclosed. By contrast, an IP who answers the same question by providing the customer with an up-to-date written discussion of spousal support laws and practices provides a superior service. This is especially true if the written materials are keyed to a number of different fact situations and present a reasonable range of support amounts appropriate for each.

Okay, let's assume that I have convinced you of the desirability of making written materials available to your customers and that you have located the necessary books, articles, or software. The next question is, how do you get them into the hands of your customers? Here are several strategies:

Sell the book: If an excellent self-help book is available in a particular legal area, such as an up-to-date, easy-to-understand, small business incorporation manual designed specifically for your state, you will want to sell it. In fact, for your own self-protection, you will probably wish to require every customer to buy it and state in writing that they have read it. Because I am a long-time publisher of self-help law books and make most of my living selling them, you may want to discount this advice as being self-interested and hence unreliable. I am convinced, however, that if you do, you are likely to regret your decision. Why? Because, again, at the risk of being repetitive, the self-help law book allows you not only to put solid information into the hands of your customers, but to lay the groundwork in advance for one of the few effective defenses available should you be prosecuted for unauthorized practice. This is simply that a customer has the right to purchase an independently published self-help law book (whose publication is protected by the First Amendment) and, using the information it contains, tell you how to prepare his or her legal forms.

If you face a particularly uptight situation with the local bar, you may not want to sell any legal material yourself on the theory that the more separate you are from the way in which your customer gets legal information, the better off you are should there be a lawyer-initiated investigation of your operations. While this extra degree of care is no longer necessary in the many states where IPs are well-established, it is still a good idea in states where stamping out unauthorized practice is still a maniacal concern of organized lawyerdom. Following this approach, you would arrange for a local book store or office supply store (many already carry legal forms), or another nearby merchant, to stock the book in volume, and then refer customers to that store.

Set up your own small library: Most IP's report that they hear the same legal questions over and over again. For example, people who are filing for divorce, and who have minor children, will often ask what rules govern child custody. If there are self-help law books available that detail these rules, you should have them in your own library. In addition, you will want to gather other legal materials suitable for use by your customers. In Oregon, Robin Smith of People's Paralegal Service keeps copies of a court decision and several articles from Oregon legal publications that clearly set out child custody rules. In other legal areas, People's Paralegal has similar materials available, thus allowing customers the opportunity to educate themselves.[3]

Use legal information phone lines: A number of companies have established legal information phone services. For two or three dollars per minute, charged to a credit card, a caller can have a lawyer answer legal questions. In theory, these services are a wonderful resource for the independent paralegal as they provide a ready source of legal information for confused customers and free the independent paralegal from the temptation of providing legal information. Sadly, a number of these phone answer services are essentially scams run by lawyers who profit not by answering questions, but by talking clients into buying their services or referring them to other lawyers for a fee. When a self-helper calls, the service tries to talk them out of handling their own action.

Fortunately, there are at least two phone services that do provide reliable, up-to-date legal information and are supportive of self-help efforts.

Tele-Lawyer: Offers information on a wide range of consumer law areas, including bankruptcy, credit problems and, for many but not all states, divorce and other family law concerns:

800-835-3529 (credit card calls in California)

900-283-5529 (credit card calls outside of California)

Divorce Helpline: A California-only service that specializes in helping people to do their own California divorces, including help in calculating child support obligations, pension fund values and the ownership interests of each spouse in marital property:

800-359-7004

Incidentally, many independent paralegals not only recommend that customers who have legal questions call these services, they arrange for them to do so from their office so they can listen in and use the information as part of their own continuing education effort.

Use the Law Library: In states with smaller populations there may be few, if any, published self-help law materials. If you face this situation, you may have no book to sell unless you work in legal areas such as bankruptcy, copyright, patent or Social Security appeals, which are under federal jurisdic-

---

[3] Nolo Press extends bookstore-type discounts to IPs who wish to stock and resell its books. For information, call customer service at 800/955-4775. In the 510 area code, call 510/549-1976.

tion, or a publisher has published a good book tracking the laws of all 50 states. And even in states where there are self-help materials available, some may be procedure-oriented, and not deal in sufficient detail with substantive law.

No matter where you are, you will also want to do your own research at the local law library and prepare a list of relevant materials for future use by your customers. Law libraries are located in most county courthouses and are open to the public. Many law school libraries, especially those at publicly-funded universities, are similarly open to all. Your main goal will be to locate the practice books or court decisions lawyers rely on to answer the same routine questions your customers will ask. The reference librarian, if so disposed, can surely put your hand on the best materials. In this context, it's worthy of note that the American Association of Law Librarians has been working hard to make law libraries more accessible to the public, and some law librarians have already collected and organized materials of interest to nonlawyers.

HOW TO IMPROVE LEGAL RESEARCH SKILLS

Independent paralegals who have attended a formal paralegal school already know basic legal research skills. For others, it's an essential skill that should be promptly mastered. Because legal materials are organized in unique ways, it's almost essential that you either take a course or spend time with good self-help teaching tools. Here are a couple of excellent ones:

- *Legal Research: How to Find and Understand the Law,* by Stephen Elias and Susan Levinkind (Nolo Press): A basic text, designed for paralegals, which follows a step-by-step approach to mastering legal research techniques.
- *Legal Research Made Easy: A Roadmap through the Law Library Maze,* by Robert Berring (Nolo Press/Legal Star): An entertaining 2-1/2 hr. video by an experienced law librarian and teacher of legal research skills that provides a comprehensive introduction to legal research techniques.

Once you have located the materials you know your customers will want to refer to, create a short reading list. Typically a list for people doing their own divorce should contain five to ten entries which focus on substantive law, such as rules governing child support and child custody and visitation. You may also want to include these information sources on your customer information sheet along with basic information, such as the amount of court filing fees and what forms are necessary to file for divorce.

Let's now look at an example of how this approach to helping your customers educate themselves might work in practice.

> **EXAMPLE:** Cathy P. is a resident of Red Bluff, California. She has been employed on a temporary basis by several lawyers as a typist and has prepared several dozen sets of divorce forms. Recently she got her own divorce, handling the whole thing herself without problem and then helped her boyfriend prepare his own divorce papers. She has just decided to set up a part-time typing service to type divorces for others.
>
> To deepen her knowledge, Cathy first attends courses in family law and how to organize an independent paralegal business, sponsored by Independent Paralegal Workshops. In addition, she follows a number of the learning techniques discussed in Chapter 8, Section A, and in the interview with Glynda Mathewson in the Appendix of this book.
>
> As part of preparing herself to deal with customers' questions about divorce, Cathy checks several local books stores. She finds several books on self-help divorce in California. One, *How To Do Your Own Divorce in California,* by Attorney Ed Sherman, is particularly good. Ir not only contains all the forms and instructions necessary for a person to represent herself in an uncontested divorce, but also the background information necessary to make sensible decisions about how to divide property and debts. Cathy decides to require every customer to purchase and read both. To make this clear, she adds a sentence to this effect to her general disclaimer form that tells people that she is not a lawyer. It looks like this:

"I have a copy of *How To Do Your Own Divorce in California,* by Attorney Ed Sherman, and have read it carefully."

_____   _____
Date   Signature

Cathy then locates additional books on divorce, especially those pertaining to California. These include:

- *A Guide to Divorce Mediation,* by Gary Friedman (Workman), a good general guide to how to turn a potentially contested divorce into an uncontested one through mediation techniques;
- *California Family Law: Practice and Procedure,* by Christian E. Markey, Jr., ed. (Matthew Bender), a thorough multi-volume treatise on California divorce law, complete with forms. Probably the best comprehensive source of information for both lawyers and laypersons.
- *California Practice Guide,* by William P. Hogoboom (The Rutter Group), a two-volume set that is excellent when it comes to explaining the procedures and paperwork requirements of divorce.
- *Continuing Education of the Bar,* California Marital Dissolution Practice, a two-volume legal text covering all basic laws and procedures necessary to dissolve a marriage.
- *Practical Divorce Solutions,* by Attorney Ed Sherman (Nolo Occidental), deals with the practical financial and emotional aspects of a divorce.

- *Divorce and Money,* by Violet Woodhouse, Victoria Felton-Collins & M.C. Blakeman (Nolo Press), explains how to evaluate such major assets as pensions, investments, family homes and businesses, and how to arrive at a division of property that is fair to both sides.

- *How to Raise or Lower Child Support in California,* by Judge Roderic Duncan & Attorney Warren Siegel (Nolo Press). Forms and instructions designed to show parents how to petition the court to either raise or lower child support.
- *Smart Ways to Save Money During and After Divorce,* by Violet Woodhouse & Ginita Wall (Nolo Press). Just as the title says, it's packed with money-saving tips for people going through a divorce, including the desirability of using an IP instead of a lawyer.
- *Second Chances: Men, Women & Children a Decade After Divorce,* by Judith Wellerstein (Ticknor & Fields). Contains a great chapter on joint custody and how children are negatively affected by their parents' squabbles.
- *The Joint Custody Handbook,* by Miriam Galper Cohen (Running Press). Good advice on the practical aspects of making joint custody work.
- *The Divorced Parent: Success Strategies for Raising Your Children After Separation,* by Stephanie Marston (Morrow). How to raise well-adjusted kids after a divorce.

C. Limit Yourself to Legal Form Preparation: Don't Give Legal Advice

Even if you include a dozen disclaimers in your promotional material and wallpaper your office with signs stating that you don't practice law and are not a lawyer, you must live up to your statements or you are likely to end up in legal hot water. In other words, if despite your assurances that you don't give legal advice you in fact advise people on how to solve complicated legal problems or help them deal with problems arising out of contested lawsuits, you may very well be charged with the criminal offense of practicing law without a license or cited by a court in a civil contempt proceeding involving the same charge.

This directly raises the question of what types of oral advice will trigger a charge of unauthorized practice of law. There is no definitive answer. The difference between explaining general consumer information and transferring legal expertise is an extremely fine one. Depending on the geographical location, the factual context, and perhaps even on the sophistication of the customer, communicating a particular type of information may be judged to be the practice of law in one prosecution and not to be in another. For example, many judges would say that telling a customer who has already completed a Chapter 7 bankruptcy that they must wait six full years to file another is general consumer information, which is widely available and hence does not constitute the practice of law. However, a few judges might still claim this information is legal in nature, and therefore, a nonlawyer explaining it to a customer is a criminal offense.

A few years ago, if an independent paralegal was prosecuted (this was rare for other reasons—see Chapter 2), a judge would normally rule that explaining any information about the law to a consumer (e.g., "you file the long white form and fill it out with black ink") constituted UPL. By contrast, today it is becoming increasingly recognized that explaining basic legal facts widely known in the community (e.g., "it's a crime to lie on tax forms, or, the speed limit is 55-mph") does not constitute the practice of law and therefore won't result in an unauthorized practice conviction. I call this the "general knowledge" exception to the rule that only lawyers can give legal advice and I believe that in the next decades it will be greatly expanded to cover wide areas of information. Logically, any information widely available to the public through self-help law books, videos, software, consumer information packets and magazines should eventually fall into this category.

Two areas where this "general knowledge" rule has already expanded the types of information an IP can transfer to a customer are bankruptcy and family law. In large part, this is because consumer reporters, consumer action columns and self-help books, to mention but a few information sources, routinely explain the basics of divorce, adoption, change of name and bankruptcy. For example, it's possible to learn that a consumer is only eligible for a Chapter 7 bankruptcy once in seven years, or that all parents who have the ability to do so must pay child support, from literally dozens of non-lawyer sources. Even lawyers' groups have begun to recognize the value of the public getting this information, to the extent that they often bestow community service awards on the reporters who prepare or present these materials.

Given this strong trend towards providing the public with better and more in-depth legal information, it seems inevitable that organized lawyerdom will be unable to successfully prosecute independent paralegals for explaining this same information to their customers. Indeed, I know of several cases that were dismissed or dropped because the prosecution couldn't sufficiently prove that the information transferred from the IP to the customer was legal in nature. (See Virginia Simons' interview in the Appendix.)

And now for a face full of cold water. Despite the trend towards liberating the law from lawyers, there is no certain way to know what information a local bar association, prosecutor or judge will regard as being general public knowledge as opposed to legal information, the transfer of which is enough to trigger unauthorized practice charges. In short, despite the broad national trend towards allowing IPs to communicate basic consumer law information to their customers, particular individuals who do so are still vulnerable.

Given this, what general guidelines should an independent paralegal follow to be in the best position to defend herself should organized lawyer-dom prosecute? As I have emphasized throughout this book, the conservative answer is to do nothing but type forms in uncontested actions, best accomplished by following the customer's instructions after providing him or her with the self-help law information materials necessary to make sensible choices. If customers still have substantive legal questions, even routine ones, the independent paralegal should religiously refer them back to the self-help law materials that discuss the areas of their concern, or to a lawyer-staffed law phone service, or directly to a lawyer.

When it comes to very routine questions about subjects that are common knowledge in the community (e.g., "Is a parent legally responsible to support his or her minor child?"), IPs who work in parts of the country where the likelihood of prosecution is low—or who receive referrals directly from courts, as is beginning to happen in several places (see interview with Virginia Simons)—may conclude that they can safely provide answers. But before an IP, even one who feels legally secure, goes too far down the road of personally providing customers with legal information, I believe she should take a hard, critical look not only at what she is doing, but why she is doing it. Is she really answering legal questions and providing legal information because this is the only efficient way to legally inform the customer, or is it because she enjoys being an authority figure and secretly yearns to be a "junior lawyer." Too often, when I have examined a particular independent paralegal's operations, I have found that the independent paralegal deliberately chose to put herself in legal jeopardy and to deny her customers access to the best legal information, because she personally gets off on the lawyer-like role (per trip) of telling the customers what to do.

Again, a good compromise between never giving oral information or answering customers' sensible questions and acting like a lawyer is to back all oral information you give with high-quality self-help legal written materials, preferably those published by someone other than yourself. For example, if you are typing articles and bylaws for profit and nonprofit corporations in Houston, Texas and provide the books *How to Form Your Own Texas Corporation* and *How to Form a Nonprofit Corporation*, both by Attorney Anthony Mancuso (Nolo Press), as part of doing every corporation, you can sensibly argue that the information you are giving orally is simply a summary of the written materials.

Legal Areas Open to Independent Paralegals

ost people who open businesses as independent paralegals have a good idea of the type of legal paperwork they want to help people with. Often they just want to continue doing what they did when they worked for a private attorney, a legal clinic, or a court clerk's office. Or, occasionally the independent paralegal has become interested in a particular area because of a personal experience with the legal system. For example, I know two IPs who got involved with handling landlord problems after several of their own tenants refused to pay the rent. One works part-time for a county apartment owner's association specializing in counseling landlords on their legal rights; the other runs a small eviction form typing service. It is also fairly common for people to get started in the divorce typing business after successfully handling their own divorce.

Because so many uncontested divorces and bankruptcies are processed each year, and because independent paralegals have been successfully preparing paperwork in these fields for some time, the majority of fledgling IPs initially choose these legal areas. This makes sense, unless the geographical area where the new IP wishes to work is already saturated with divorce and bankruptcy typing services, as is the case in a number of West Coast communities.

However, just because a number of independent paralegals have done well doing divorces and bankruptcies, don't be fooled into thinking that to be a success in the independent paralegal business, you are limited to helping people fill out these types of forms. There are, in fact, dozens of legal areas open to you. Before listing a number of these, let's take a moment to understand why some types of legal tasks offer great potential to independent paralegals, while others do not.

A. Avoid Contested Cases

As I repeatedly emphasize throughout this book, a basic rule for survival as an independent paralegal is normally to refrain from working with customers who have contested disputes or whose disputes are likely to become contested. (See the sidebar, below, for an exception.) Legal literacy in the U.S. is so miserably low that the average citizen doesn't know enough about the law or legal procedures to handle a contested dispute without considerable help. If, as an independent paralegal, you are the nearest thing to a legal expert in the life of a person who is confused, and perhaps intimidated by a contested

lawsuit, she will almost inevitably ask you for legal advice and information. This in turn will put you in an awkward position. Unlike uncontested actions, such as bankruptcy, where there are high-quality self-help law materials to which you can refer your customers, few, if any, reliable materials exist to help nonlawyers cope with a contested lawsuit, especially if the other party is represented by a lawyer.[1] If in attempting to respond to your customers' anxious questions you provide legal information, you run a substantial risk of being charged with practicing law without a license. On the other hand, if you refuse to provide customers with the information they think they need to deal with an immediate problem, they are likely to become demanding and perhaps angry. At the very least, trying to deal with this will be a drag on your business. And, of course, there is always the risk that an unhappy customer will complain to the bar association or a consumer agency.

---

[1] An exception is *Represent Yourself in Court: How to Prepare & Try a Winning Case*, by Attorneys Paul Bergman & Sara J. Berman-Barrett (Nolo Press), which does an excellent job of showing the reader how to handle a contested civil court case.

The best and probably the only way to avoid this sort of problem is to strictly limit your work to uncontested actions, unless, of course, you work in a cause-related, nonprofit setting, such as advising women on how to collect child support, trying to defend the environment or helping tenants deal with a local rent control ordinance. As I discuss in more detail in Chapter 14, IPs who work in a nonprofit setting, even one that involves contested cases, are at less risk of being challenged by the bar, at least in part because lawyers don't get much in the way of fees from these areas and so are less concerned about nonlawyers getting involved.

SIMPLIFIED COURT PROCEDURE ALLOWS IPS TO PREPARE PAPERWORK IN CONTESTED CASES

In California, where over 60% of divorces are handled pro per, courts have begun establishing simplified procedures to handle contested disputes over issues such as child custody, property division, child support and visitation. Operating in this consumer-friendly atmosphere, IPs find they can type the paperwork necessary to get both spouses in a contested divorce case into court. Here is how Bakersfield IP Virginia Simons puts it: "The fact that the court has set up a way for people who are representing themselves to present their contested case means the consumer is much less apprehensive. When they come to me asking if I can help them with a contested divorce, I tell them I just type the papers and don't give legal advice. Since there are good self-help law materials available, people who argue about child support and custody without a lawyer really do fine, now that the courts make them welcome.

Fortunately, deciding to limit your work to uncontested matters does not involve much sacrifice, as the great majority (surely over 80%) of all legal matters presented to American courts and administrative tribunals do not involve a dispute. For example, despite the impression you may have gained from watching daytime TV dramas, where every divorcing couple has a small mansion, two BMW's and a herd of horny lawyers who make house calls, the great majority of modern divorces are not contested and do not require expensive lawyers or, for that matter, in most instances, any lawyer at all. This makes sense when you remember that the majority of people who divorce are relatively young, don't have much property, and often don't have children.

With little to fight about, most avail themselves of the opportunity that no-fault divorce laws and standardized divorce forms offer to end their legal relationship with as little hassle as possible.

This isn't to say that every divorce is uncontested. Obviously, the trauma of a couple separating can occasionally be so powerful that it spills over into the legal arena. Indeed, several established divorce typing services report that about 5% of the seemingly uncontested divorces they prepare end up being contested, at least to some degree. This points up the need for independent paralegals working in the divorce area to emphasize in their promotional material that they only handle uncontested actions. Even more important, it indicates the necessity for tight customer screening at the initial customer interview, designed to weed out cases that are likely to become contested. Finally, the IP should plan in advance to efficiently deal with those few customers who, despite good screening, end up involved in a fight. (See Chapter 7, Section A.) For example, here is an excerpt from a flyer used by one divorce typing service.

DIVORCE YOURSELF

A NONLAWYER DIVORCE TYPING SERVICE!

With our form preparation help, you can file your own uncontested divorce. To be uncontested, you and your spouse must agree on the main issues of divorce, including:
- Custody of the children
- Visitation Rights
- Child support
- Spousal Support
- Division of Property

Important: We do not work with people involved in contested divorces. If you believe that your divorce is likely to be contested, please see a lawyer. If after you engage our services to help you prepare your uncontested divorce, your spouse files court papers to contest it, we reserve the right to refer you to a lawyer.

In addition to adopting written policies stating that you don't handle contested actions, it's important that you learn to recognize and respect the almost inevitable warning signals that will alert you when a contest is likely. For example, if a potential divorce customer tells you he doesn't plan to pay child support, wants to make his spouse pay all the bills, and that if she gives him any trouble, he will find a way to convince her, you will want to decline to type the papers. In this situation, the couple obviously hasn't agreed on much, and the other spouse is almost sure to end up with a lawyer to protect her interests.

Turning away customers can be a tough task for the new businessperson who is understandably anxious to develop business quickly. The danger is, of course, that a business-hungry IP will talk himself into helping a customer prepare paperwork in situations in which a later contest is likely. Unfortunately there is no detailed advice I can give you except to pay attention to any warning signals your customers give. You will lose much more than you gain if you take on a customer who has a messy contested problem.

Consumer bankruptcies are another area in which most filings are not contested. In bankruptcy, the underlying problem is normally painfully simple—the debtor owes a lot of money and has very little. Because there isn't much to discuss, except the holes in the debtor's pocket, few creditors are likely to challenge the bankruptcy. Very occasionally a creditor will surface with a claim that must be defended. One that is not too unusual is a creditor's assertion that the debtor submitted a fraudulent financial statement to get credit in the first place. If this occurs, or indeed, if a similar legal hassle develops in any other area in which you are working, whether it be divorce, incorporation, or probate, you will want to be able to refer your customer to a lawyer.

B. Type Legal Forms in High Demand

In addition to avoiding contested actions, you obviously want to work in areas of legal form preparation for which there is steady consumer demand. Fortunately, there is an added benefit in doing this for legal areas where the volume of paperwork is high—the legal bureaucracy has almost always worked out step-by-step protocols for handling that paperwork. Think of it this way: If a state court gets one stepparent adoption filing per calendar quarter, they may informally make up at least some of the paperwork requirements as they go along. But if they receive 20 a week, you can be sure that rules for forms and procedures will be clearly defined. And once they are, it's not difficult for the IPs to help their customers conform.

At this point you may be wanting to interrupt and ask something like this: "Doesn't each person's unique legal problem require a high degree of customization when it comes to filling out paperwork?" The simple answer is "No." Whenever a society has to deal with a great many people who need to accomplish the same task, whether it's applying for a driver's license, filing income tax, or applying for a business permit, the only cost-effective approach is to reduce the procedural steps to rote. This generally amounts to requiring the person who wants to accomplish the particular task (or their lawyer or typing service) to insert "magic words" in boxes and blanks on forms. And this is exactly the same approach courts use when it comes to filing for divorce or a change of name. The fact that lawyers think of divorce and name changes as "legal tasks" does not change the fact that, in uncontested situations, if you put the correct words in the correct boxes and blanks, you get the result you desire, and if you don't, you don't.

To sum up, in deciding whether a particular legal area is a good one for a paralegal approach, determine if:

- most filings are uncontested,
- volume is reasonably high,
- the paperwork is routine,
- you can charge enough to make a living (see Chapter 9), and
- resources are available for you to educate yourself as to how to do the particular task. (See the interview with Catherine Jermany in the Appendix).

C. Legal Areas Open to Independent Paralegals

Now let's examine some of the specific legal form preparation tasks that have worked well for independent paralegals. As mentioned, divorces and bankruptcies have long been popular with IPs because there are a lot of them and because many people who need one or the other can't afford to pay a lawyer. But these aren't the only areas where an IP can prosper. Consider that every year there are more than a quarter million evictions, at least half a million small business incorporations and, taken together, hundreds of thousands of step-parent adoptions, name changes and conservatorships for people (most of them elderly) who aren't competent to manage their own financial affairs. In addition, hundreds of thousands of copyright applications are filed, millions of wills and living trusts are prepared, a substantial number of Social Security disability appeals are filed, and the estates of the majority of people who die must be probated. All of these legal areas and lots more are suitable for the independent paralegal because, for the most part, they involve the preparation of routine, and usually fairly repetitive, paperwork.

Here is a list of areas in which paralegals currently practice.

- **Divorce** (and annulments). This is the big one, with about 90% of IPs handling divorce petitions.
- **Bankruptcy** (Chapter 7 and Chapter 13). Nationally, this is the fastest growing IP area. Almost 1 million bankruptcies are filed in the U.S. each year, and pre-printed forms and easily available self-help law books make doing the paperwork routine.
- **Evictions and other landlord services.** This is a fast growing, high-profit area that paralegals may well take over almost entirely. (In California, state law requires that people who assist nonlawyers prepare evictions—called unlawful detainers—must post a bond. (Business & Professions Code 6400 et seq.)
- **Guardianships.** This usually routine legal action gives a grandparent or other relative or friend, who typically already has physical custody of a child who isn't their own, legal status that is often demanded by schools, hospitals, banks and others. About 25% of IPs handle guardianships.
- **Civil paternity actions.** When unmarried couples separate, a judicial decree of paternity is a necessary part of getting a court order for visitation and custody. Preparing the paperwork necessary to establish a parental relationship under the Uniform Parentage Act makes up a significant portion of the business of many IPs.
- **Conservatorships.** A usually routine action brought by family members when an older person can no longer handle their own business and financial affairs.
- **Tenants' rights.** Most opportunity in this area is with nonprofit tenants' advocacy organizations, or public agencies such as rent boards or mediation services.

- **Probate.** Absent a probate-avoiding living trust or other pre-established plan to avoid probate, probate is normally required to get necessary court approval to transfer assets from the deceased person to his inheritors.
- **Debt collection.** An established industry that unfortunately never lacks growth potential—not my personal favorite. In most states, bill collectors are regulated, so don't choose this one until you check out your state's rules. Still, there can be good opportunities in helping pro pers enforce their own money judgments.

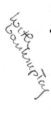

- **Debt counseling.** Many debtors don't know how to take advantage of legal protections while they reorder their affairs and get back on their financial feet. As Catherine Jermany reports in her interview in the Appendix, a number of IPs are meeting this demand by successfully combining credit counseling with the preparation of bankruptcy forms.
- **Immigration.** Using materials such as Nolo's *How To Get a Green Card: Legal Ways to Stay in the USA*, by Loida Lewis, many paralegals provide immigration information and form preparation services. In some states, such as California, providers must comply with regulatory laws. (Business & Professions Code § 2240-22446.5)
- **Incorporation.** Helping small businesspeople incorporate is an area of almost unlimited potential for the independent paralegal who can afford to computerize the form preparation. (See Chapter 11.) If you doubt this,

consider the view of William K. West, writing in *Case and Comment,* Vol. 90, No. 5, 1985, a publication which calls itself the "national magazine for practicing lawyers":

One area that normally calls for a standardized approach is incorporation. With more than 600,000 new corporations established in the United States in 1984 alone, it is a high-volume business. And yet much of it can, and should, be handled by paralegals, not lawyers. This is particularly true because standardized incorporation kits are available from a number of vendors. With proper training, a paralegal can take over the bulk of the paperwork involved in setting up a corporation, referring to the attorney only when the incorporation in question differs from routine.

- **Deed and other real estate transfers.** In many states, real estate people, title companies and other nonlawyers already control this business when residential and commercial property is bought or sold. However, consumers often need help in arranging private real estate transfers between friends and family, and this is a potential area for IP involvement.

- **Adoptions.** Many IPs prepare adoptions that occur when a parent with custody of children from a former marriage or living together relationship remarries and the new spouse wants to legally adopt the children. If the absent natural parent consents, or is out of the picture, the paperwork is routine.

- **Small claims court procedures.** Many IPs who currently work in this area concentrate on running group seminars and classes aimed at small business people who use the court regularly. The idea is primarily to teach them how to use small claims court to sue customers who have failed to pay bills. But as small claims dollar limits increase in many states, the small claims counseling business is beginning to focus on helping individual consumers prepare their cases. Yes, this raises the issue of an IP helping a consumer prepare for a contested action, but since it's in the context of a court where people are encouraged to represent themselves, nonlawyers should be able to provide this information free of unauthorized practice of law charges.

- **Child support increases and decreases.** In many states, parents are entitled to petition for increases based on inflation or changed circumstances. In some states, court personnel will help with those petitions, and in many others, women's groups provide help through nonprofit organizations. But in lots of communities, IPs prepare much of this mostly routine paperwork.

- **Restraining orders.** As with child support increases discussed just above, many women's groups provide this help. But especially when a customer is filing for divorce, IPs often prepare these protective orders in addition to typing divorce papers.

- **Simple wills.** Using *Nolo's Simple Will Book* (Nolo Press), or software such as *WillMaker* (Nolo Press), many IPs are helping customers prepare their own simple wills. (See Ch. 11 for more on using computerized legal form preparation software.)

- **Living trusts.** Lawyers advertise these probate avoidance devices for $1,500-$4,000. Many IPs will prepare them for $200-$400, often relying on books such as Denis Clifford's *Make Your Own Living Trust* (Nolo Press) or software such as *Living Trust Maker* (Nolo Press) to inform the customer and protect the IP from charges of unauthorized practice. However, in several states, nonlawyer living trust providers have been charged with unauthorized practice.[2]

- **Name changes.** These are truly routine and easy. There are lots more of them than you might expect—check the number with your state court's office or Department of Vital Statistics.

- **Social security disability appeals.** A number of nonprofit groups who work with seniors and the disabled do this work using paralegals. In addition, many IPs are establishing their own for profit businesses in this area (see interview with Glynda Mathewson in Appendix).

- **Copyright applications.** This is a routine, by-the-numbers job already handled by nonlawyers at most publishing companies. It's an area paralegals are sure to invade soon.

- **Partnership agreements.** Nolo Press publishes a book entitled *The Partnership Book: How to Write a Partnership Agreement,* and software, *Make Your Own Partnership Agreement,* that make it easy for IPs to help small business people prepare their own partnership agreements.

---

[2] The Florida Supreme Court in Case No. 878,358, *The Florida Bar Re: Advisory Opinion-Nonlawyer Preparation of Living Trusts,* has ruled that it's UPL for a nonlawyer to prepare a living trust, but not UPL to gather information necessary to do the preparation.

- **Nonprofit corporations.** Several groups that work with arts groups are active in this area, but there is room for lots more paralegal form preparation work.

- **Workers' compensation.** Many lawyers have abandoned this area because, by their standards, fees are low. The result is a shortage of providers—a vacuum being filled by IPs who help people help themselves.

- **Patents.** A number of IPs work with self-help patent filers to help with the tricky task of drafting patent claims. To get customers, they list their services in publications read by independent inventors. Nolo Press publishes a book, *Patent It Yourself*, and software, *Patent It Yourself*, that IPs can use to help prepare and file patents.

CAN INDEPENDENT PARALEGALS REPRESENT CUSTOMERS APPEARING BEFORE ADMINISTRATIVE AGENCIES?

The Federal Administrative Procedure Act (see Chapter 2, Section C) allows Federal agencies to specifically permit nonlawyers to appear before them. Many do. For example, Social Security disability appeals, Medicare appeals, Veterans' programs and Federal housing programs can be handled by nonlawyers. State UPL laws can apply to Federal agencies and programs. If the agency has not explicitly stated that nonlawyers may appear before it, check in your state to see what the situation is.

At the state agency level, things are more confused. In some states, nonlawyers have the right to appear before many types of administrative agencies under state law. In others, only lawyers can appear before most agencies. In a few, state courts have used the inherent powers doctrine (see Chapter 2) to restrict the right of state legislatures to empower nonlawyers to appear before agencies. This means you will have to check individually with each agency you are interested in to see if nonlawyers are allowed.

After reading this list you may be tempted to prepare several types of paperwork. There is nothing inherently wrong with this, as long as you have the detailed knowledge to handle each and don't spread yourself too thin. Especially if you are new to the business, however, it's best to concentrate on one area, learn it thoroughly and then branch out.

When you are ready to expand, look for areas that are a natural extension of the one you already handle. Not only does this facilitate your learning process, but it makes it much easier to market your services as a coherent package. For example, Irene Zepko, a long-time paralegal in Fresno, California, defines her form preparation business around family problems. Thus, she types guardianships, conservatorships, stepparent adoptions, name changes, minor's emancipation petitions, child custody and support modifications, and paperwork to establish a parental relationship for unmarried couples, as well as divorces. Indeed, divorce typing, which once made up the great majority of Zepko's business, now amounts to no more than half. Zepko takes pleasure in this diversity, both because her work is now more varied and interesting, and because, with 20 competing IPs working in Fresno, there isn't enough divorce typing to go around.

At a glance, it sounds as if Zepko has taken on a lot. But since all her work is family-related, and California has adopted easy-to-use pre-printed forms, there are many similarities and procedural overlaps from one type of action to the next. Zepko is also aided by the fact that Nolo Press publishes step-by-step guides for completing paperwork in most of these areas.

CHAPTER

5

Naming Your Business

Naming a new business is fun. You free your imagination, let your creative juices flow, and come up with a name that tells the world exactly who you are. Right? Unfortunately, things are usually not that simple, especially when it comes to naming an independent paralegal business.

If you choose a name that describes the services your business offers (for example, "Probate Form Typing Service"), people will know what you do. However, since the name isn't unique, you may have difficulty preventing a competing business with a similar name from opening up in the next town. If your name sounds too much like a lawyer's ("Divorce Law Consultants") you are likely to have the organized bar on your case in a hurry. If you pick a unique name that has nothing to do with lawyers ("Unicorn Enterprises" or "XYBOR Form Preparation Service"), your name will be easy to protect from use by competitors and will probably not trigger hostility from organized lawyerdom, but most people won't have a clue as to what you do.

HOW TO TRADEMARK YOUR NAME

In this chapter, and especially in Section G, I briefly discuss basic concepts of trademark law. I don't have the space here to show you how to protect a name under Federal and state Trademark law. Doing this involves a number of steps, including choosing a protectible name, conducting a trademark search and formally registering your name. If you plan to operate in more than one state, you will probably want to register your name with the Federal Patent & Trademark Office. Nolo Press publishes a step-by-step guide to show you how to accomplish this entitled *Trademark: How to Name Your Business and Product*, by Attorneys Kate McGrath & Stephen Elias (Nolo Press).

As you can see, coming up with a good name for an independent paralegal business involves juggling a number of variables. Here are a few suggestions.

A. Avoid Buzz Words That May Antagonize Organized Lawyerdom

As you should now clearly appreciate, the ability of an independent paralegal clinic to survive depends in large part on the ability of the operator to avoid the wrath of organized lawyerdom. The first place to practice this skill is in the selection of your name. The best way to avoid grief with the legal profession is to choose a name that carefully avoids such lawyer buzz words as "lawyer," "attorney," "counsel," "counselor," "legal," "legal services," "legal information," "legal resource center," "legal clinic," "law" or "paralegal." There is an obvious reason for my advice. It amounts to illegal misrepresentation to use a name that suggests you are a lawyer if you are not.

When Ed Sherman and I initiated a group of self-help divorce typing services in California in 1973, we used the name "Wave Project." While this name was a little too fanciful for the taste of some of the people we worked with, and was eventually changed, it had one great advantage. By choosing a fanciful name rather than a descriptive one, we allowed the divorce typing business to define the "Wave Project," with the result that organized lawyerdom could never claim that our name misled the public into thinking that we provided attorney services.

When the Wave Project members changed their name, many chose "Divorce Centers of California," a name they have now successfully used for over 15 years. While it's hard to argue with success, I wouldn't have chosen this name because it doesn't sufficiently emphasize self-help. In more tradition-bound areas of the country, organized lawyerdom might claim that potential customers could be misled into thinking that Divorce Centers offered attorney services.

B. Choosing a Name That Emphasizes Self-Help Law

In my opinion, the best approach to naming your business is to adopt a name that emphasizes that you prepare paperwork for people who are handling their own legal affairs. In this context, the Latin terms for self-representation—*"In pro per"* (in one's own person) and *"pro se"* (on one's own behalf)—have been used by several independent paralegals. Although technically accurate, using somewhat obscure terms such as these is counterproductive for three reasons. First, many potential customers don't know what these Latin phrases mean. Second, some wrongly believe such phrases have something to do with lawyers, and may even wrongly conclude that you provide legal advice. Third, and most important, because Latin gobbledygook is negatively associated with lawyers and their seeming addiction to hiding behind jargon, at least some potential customers are likely to be turned off.

By pleasant contrast, however, the rough English equivalents of "in pro per" and "pro se," such as "self-representation," "self-help" and "do your own," work well as names when combined with a description of the actual service offered. Thus, "Self-Help Bankruptcy Typing Service" and "Do Your Own Divorce Typing Center" are both relatively safe and informative names.

It is not wise to use the word "help" without further defining it by adding a word such as "self." Otherwise, names like "Divorce Help" or "Bankruptcy Help" make it sound as if you provide legal expertise and information in these areas. Since doing this risks a charge that you are practicing law without a license, these are counterproductive names.

C. Using Descriptive Names

I have suggested that names that accurately describe what you do have an advantage from a marketing point of view and also help keep you out of trouble with organized lawyerdom. Thus you might end up with "South Boston Divorce Typing Service" or "Quality Incorporation Form Typing Service." Rosemary Furman, the pioneering Florida paralegal (see interview in the Appendix), who did business for years in Jacksonville, Florida under the nose of a hostile bar, called her business the "Northside Typing Service." The point of this approach is, of course, to let potential customers have some idea of what you do, but to avoid giving organized lawyerdom a convenient stick with which to beat you. In this context, remember, as I discuss in detail in Chapter 2, there is no law against simply typing forms for customers who wish to represent themselves in court, as long as it's the customer who makes all significant decisions.

The downside of using a descriptive name is that, under trademark law, descriptive names can be difficult to protect from use by potential competitors. For example, terms such as "typing," "form preparation," "word processing," "stenographer," and "secretarial" are in such general use that they are considered to be in the "public domain," and can be used by anyone, except in a few limited situations in which they are likely to result in customer confusion. (I discuss this concept in more detail in Section G, below.)

D. Combining a Unique and Descriptive Name

A good approach to naming an IP business that gets around the problem that a descriptive name is often hard to protect legally is to combine a unique or fanciful name with descriptive terminology. Thus, White Rose Divorce Typing Service would be protectible as a trademark if no one else had previously claimed or used it, and at the same time it tells your customers what you do.

E. Using Your Own Name

Yet another approach to naming your business is to use your own name, perhaps combining it with a term that describes what you do. Thus, Kwan Lee might use "Lee Probate Form Preparation Services."

One advantage of using your own name is that, in many states, it eliminates the need to file a fictitious business name statement. On the other hand, a potential disadvantage is that you can't claim exclusive use of your name under the trademark laws should someone else with the same name also want to use it, unless over a period of time it has become so well-known and identified with your business that it clearly defines it in the public mind. (See Section G, below.)

This means if your own name is a common one, you may wish to choose a more distinctive name for your business. However, if your name is somewhat unusual, such as Pladsen, Hodovan, or Ihara, using it as part of your business name is probably fairly safe, since the chances of another independent paralegal with the same name going into competition with you seems fairly remote. For the same reasons, you might call yourself the P & K Lee Probate Form Preparation Business, a name that would likely be distinctive even if another person named Lee opened a similar business.

What about using your own name along with a vague-sounding term such as "Associates," "Consultants" or "Organization?" This is often a poor idea for two reasons. You are likely to end up with a name that sounds like a law firm, at the same time that it doesn't inform potential customers about what you do. For example, "Jones & Lee, Associates" may sound prestigious, but it is a lousy name for a typing service that helps people prepare their own wills and living trusts. Also, without a qualifier like "Jones & Lee Typing Service," or the addition of initials, you run the risk of infringing the trademark of some other business already using that name, especially if your name is similar to a famous one, like Firestone, Sears or Champion.

If, despite my advice, you are determined to use a vague term like associates, you can make it far more safe and effective by using it in conjunction with a term that describes what you do. Thus, if Jones and Lee, Associates adds "A self-help typing service for wills and living trusts," their name fairly and accurately describes their business. Of course, they may find that this is a bit cumbersome and expensive, when it comes to listing their services in classified ads.

F. Using "Paralegal" as Part of Your Name

Let's now briefly discuss "paralegal," the term many, if not most, nonlawyers who run legal form typing services use to describe themselves. Like "midwife," "computer consultant" and "financial planner," "paralegal" can mean almost anything. Because most states have no official certification programs for paralegals, people with all sorts of training and experience quite properly and legally use this term. Some base their claim to be a paralegal on the fact that they took several paralegal courses at a business school. Others have a degree in paralegal studies from a university or college that requires several years of study and which may or may not be accredited by the American Bar Association or some other group. Still others are former law firm employees who establish their own business to market specialized "freelance paralegal" services to lawyers. (See Chapter 13.) And, of course, there are also many "independent paralegals" who teach themselves how to type and market legal form preparation services directly to the public.

So far, so good, you are probably thinking. If the term paralegal can mean a variety of things, why shouldn't I use it to describe my independent typing service? Simply put, because the great majority of people who call themselves paralegals currently work for lawyers. This means that in the view of organized lawyerdom, shortsighted though it may be, paralegals are an extension of their empire. Your use of the term may give rise to their charge that you are representing yourself to the public as working under lawyer supervision. If this is hard to swallow, consider the parallel reality of the medical profession, where many doctors believe that "nurses" are people put on the earth to serve them, and the very word nurse conjures up, in the public mind, the image of a person who takes orders from a physician.

At least one trial court decision, *State Bar of Nevada v. Johnson,*[1] has specifically disapproved of the use of "paralegal" as a name for a legal typing service. In establishing guidelines for typing service operation, that court stated:

>...*The court probably cannot keep the defendants from appropriating a business name [Paralegal] which is not elsewhere prohibited in an as yet unregulated field. The court does feel, however, that it is within its power to limit advertising a status as "paralegals," as well as advertising the firm's ability to furnish "paralegal" services, because the term misleads the public into believing that the defendants are in the business of providing legal and non-scrivener services.*

What about attempting to define the term paralegal with a second term, such as "Everyone's," "People's" or "Public," to eliminate the suggestion that lawyers are involved? This helps, but I would still advise avoiding a term that is likely to annoy lawyers. At this point, you may wonder what difference this makes, if lawyers are out to shut you down anyway. I don't have a definitive response to this query, except to suggest that whenever you deal with a large, unpredictable beast with long claws, it makes sense to avoid needlessly pulling its tail.

G. Legal Protection Against Copiers

So far I have briefly mentioned the legal concept of protecting your business name from use by competitors. Now let's look more thoroughly at the legal rules that are relevant to protecting the name of any business, including yours.

---

[1]Case No. CV89-5814 (Nev. 2nd Dist. Ct., April 12, 1990)

As part of doing so, it will be necessary for you to read the following material on both trade names and service marks before drawing any conclusion.

1. Trade Names

The name that you select for your business is considered your "trade name." Trade names are subject to one major restriction. Your trade name can't be so similar to another trade name used by the same type of business in your area as to cause customer confusion. For instance, if "Speedy Divorce Form Preparation Service" has been open down the street for a year or two, you cannot legally open your own business under this, or a very similar, name.

What this often means, in practice, is that if you form a corporation, your proposed trade name will be reviewed by the state agency in charge of corporate registrations to see whether it is too similar to existing corporate names. If it is, it will be rejected and you'll have to come up with another. Likewise, if you have a sole proprietorship or a partnership, you will have to file a fictitious business statement with the county (or the state, in some places). Your proposed name will be checked against other names in your county and rejected if it is identical or too similar to an existing one.

In addition, unincorporated businesses can defend their trade names from use by others under state laws prohibiting unfair competition. These laws generally only require that businesses not engage in conduct that creates a likelihood of confusion. Thus, assuming you (or a competing business) isn't incorporated, if another "Speedy Divorce Form Preparation Service" opens up in another part of your county, or maybe even your state, you probably could challenge them under unfair competition laws, if you could show the likelihood that some of your customers would be confused by the new business's identical trade name. And the same laws can be applied against you if you select a name identical (or too similar) to a rival's.

2. Service Marks

Now suppose you chose a highly distinctive name, such as White Rose Divorce Typing Service. As a result of one of those sleights of hand for which the law is famous, a distinctive trade name such as this is entitled to much more protection than a descriptive trade name the instant it is used to identify the services being offered by the business. Why? Because when a trade name is used to identify services, it magically becomes a service mark, and distinctive service marks, as I explain immediately below, are fairly easy to protect against use by others.[2]

This need not be confusing, because your trade name (that is, the name you select for your business) will most likely be the same as your "service mark" (any name or symbol that is used to market a particular service). For instance, "Hyatt Legal Services," is both the name of the business and its service mark. Or, to take a more relevant example, if you use "South Bay Probate Typing Specialists" to market South Bay Probate Typing Specialists form preparation services, you have chosen both a trade name and a service mark.

In practice, your trade name becomes your service mark as soon as you use it to market your services. The only difference between them as far as you

---

[2]While trademarks refer to products and service marks refer to services, they mean the same thing for purposes of this discussion.

are concerned is that trade names are entitled to slightly less and different protections than are service marks. So while trade names have protections under unfair competition laws, service marks have both that *and* protection under trademark laws, which are stronger and provide stiffer penalties for infringement.

The wrinkle is that only service marks and trademarks that are distinctive or unique get protection from copiers under trademark laws. To return to the "Speedy Divorce Form" example, because Speedy is a common promotional term, and because Divorce Form says what the business does, the mark is too descriptive or not unusual enough to get protection as a trademark. Other words that are not unique enough to act as trademarks are common surnames and geographic terms, unless they gain secondary meaning. (See box, below.)

On the other hand, White Rose Divorce Form Typing Service is distinctive because it applies a term not usually associated with such a business. That makes it unique, and therefore fully protectible as a trademark. Other ways to create a unique service mark are to make up a word (like Zoline Forms Preparation), or to use a term in a suggestive way (like Ethereal Probate Services), as long as it's not too close to the subject matter of the services to become descriptive. Distinctive or unique marks are registrable with the state trademark office (or the federal office, if you do business across state lines). Once registered, the mark is exclusively yours to use within the state (or the country).

A SECONDARY MEANING RULE:
Descriptive Business Names Can Eventually
Become Protected As Service Marks

A service mark that starts out in the public domain because it is descriptive or already in common use, including surnames or geographic terms, can sometimes gain the right to legal protection later. Called the "secondary meaning" rule, this legal concept allows a business to gain exclusive use of a descriptive or other common mark once the business becomes so well known by that name that the name comes to signify the business in the public mind. For example, McDonald's is no longer a common surname to most people; instead, we all know it as a trademark for the fast food chain. Likewise, "Ace Hardware" is protectible as a trademark because it has become so famous that we know exactly what stores the mark refers to. But note: Proving that your mark has acquired secondary meaning can take years and cost lots, due to customer surveys and attorney fees. This concept is discussed in detail in Nolo's book, *Trademark: How to Name Your Business and Product*, by Attorneys Kate McGrath & Stephen Elias.

3. Improper Use of the Name of a Well-Known Business

There is one more factor to consider when you're thinking about service marks: "dilution" of famous marks. For example, suppose that you decide to name your independent paralegal clinic "Tiffany Scriveners." As it happens, the trademark "Tiffany" is owned by the company selling Tiffany jewelry. Under general trademark/service mark law, you would only be prevented from using the Tiffany mark if customers would be likely to confuse your product or service with that attached to the mark. However, another legal rule, which operates in a number of states, allows the owner of a mark to prevent its use by another if the qualities associated with the mark would be diluted in some significant way. For instance, if a company called "Tiffany Chimney Cleaners," or "Tiffany Bankruptcy Form Preparation Service," opened its doors, the first person through them would probably be a lawyer representing the Tiffany jewelry company, with court papers alleging dilution of the Tiffany mark. In short, our advice on this one is simple: don't use or play on the unique trade name or service mark of a large business. For example, Godiva Chocolates made Dogiva Dog Biscuits change its name under this rule.

4. Summing Up the Law of Trade Names and Service Marks

Suppose Speedy Divorce Form, a sole proprietorship, was the first to use this name in connection with a divorce-form typing business that only operates within one state. If it used its name locally and just filed a fictitious business name statement, Speedy Divorce Form would be entitled to protection only against other businesses operating in the same area because of the likelihood of consumer confusion. If Speedy Divorce Form were able to register its name as a service mark with the proper state agency, it might be able to prevent a rival business from using the same mark anywhere in that state. However, this would depend on the law of the particular state. The term might be viewed as too descriptive to gain even statewide protection.

If Speedy Divorce Form operated in at least two states, then it might be entitled to some national protection for the mark by registering it with the U.S. Patent and Trademark Office. Again, because this name is so descriptive, courts would be much less willing to protect it against use by others than if it were highly distinctive, such as, say, "Klingon Divorce Typing Service" or "White Rose Self-Help Bankruptcy Typing Service."

H. Summing Up: Names You Shouldn't Use

So far, we've covered factors you should try to incorporate into a business name—the degrees of distinctiveness and descriptiveness. We have also discussed why it's a good idea to identify your business in a way that prevents lawyers from claiming you are misleading the public into thinking you are a law office or provide legal advice or help. Now, let's summarize this information in a list of "don'ts." Remember, it's worth the time it takes to choose a name carefully, because if your business becomes a success, your name will be one of your most valuable assets, and you won't want to have to change it.

- Do not use a name that uses words like "law," "legal services" or "paralegal." (See Section A for other words to avoid.)

- Do not use the same name as an existing business that operates in your area.
- Do not use a name that can be easily confused with that used by any business in your area. For example, if you call your business "How to Do Your Own Divorce Associates" and someone else in your city is using the term "Divorce Yourself Associates," you are asking for legal trouble because your name may mislead or confuse the public.
- Don't use a name other than your own (or, if you are incorporated, other than the name your corporation is registered under) without first filing a fictitious name statement (in most states). Contact your county clerk's office for information.
- If you plan to incorporate, don't use a name without first checking with your state's corporation commissioner or secretary of state. If the state finds your name is the same or confusingly similar to one already used by another corporation, you will probably be required to choose another.
- Do not use the name of a large national corporation, even if incorporated in another state.
- Do not use a name that could easily be confused with a service mark that you have reason to believe is federally registered (you can tell by the "®" that accompanies the mark) or registered in your state.
- Register your name with your state's trademark office or, if you will use it across state lines, with the Federal Patent & Trademark Office. For how-to information see the book, *Trademark: How to Name Your Business and Product*, by Attorneys Kate McGrath & Stephen Elias (Nolo Press).

Establishing an Office

People have successfully begun independent paralegal businesses from all sorts of places, including the kitchen table. When you are just starting out, your decision about where to carry on your business will probably be determined in large part by personal economic considerations. Although I believe on balance that it's usually easiest to rent a modest office as opposed to operating from your living space, this may simply not be practical. There is nothing inherently wrong with starting small, even if this means operating out of a spare bedroom or converted garage—unless you are in an area in which zoning laws prohibiting home-based businesses are strictly enforced or you can't get the motor oil off the floor of the garage.

A. Opening a Home-Based Business

There can be an advantage to operating a business from your home if you live in a state or city where organized lawyerdom is likely to try to put you out of business if it can find you. If you are able to attract enough customers via word of mouth or other semi-underground methods, you may be able to run a home-based paralegal business successfully for some time without organized lawyerdom even knowing you exist.

Operating from home seems hugely attractive to many people, especially those who have spent years battling their way to work at rush hour. It usually isn't quite that wonderful. Take it from someone who has done it for years—the joy of being only one step from work can quickly turn into the anguish of never seeming to be able to get more than three steps away from it. In addition, anyone who runs a home-based business must deal with the fact that some potential customers are mistrustful of a business not located in a conventional office setting. Normally, however, you can defuse this problem in advance. I ran both a small legal clinic and a publishing business from my home by taking most of the steps outlined below—but then, in fairness, I should point out that I had one big advantage. I was living in Berkeley, California, where to be a little bizarre was normal and to be conventional meant you had already moved away.

If you plan to operate out of your home, here are a few suggestions based on my own experience that should go far towards reassuring your customers that you run a quality business:

- Set up a defined work area separate from your living space. A good-sized room is best, but a corner of a larger room will do in a pinch if it is carefully screened or partitioned. Furnish your workspace like an office and, if possible, provide a small waiting area for customers should appointments overlap. You will need a desk, a couple of sturdy chairs for customers (so you don't have to bring one in from the kitchen), a file cabinet, word processor (or typewriter), and a supply of standard office supplies. It will help greatly if you can also afford a small photocopier and a FAX machine.

- If you live with others, absolutely insist that they respect this work area. This not only means that it's kept free of personal belongings, but that it's quiet and private when you are working with customers.

- See customers only by appointment. When you talk to them by phone to make an appointment, inform them you operate from a home environment so they won't be surprised when they arrive. Some home-based independent paralegals often add that they do this in order to keep overhead, and therefore prices, down.

- Establish a business phone with an answering machine—preferably one that lets a caller talk for as long as he wants. Having a separate line allows you to instantly distinguish between business and personal calls. Answer your office phone only during working hours and always state your business name.

- If your situation allows, establish a separate business entrance. I did this when I ran my home-based business and it worked extremely well. The people who came to see me on business never saw anything but the office.

- Have your office and waiting area reflect what you do. Displaying framed copies of newspaper articles about you and your business is one way to do this. For example, the waiting room of the Superior California Legal Clinic in Sacramento has several *Sacramento Union* newspaper articles about self-help law clinics mounted on the wall. Another effective means of doing this is to display a collection of self-help law materials. Also, as discussed in Chapter 3, you should provide customers with printed information making it clear that they are representing themselves and that you are not an attorney. A description of your basic self-help philosophy would also be helpful. Here is an edited version of one used by the Superior California Legal Clinic:

DIVORCE HELP

DO YOU NEED LEGAL ASSISTANCE
OR A NONLAWYER TYPING SERVICE?

An alternative to hiring a lawyer to do your divorce is to "do it yourself."
SUPERIOR CALIFORNIA LEGAL CLINIC'S trained nonlawyer personnel
will help you prepare all forms necessary to do your own divorce.

- You can handle your own legal form preparation needs with a little
  help from us.

- Many people already know the basic information necessary to obtain
  their own divorce or accomplish other basic legal procedures. What
  they don't know is how to complete the necessary forms.

- Our service is based on the idea that everyone should have the
  opportunity to handle their own case efficiently, simply and at an
  affordable price.

CAUTION:

Representing yourself can work well for routine uncontested actions.
However, if you expect a legal battle, you should not do your own
divorce without attorney representation or assistance.

- If you live with others, discuss your needs in detail and make sure they
  are supportive of your home business. If your family or housemates have
  doubts about your enterprise, don't embark on it until all their concerns
  have been positively resolved. For example, if your spouse is concerned
  about how you will cope with your customer's children or about customers who smoke, or perhaps about who will care for your own child
  while you are interviewing customers, don't brush these worries aside.
  Failure to come up with mutually acceptable solutions to these problems
  risks having the efficient operation of your business negatively affected.

- Consider the needs of neighbors. In many areas where home-based businesses are technically illegal, municipal officials won't hassle you unless a complaint is filed. This usually occurs because neighbors are angered over losing their parking space or fearful because they don't know why so many people are coming and going. A little communication (for example, "I type divorces, I don't deal drugs") and courtesy can work wonders. For example, if you have a driveway, keep your own car in the garage and ask customers to park in your driveway rather than in front of your neighbors' homes.

GOOD INFORMATION ABOUT RUNNING A HOME-BASED BUSINESS

For more information about running a business from your home, I recommend the following books:

- *Working From Home,* by Paul and Sarah Edwards (Jeremy Tarcher): This book offers a good overview and sound advice about living and working under the same roof. I particularly like the discussions on how to keep your personal and business lives separate and avoid loneliness.
- *The Home Office: How To Set Up and Use Efficient Personal Workspace in the Computer Age,* by Mark Alvar (Goodwood Press): As the subtitle indicates, this book focuses on the physical details of establishing a home office. Issues covered include choosing a suitable space, selecting furniture, and buying office equipment—including computer hardware and software.

Despite the advantages of a home-based business, all independent paralegals I know who started this way eventually moved to a formal office setting. Many, of course, were glad they started at home because it allowed them to both hide their existence from organized lawyerdom and test the financial waters of their new business without feeling that they were betting their whole economic future on its immediate success. Indeed, I know several who held on to their jobs until their independent paralegal business (operated from home mostly during evening hours and on weekends) started generating enough money to allow it to be a full-time occupation.

People's reasons for eventually moving their business to a commercial office space vary, but an important one is often the realization that the cost of office space is significantly less than that for living space. The fact that it was initially cheaper to start at home (you already own or rent it), becomes less important as your business expands and you require more room. Then it usually becomes cheaper to find commercial office space, as opposed to getting a bigger living/work space.

Wanting to get away from living with a business is another important reason why many home-based IPs eventually move to an office setting. In this context, several paralegals mentioned that it's one thing to share hearth and home with a little start-up business, but quite another—and much less desirable—to cohabit with a growing one.

Finally, some IPs report that the patience and support of family members, housemates and neighbors can eventually wear thin. The fact that they are willing to cooperate with your needs for a few months or years while you are getting started doesn't mean they will do it forever.

B. Running an IP Business From Commercial Space

If you do decide to operate from a business space, you have some choices to make. One is to simply rent an office and put your name on the door. Another is to share space with an established business. Doing this can be a sensible half-way measure between moving your business out of your living space and opening your own office. This can be particularly desirable if you are on a tight budget, since sharing a business space costs a lot less than opening your own office.

It's not hard to find space to share. All sorts of businesses, including real estate and insurance agencies, business consultants, financial planners, and tax preparers, commonly have extra room. For a modest monthly rental, you can often arrange to put your desk and typewriter in a partitioned-off corner of a big office, or better yet, a small separate room. A big advantage to this sort of arrangement is that you gain the respectability an existing business provides without either the trouble or expense of renting your own place.

Another space-sharing alternative is to work out a cooperative arrangement with a nonprofit or other group that works in the same field that you do. For example, in exchange for free or low-cost space at a local women's organization, you might, in addition to typing divorces for a reasonable fee, agree to help low-income women prepare the paperwork for restraining orders for free. Similarly, if you want to do work for landlords, you might discuss your space needs with the county apartment house owners' association. In exchange for your offering members your services at a discounted fee, the association might be willing to provide you with free or low-rent space. (I discuss how IPs can work with nonprofits in more detail in Chapter 14.)

Sooner or later, however, you'll probably want to rent your own office space. There are loads of different types of office settings available, many of which are discussed in my interviews with Glynda Mathewson, Robin Smith and Jolene Jacobs in the Appendix. Here are some considerations about locating an IP business:

- You don't need or want a fancy office in a posh location, so it's fine to keep your rent budget relatively low.
- Location is important, but not nearly as critical as it can be to a retail store or restaurant. Most of your customers will be referred to you by others, so any easy-to-reach location will work. There is no need to locate in a high rent district or an area with lots of pedestrian traffic.
- Access is important. Always ask yourself where customers will park. Also, check out public transit routes. Yours is not an affluent clientele and you'll do better if you're near a bus stop.
- Safety is important. Don't locate in an area people will think twice about coming to. Your customers will be working folks, many of whom will

want to come by in the evening. If your neighborhood is scary after dark, a good number of people won't come.

- Older but still respectable business buildings like those recently abandoned by lawyers and doctors for fancy new office complexes are often a good choice, especially if they're located near courts and other city services. (See Glynda Mathewson's interview.)
- Older shopping centers and strip malls often have offices upstairs, over the shops, which are available at very reasonable rates. Since these areas are usually located on busy streets, have parking lots and are near public transportation, they can be a good choice.

In addition to location, you will need to think about how much space you'll need. It's my experience that working out of one room is difficult. Customers who are being interviewed or filling out paperwork appreciate a private area away from your reception space, which will often necessarily double as a child's play area. So rent at least two small offices, or a room big enough to be divided. If you can afford it, renting three work areas is even better: one for reception, one for customer interviews and one for form preparation. I recommend a separate area for form preparation, not only because your computer, typewriter, photocopy and FAX machines take up space, but because you will want easy access to them at all times, something that may be difficult if you are conducting interviews in the same location.

C. Negotiating a Good Lease or Rental Agreement

When you rent an office, you not only must worry about the amount of rent and the location and size of the space, you also must negotiate a lease or month-to-month rental agreement. Do you want to try and lock in a space for years or choose the shortest time period possible? There are no right answers —it depends on how established your business is, how fast it is growing and whether you are likely to be challenged by organized lawyerdom, among a host of other factors. Here are some general, and at times conflicting, factors you will want to consider:

- Renting moderate-priced office space is usually easy in most areas because the market is glutted. This means there is little need to lease a particular space for a long time. In the unlikely event you are asked by the landlord to move, there will be a wide choice of other available locations.

- When you first open, you'll be doing many things to get your business known in the community. One of these will be to inform people where you are located. It follows, then, that assuming it turns out you have picked a good location, you will want to stay put for a while. If you do, you may want the security that comes with a lease.

- If your business prospers, you may want more (or perhaps better-located) space. Unless it's likely to be available at your first location, this means you won't want a long lease that will make it difficult or expensive for you to move.

Fortunately, there is a way to at least partially resolve the conflicts between wanting the security of knowing you can stay put and the freedom to move on. This involves renting an office space for a relatively short period with an option to renew for a longer period. For example, you might lease two rooms in a business building for six months or a year, with an option to renew at the end of the tenth month for an additional year or two at a pre-established rental amount. This allows you to see how things work out and make your decision accordingly. Because granting you an option potentially ties up a landlord's property, she may ask you for an extra payment in exchange. As long as the amount is modest, this request is reasonable and you may want to go along.

But suppose a landlord refuses to consider a short lease period with an option to renew and demands a lease for two or three years? Unless your business is well-established and you are absolutely sure you will stay there for that period, just say "no." Again, as I emphasized earlier, most communities have a glut of small- and moderate-priced offices in older buildings, and you should have no trouble finding one, with a landlord who will accommodate your needs.

D. Good Information on Small Business Operations

This book is primarily about how to run an independent paralegal business, not about small business skills generally. Just the same, when your thoughts turn to establishing an office, it's a good time to consider lots of other details of running a quality small business. Some of these are fairly mundane, such as getting a business license, buying appropriate equipment and establishing a good bookkeeping system. Others are more complicated, such as creating realistic financial projections and a sound marketing plan. In this regard, Independent Paralegal Workshops, based in Southern California (see interview with Lois Isenberg in the Appendix), offers excellent training seminars that address all of these areas.

In addition, there are several excellent books on how to accomplish these (and many more) small business tasks. I highly recommend the following:

- *Small Time Operator,* by Bernard Kamoroff (Bell Springs Publishing). This handy guide, which is updated yearly, has been popular for over twenty years for excellent reasons. It gives you essential information about the paperwork you'll have to deal with, including keeping books, paying taxes, becoming an employer, etc. The book also contains excellent information on how to efficiently use computers and other electronic equipment in your business. In fact, it is so detailed, it even tells you the type of calculator to buy. If you never buy another business book, buy this one.

- *How to Write a Business Plan,* by Mike McKeever (Nolo Press). This easy to use guide shows you how to raise money for your new business, including tips on how to arrange loans from both family members and conventional lenders. As part of doing this, it helps you prepare a detailed financial plan for your proposed business. In my experience, doing this may demonstrate that even using your best case assumptions, your proposed business won't produce the financial rewards you expect. In short, this book not only will help you prepare to borrow money to get a business started, it gives you the financial tools necessary to realistically assess your business idea.

- *Honest Business,* by Michael Phillips and Salli Rasberry (Random House). This book might as well be entitled, Zen and the Art of Small Business Success. Although it's now a few years old, this remarkable book, which focuses on the personal and psychological qualities it takes to succeed in a small business, fills a niche occupied by no other. Much of Phillips' and Rasberry's advice stands conventional small business wisdom on its head. For example, they explain why having plenty of capital can be much worse for a new business person than not having enough.

- *Marketing Without Advertising,* by Michael Phillips and Salli Rasberry (Nolo Press). The same authors demolish the myth of advertising effectiveness and outline practical alternate ways for a small business to market its products and services. As I further develop in Chapter 10, "Marketing Your Services," creating a marketing plan that does not rely on expensive advertising is usually a key to success as an independent paralegal.

- *The Legal Guide for Starting & Running a Small Business,* by Attorney Fred S. Steingold (Nolo Press). The legal ins and outs that every business owner needs to know to establish and run a small business. Topics include: deciding whether to form a sole proprietorship, partnership or corporation, buying a franchise or existing business, negotiating a favorable lease, hiring and firing employees, working with independent contractors, creating good contracts and resolving business disputes.

How to Establish a Good Relationship With Lawyers, Mediators and Judges

There is no need to elaborate on the fact that organized lawyerdom has done a miserable job of providing routine legal services at a reasonable price to the American public, and that this is one reason for widespread public anger towards the profession. Indeed, many paralegals enter the legal form preparation business at least in part because of their own hostile feelings toward lawyers. However, even though antipathy to the legal profession by IPs is reasonable, especially when you consider you must compete with a group that commonly wants to put you in jail, paradoxically, it is often to the advantage of both you and your customers that you work closely with one or more lawyers.

A. Working With Lawyers

Think of it this way—should you ever need to ask for help or advice, wouldn't it be nice to have access to a sympathetic legal expert supportive of the idea of self-help law and your role in it? And wouldn't it be great to be able to refer customers who need legal expertise you can't safely provide to a lawyer who is both reasonably-priced and competent. And, while we are playing a fantasy game, wouldn't it also be terrific to know one or more lawyers willing to go to bat for you and your business should their less flexible brethren accuse you of unauthorized practice?

If your answer to any one of these questions is "yes," you're ready for the big question: "How do you find supportive lawyers, or at least one of them?"

Before I suggest ways to do this, a few more words about lawyers are appropriate. Throughout most of this book, I have pictured organized lawyerdom as a monolithic group almost universally hostile to the idea of nonlawyer competition. While viewing the legal profession as a monolith is necessary to focus your attention on necessary survival techniques—it is also an oversimplification.

If instead of looking at the entire legal profession with what amounts to a wide-angle camera lens, you instead employ a zoom lens to focus on individuals, you will immediately see that lawyers don't have a monolithic view of anything—even their own divine right to dominate the delivery of legal services. Or, put another way, many individual lawyers understand that their profession is out of touch with the legal needs of millions of ordinary Americans and are embarrassed by it. While the traditional view that lawyers should preserve their monopoly at all costs still dominates most state and local bar associations and county courthouses, even in these places, the notion that independent paralegals should be squelched under all circumstances is slowly receding.[1] And once you get away from lawyers associated with the delivery of personal legal services and instead canvass those who work for big firms and public agencies, you'll find a good number who are actually supportive of efforts to make high quality, low-cost legal form preparation services widely available. The fact that not all lawyers buy into the traditional views of organized lawyerdom should not be surprising when you consider that one-third of American lawyers have been admitted to practice in the last decade.

If you still doubt that fair-minded lawyers exist, consider the views of Bob Anderson, an attorney in Berkeley, California who operated a divorce typing service as a paralegal prior to becoming an attorney:

While running the Divorce Center, I developed a list of friendly attorneys for advice and referral (whenever I made a referral I attempted to name at least two attorneys, so that the customer could make a choice). A number of positive effects flowed from this relationship as far as I was concerned. First, by referring questions to attorneys I greatly reduced the risk of my practicing law without a license. Second, I provided a better service to the customer in that s/he had questions answered that were beyond my knowledge. And third, I was able to refer people who called but could not use a self-help service for one reason or another to attorneys who were less likely to rip them off, but who would provide the required service. Now, as an attorney, I refer qualified cases to self-help typing centers. I get satisfaction from seeing that the self-help movement is continuing because (especially in California divorces) there is increasing recognition among us (attorneys) that we cannot properly service the typical self-help case because of the dollars involved versus the fees we have to charge.

On the other hand, there are some negatives to the self-help center operator/attorney relationship. The first is that it is hard to find attorneys

---

[1]For example, in a *California Lawyer* magazine fax poll of February 1993, 59% of lawyers responding said nonlawyer legal technicians should not be able to handle any legal work, while a surprising 41% disagreed and favored at least some nonlawyer practice.

who will be willing to take on this responsibility, at least partly because of fear of malpractice suits (this is to be read as difficult, not impossible. My experience was that there were and are such attorneys.) The second is that one takes a risk of losing the customer every time you send him/her to an attorney. This is warranted if the situation is too difficult to be handled by a self-help operation, but there may be times where the lawyer wrongly convinces the customer that the case is too difficult and takes the case away. I ran into this problem; but by following up on referrals and by constantly looking for sympathetic attorneys to add to the list, I minimized the problem.

B. How To Find Supportive Lawyers

Locating a lawyer or lawyers who will support what you are doing can be a huge help when it comes to dealing with (or fending off) those who don't. Remarkably, if even one or two lawyers in your community know what you are about and approve your work, you are less likely to be prosecuted. Indeed, just one friendly lawyer may even be able to stop a prosecution that is in the works. I have seen this happen on at least three occasions. In each instance, after either one or several local attorneys quietly let it be known that they would go to bat for a particular independent paralegal who was threatened with an unauthorized practice charge, the planned prosecution was dropped. How can one, two, or even a small group of lawyers stop organized lawyerdom so easily? Because prosecutors know they are less likely to win the battle for public opinion if local lawyers are willing to take the witness stand or make public statements saying that the particular independent paralegal is not practicing law and is an asset to the community.

In addition to making contact with sympathetic lawyers for self-preservation reasons, you will also benefit from an alliance with at least one lawyer familiar with the legal subject or subjects you deal with for at least two reasons. First, if you pick a truly experienced lawyer, this person will probably know more than you do about the legal paperwork you are preparing. If you can occasionally call this person for advice when you face a difficult problem, it will be a big help.

Second, and at least as important, a relationship with a local lawyer will mean you have someone to whom you can refer customers who need formal legal advice, or whose problem changes from uncontested to contested before your horrified eyes. If you don't have the ability to do this, you may be tempted to try to help your customer solve a problem that you are not equipped or trained to deal with. Aside from the risk of being charged with the unauthorized practice of law inherent in giving any legal advice, you also assume the risk (to your customers, at least) of giving bad or incomplete advice.

But, suppose you are just starting your business in a section of America where most lawyers are still maniacal about defending their monopoly. How do you find lawyer allies without making yourself so visible to organized lawyerdom that you do more harm than good? There is no one right way to do this, but here are some hints. Please realize that like most general rules, each of these has its exceptions, and it will be up to you to creatively apply them to your situation:

- Avoid attorneys closely-associated with local bar associations and bar referral panels. They tend to attract just the sort of small office traditionalists who will feel most threatened by your business and will want to close you down.

- Attorneys with strong pro-consumer records are good people to feel out. Also, lawyers who work in the emerging field of mediation often tend to be predisposed to helping people help themselves.

- Lawyers in private practice who have worked for federally-funded legal services (often called "legal aid") programs can also be good bets, as they have already worked in a clinic-like context where the same sorts of legal tasks you handle are accomplished by paralegals. In addition, many lawyers who are attracted by legal aid work in the first place are sympathetic to the needs of the legally underserved. Current legal services intake workers, secretaries, and paralegals should be able to suggest some likely former legal services lawyers.

- Do not assume that a progressive political stance on social issues, such as the environment, women's rights, minority hiring, or disarmament means a lawyer will be sympathetic with what you are doing. To the contrary, in my experience, it is often people who are fairly conservative politically who are the most pro-self-help law. This isn't so surprising when you realize that many conservatives take seriously the traditional right of every American to have good access to the legal system at a reasonable cost. Paradoxically, many personal injury, criminal defense and other lawyers who often favor all sorts of reforms for society typically oppose long-needed legal reforms such as adopting no-fault automobile insurance, abolishing probate and licensing independent paralegals. They fear change in these areas because it will negatively affect their monopoly over the legal system and, as a result, the girth of their wallets. Again, the point is, do not bare your soul to a lawyer just because you respect the stance that person took on an unrelated social issue.

- Personal friends and acquaintances (or, if necessary, friends of friends) can be a good source of possibly helpful lawyers. If you worked previously at a court clerk's office, or a local law firm, you probably know at least a few lawyers you respect. If you don't have these contacts, think about whether you know anyone whose judgment you trust who can suggest lawyers who are likely to be sympathetic.

In an effort to create a network of lawyer supporters, start by locating one lawyer to whom you can refer customers with problems more complicated than you can handle. As a significant percentage of almost one million lawyers in the U.S. are under-employed, there are plenty of likely candidates. Some of these lawyers are likely to be interested in (and often threatened by) the growth of the self-help law movement and want to get in on the action. One way for a lawyer to do this is to set up a paralegal division within their own office; another is to work closely with one or more self-help legal typing services.

When you locate someone who you think is a potential supporter, approach her carefully. Start by soliciting their general views on the desirability of opening up the legal system to more participation by nonlawyers. If they are hostile or extremely worried, back off. If they express an openness to the independent paralegal movement, but seem tentative, go slow and don't presume too much at the start. Always remember that all lawyers, even your friends, have undergone a remarkably homogeneous educational experience which has repeatedly emphasized the fact that only lawyers are competent to practice law. This is a hard burden for even the most enlightened lawyer to completely put down and you are likely to find that even a genuinely supportive lawyer will experience moments when he doubts whether your profession should exist. Try to anticipate this and help your lawyer friend come to terms with and conquer these occasional attacks of professional paranoia. No matter how highly she was recommended, or how much you respect her for other reasons, go slowly when it comes to disclosing what you are doing or plan to

do. Again, if you are greeted with hostility, or even a lot of obvious nervousness, don't argue—back off quickly.

Assuming the lawyer seems genuinely open to working with you, ask if it will be okay if you occasionally refer customers who wish to handle their own legal affairs, but need some legal advice as part of doing so. If the lawyer wants to know more about your business, be prepared to demonstrate that you really run a self-help legal typing service and do not provide legal advice. (The best way to do this is to follow the techniques I discuss in Chapter 3.)

Again, assuming all signs are go, send over a few people. Check back with your customers to find out how they were treated. If you find they got good service at a fair price, you will want to try to gradually establish a closer relationship with the lawyer. The best way to do this is to make yourself valuable to the lawyer by continuing to refer appropriate customers to his office. As the lawyer comes to see that you are a responsible business producer, you can begin to discuss some of your needs. Over time, you will want to work out an informal understanding with the lawyer that in exchange for the business you produce, he will answer your occasional questions and go to bat for you if you are accused of practicing law without a license.

In Bakersfield, California, a group of local independent paralegals has taken this sort of relationship a step further. A local lawyer, who believes strongly that IPs should be trained to do an excellent job, volunteers his time to help train the independent paralegals on how to do a better job typing divorce and bankruptcy forms. (See Virginia Simons interview in the Appendix.)

C. Make a Lawyer Your "Partner"

So far, I have assumed that you want to open your own business and relate to lawyers only as you need them. I have also extensively discussed the fact that operating independently makes you vulnerable to the charge that you are practicing law without a license. For some readers, beginning a new business (which is never easy), at the same time that you may be attacked by hostile lawyers will be too much to cope with.

One way to reduce the fear that you will be prosecuted for unauthorized practice is to work directly for a lawyer as a freelance paralegal. (See Chapter 13.) Another is to have a lawyer work very closely with your business. In other words, instead of working for a lawyer, encourage a lawyer to work with you. Before you dismiss this idea as silly, consider the fact that bill collectors have used this approach for years, often working with one lawyer in a stable long-term relationship that in all but name amounts to a shared business. Major portions of the medical profession also seem to be heading in this direction with business people increasingly owning hospitals, clinics and emergency treatment facilities, and hiring doctors and other professional care providers to work for them.

More to the point, I know of several divorce and landlord eviction services run by independent paralegals who have a lawyer directly associated with their practice. In exchange for having the lawyer available to provide reasonably-priced legal advice to the paralegal's customers when necessary, the independent paralegal typically refers all customers with contested cases and legal questions to the lawyer. Again, the advantage to this sort of arrangement to the lawyer, the paralegal and the customer is obvious.

The desirability of establishing an independent paralegal business that works very closely with a lawyer must, of course, be weighed against the fact that having a lawyer closely associated with your business may negatively affect the way you work. Remember, one reason why independent paralegal services are so popular is that they allow customers the right to simplify their legal problem. Lawyers, of course, commonly do the opposite, burdening even the most routine legal tasks with layers of often unneeded complexity—a process that, in the eyes of many legal reformers, all too often seems to continue exactly as long as the client's money holds out. In short, if you have a lawyer associated with your operation, you want to be sure that her lawyerly tendency toward high-cost obfuscation doesn't end up emasculating your business.

Another potential problem for independent paralegals and lawyers who work closely together are state laws and state supreme court opinions that state that every business offering legal services to the public must be owned and controlled by lawyers. Specifically, these statutes make it illegal for non-lawyers to participate in the ownership of a law practice (Washington, D.C. and North Dakota are limited exceptions) or to split legal fees with lawyers.

In the long run, I suspect that many of these laws will be struck down as being illegal restraints of trade under the Sherman Anti-Trust Act, but as this edition goes to press, they are still firmly on the books. Fortunately, if you engage in a little creative business organization, they shouldn't prevent you from working closely with a lawyer. One good approach is to keep the two businesses structurally separate. This not only means you should not formally hire the lawyer or split fees, but that each business should be an independent legal entity (that is, if you occupy the same office, put both names on the door, get separate business licenses and don't treat the lawyer as an employee or independent contractor). If a customer uses the services of both you and the lawyer, she should pay with separate checks. Yes, when an IP and a lawyer work closely together on a regular basis, respecting this somewhat artificial business division can be cumbersome, but if you're investigated by organized lawyerdom, you'll both be glad you took the trouble.

D. Working With Mediators

In some legal areas, a certain percentage of an independent paralegal's customers are likely to have, or develop, a contested dispute about a factual issue with another party. Divorce is the most obvious, where arguments over property division, support, child custody and visitation are fairly common.

If you are typing a divorce or paperwork for another domestic action, such as a step-parent adoption, and your customer tells you that he and his former mate are having a serious dispute about a factual matter, your best bet is to encourage them to see a private or, if such a program exists in your area, a court or other publicly-run mediation service.

Mediation is a process by which a third party (the mediator) helps people with a dispute arrive at their own solutions. Precisely because it is non-coercive—the mediator, unlike a judge or arbitrator, has no power to impose a decision—mediation often works brilliantly to settle domestic disputes. The idea is normally for you to refer the disputing couple to the mediator, have them work out their dispute (and write down the agreed-upon compromise) and then have your customer return to your office to complete the other paperwork.

The question then arises, what type of mediator should you work with? Here are some thoughts:

- Most of your customers will be on a tight budget. You'll need to find a mediator who charges a reasonable fee (often in the range of $75 per hour) and is result-oriented. A mediator who expects to help customers probe their psyches for many hours, at $200 per hour, may be fine for the BMW set, but would not be a good choice for most of your customers.

- In many states, mediated agreements to divide property as part of a divorce can be submitted directly to a court as part of the divorce paperwork you type. If so, you will want to work with a mediator who knows how to prepare the necessary forms.

- This raises the question of whether the mediator should be a lawyer. My answer is not necessarily. Although lawyer mediators will normally be adept at preparing necessary paperwork, they often aren't able to shed their "lawyer in control" attitudes and truly let the parties arrive at their own solutions. In addition, many charge more than most of your customers will be able to afford. In my experience, nonlawyer mediators, whose fees are often more modest, are typically more open to allowing disputants to find their own solutions.

E. Working With the Courts

In some parts of America, court clerks and judges are implacably opposed to the self-help law movement and, by logical extension, to IP's. However, in many states, including large portions of Florida, Texas and most of the West

Coast, the legal profession's outright hostility is beginning to be replaced by grudging acceptance and, in some instances, guarded support for independent paralegals. For example, in Napa, California, Sharon Goetting, who prepares forms for divorces, guardianships, stepparent adoptions, and child support and custody modification orders, was instrumental in getting the courts to hand out a free referral publication which informs the public about the existence of IP services.

Whether judges and court clerks are hostile or friendly, you may as well get used to the idea that you'll have to work fairly closely with them. Even if you never set foot in the courthouse, they will quickly come to recognize your paperwork, even though your name appears nowhere on it. Given this, I recommend that you try to form as positive a relationship as possible with key people at the courthouse. Here are some suggestions:

- Court clerks are often burdened by nonlawyers (and more often than you would guess, lawyers) filing incorrect and incomplete paperwork. Assuming that you really do know what you are doing, the papers your customers file will likely come as a welcome relief. This may result in your getting positive feedback from a court clerk. If so, use this as an opportunity to better introduce yourself. Make it clear that you only type paperwork and don't practice law. Then ask the clerk if she can suggest ways your work can be improved. One opportunity for this type of contact to take place is at the filing window, assuming, of course, you occasionally file paperwork yourself. In fact, in many communities, contacts at the filing window have lead to such a positive independent paralegal-court clerk relationship, that the clerk actually starts referring customers to the IP.

- If possible, get to know one or more local judges, who often review your paperwork. Sometimes this can be done through a civic organization or, if the judge must run for re-election, as part of her campaign. In other instances, a judge who is genuinely concerned about legal access for a particular group, such a single mothers, older people or minorities, may be willing to counsel you on ways to improve your work. If you are a member of an IP association, consider asking the judge to meet with your group. (See Glynda Mathewson's and Rose Palmer's interviews in the Appendix.) Obviously, in all meetings with judges it pays for IPs to go to great lengths to indicate that they do not give legal advice to customers.

How to Run a Quality Business

A ll of the advice in this book about how to prosper as an independent paralegal assumes one crucial thing: that you do excellent work. It is appropriate, then, to take a minute to touch on some basic business practices and procedures.

Before you even open your doors, it is essential that you do at least three things. The first is to make sure that you are thoroughly familiar with how to prepare all the legal forms and, if relevant, with the agency procedures that you will handle. The second is to understand how to run your business without engaging in the unauthorized practice of law. (See Chapter 3 for a thorough discussion.) Third, it is essential that you establish a number of ordered business procedures to ensure that every customer in fact receives quality error-free help.

A. Training

Some readers, who have worked for lawyers for years, typing the same forms they plan to prepare as an independent paralegal, will already have the technical form-preparation expertise they need. However, many others will need basic training on how to prepare legal paperwork. How to get this is ably discussed by Catherine Jermany in the interview that appears in the Appendix.

Prospective independent paralegals typically need both skills training and practical experience. Let's use the preparation of probate forms as an example. Your first step is to study all available materials on the subject that are relevant to your state. In California, Nolo Press publishes *How To Probate an Estate,* by Julia Nissley, a very accessible and easy-to-use resource. However, in most states, you won't find how-to books written for nonlawyers and will have to rely on materials aimed at lawyers. To locate these, you must become familiar with the law library, and especially with the practice books designed to show lawyers and paralegals how to probate an estate. These are published for all populous states. To locate the probate materials for your state, your best bet is to visit a good-sized law library at a non-busy time and ask the reference librarian for a list of the materials she considers most helpful in the probate area.

Once you have studied these and are thoroughly up to speed on the basics of form preparation, you will need some real world experience before you market your services to the public. Here are several ways to get it:

- Find a lawyer (usually a sole practitioner or member of a small firm) who needs help preparing probate paperwork but doesn't have a lot of money. In exchange for your freelance help at a very reasonable hourly fee (or maybe even initially as a volunteer), she can supply you with the necessary paperwork to learn on, as well as the guidance to make sure you do the work correctly.

- Study probate files at your local courthouse. Court records are public and your courthouse will have a procedure to check out files. You'll want to closely examine a good-sized pile. Court clerks may be hostile if you explain exactly what your purpose is, so if anyone asks, it may be best to state that you're doing a research project and leave it at that. (Glynda Mathewson discusses how she used this learning technique as part of training herself to type California divorces in her interview in the Appendix.)

- Work with, or for, a freelance paralegal who already prepares probate forms for lawyers. As discussed in Chapter 13, in many states, freelance paralegals do a large percentage of lawyer form preparation work. Your county paralegal association may be able to supply a list of freelancers working in your area. Obviously, you'll have to convince any freelance paralegal you call that your plans to ultimately sell form preparation services to the public will be non-competitive.

- Take a paralegal course that deals with probate specifically. The problem with this approach is that many paralegal schools won't allow you to take just the courses you are interested in but will want you to enroll for their entire program. Don't take no for an answer. Visit schools that offer hands-on probate form preparation courses and explore different ways you can get the help you need. At a minimum, find out what books and other materials the teacher uses and purchase them directly from the publisher.

- If possible, join local paralegal organizations, especially those that offer hands-on training. Some paralegal groups may not let you join unless you have already worked in the field or had formal training, but others aren't so fussy. There is no universally-used definition of the term "paralegal," and in many areas, self-taught people are accepted.

- Investigate to see if computer programs exist in your state to facilitate probate form preparation. Increasingly, legal publishers are publishing these for lawyers and freelance paralegals. These programs are designed to complete forms, not as a teaching tool, but there is obviously a lot you can learn by working with such a program.

INDEPENDENT PARALEGAL TRAINING COURSES

A few community colleges, adult education schools and private business schools are beginning to offer legal form preparation courses geared to the needs of IPs. Check locally to see what is available in your area.

Independent Paralegal Workshops, based in the Los Angeles area, offers skills training in a number of legal areas. For example, people regularly come from all over the country for their bankruptcy workshops. For a list of training courses, call 213-655-6141.

HOW TO GET TRAINING TO APPEAR BEFORE
ADMINISTRATIVE AGENCIES

As noted a number of times in this book, many independent paralegals are beginning to specialize in representing people before federal and state administrative
agencies, such as the Social Security Administration, which does not require advocates to be lawyers. As a result, I am often asked how a prospective IP can learn to
do this. To my knowledge, there are no available courses; most IPs who currently
represent people before agencies have learned either by working for the particular
agency or for organizations such as a Legal Services Program, which regularly
represents people who appear before the agency. (See the interview with Glynda
Mathewson in the Appendix.)

B. Avoid Unauthorized Practice of Law

This subject is thoroughly discussed in Chapter 3.

C. Good Office Management

The third attribute of a good paralegal operation requires that you run a top-
notch business operation. This involves doing at least the following things:

- Run a clean, well-organized office from a good location. (See Chapter 6.);
- Learn good telephone skills so you can screen out inappropriate cus-
  tomers;
- Provide your customers with accurate and thorough information necessary
  to make their own decisions about the legal task they are concerned with;
- Use a typewriter or computer to prepare all necessary forms promptly and
  accurately;
- Make sure your customers thoroughly check your work to ensure it's
  accurate before it is submitted to a court; and
- Document that you have done all of the above.

Let's now briefly look at how to do this by tracking a customer from her
first contact with your business through the preparation of all the necessary
forms.

Step 1:　Initial Contact with a Potential Customer

Assume that you prepare the forms necessary for small businesses to incorporate. You receive a phone call from Alexis Elmore, who wishes to incorporate her business, which consists of two children's shoe stores. Your first job is to tell Elmore what you do, at the same time that you find out whether her situation is appropriate for your incorporation typing service. Accomplishing both of these tasks efficiently and quickly is a real skill, especially given the fact that you are solely in the business of typing legal forms, not of transferring legal expertise.

Specifically, you would want to ask if Elmore has a pretty good idea of what a corporation is, what's involved in preparing the paperwork, who's going to own it and how many shares of stock will be issued. In short, you need to be sure Elmore knows enough about incorporation to sensibly provide you with the information necessary to incorporate her business. If Elmore replies that her accountant recommended that she incorporate and she has discussed the tax advantages with him and has read a self-help book on the subject, she is probably ready to go ahead. However, if she seems confused about what a corporation is, or is unsure that her decision to incorporate is wise, she has more work to do before she uses your typing service. You might suggest she read several good books[1] on the subject and consult a tax or small business adviser before going ahead.

Assuming Elmore's answers make sense to you, or she takes your advice, learns more and then calls you back, you will want to briefly tell her how your form preparation service works and how much you charge. Assuming this sounds good to her, it's time to make an appointment.

Step 2:　Initial Office Interview

When Elmore comes to your clean, well-organized office for her first appointment, she should first encounter a reception room or area that contains

---

[1] At the risk of plugging Nolo Press too much, the best hands-on incorporation books I know of are *How To Form Your Own California (New York, Texas, or Florida) Corporation* by Anthony Mancuso. Nolo also publishes computer software to prepare incorporation paperwork in California, New York and Texas.

material about self-help law in general and your incorporation form preparation service in particular. A small library of good small business operations books is also valuable. If Elmore must wait a few minutes, she will be surrounded by material that tells her more about what you do. Not only will it make a good impression, but you'll have excellent materials close at hand should you want to refer Elmore to good sources of more information. And don't forget to keep a few toys on hand just in case Elmore brings little Barbara.

Step 3: Open a File

Your first task at the interview is to open a file. First, have Elmore read and sign a statement that describes your self-help form preparation service and clearly states that you are not a lawyer. (This is discussed in detail in Chapter 3.) Assuming you have a computer, you will probably want to enter Elmore's biographical information and instruct the computer to generate the intake sheet. If you have the proper software, this will allow you to simultaneously add the customer's name to your master list for later use in keeping track of her file and communicating with her by phone and mail. At this stage, it is also appropriate to again verify that your customer knows how much your service costs and to establish how she plans to pay. Many independent paralegals appropriately ask for a substantial portion of their fee at the first interview. As discussed in Chapter 3, I recommend setting your basic fee to cover the cost of necessary self-help law books or kits, rather than trying to sell them separately. If Elmore has purchased the necessary material separately, you can offer her a small discount.

Step 4: Gather the Necessary Information From the Customer

Assuming that, like most business people, Elmore has done her homework and has a pretty good idea of what incorporation entails, your next task is to gather the information necessary to prepare the paperwork. The best way to do this is to have Elmore fill out a detailed information form. Incidentally, because this form is probably the most important tool you will use in your business, care should be taken to ensure that it is complete, well-organized and attractive. Creating a good information sheet is so important that a short digression on how to create one is appropriate.

Think of it this way—forming a corporation, or for that matter, preparing any other routine legal paperwork, consists of properly arranging a number of "pieces" or "bits" of information. Despite what lawyers might wish you to believe, no magic and precious little art is necessary. You simply need to identify all the information necessary to prepare a particular form and then create the best possible questionnaire to gather it. Many form books written for attorneys contain useful questionnaires and checklists of information necessary to fill out routine incorporation forms. Or you may want to purchase questionnaire forms from an independent paralegal who already works in this area.

Start by identifying the many "pieces" of information that are standard to all small corporations (or divorces, bankruptcies or whatever else you handle). Most of these will have long since been reduced to formula language, called "boilerplate" in law biz slang. Often you will find that sample Articles of Incorporation forms containing this boilerplate are printed by your state's Secretary of State or Corporations Commissioner, along with filing instructions. In addition, in many states, incorporation forms are sold by private legal printers.[2] Some incorporation forms are also commonly published in legal form books and self-help law books.[3] You will want to buy all the available forms you will need for your particular operation or create your own. Obviously, if you design a form, you will want to be sure it is acceptable to the court or agency you will file it with.

Step 5: Help Your Customer Fill in the Information Sheet

Assuming now that your questionnaire is written and you know that it works, you are ready to work with Alexis Elmore. You'll want to get as much information as possible from Elmore in her own handwriting. This way, if you are ever investigated, it's easier to demonstrate that you were typing forms under her supervision, and not engaging in the practice of law. In addition, you will probably want to interview Elmore to be sure the information she has supplied is complete. For example, your form will probably ask whether Elmore wants to elect "S corp" tax status (which would allow her business to be taxed as a partnership for federal tax purposes) as opposed to conventional federal corporate tax status. If she hasn't considered this question or seems confused, you will want to guide her to good written information on the subject, and perhaps suggest that she discuss the issue with her tax advisor before continuing.

Step 6: Review the Information Form With Your Customer

After Alexis Elmore has carefully reviewed and completed the information sheet, have her sign a statement at the bottom of the form that says that it is

---

[2] Legal printers operate in all states. Many office supply stores carry these state specific forms. One of the largest and best of these national companies (especially strong for east coast states) is Julius Blumberg, Inc., 62 White St., New York, N.Y. Blumberg's also produces excellent bankruptcy forms.

[3] Form manufacturers and publishers take the position that copying their forms, especially in a business context, is a copyright violation. If you use a particular publisher's materials, you should buy (not photocopy) them.

complete, correct and reflects her desires. Keep a signed copy of this form for your files. It is essential that you do this for two reasons. First, you need to protect yourself should Elmore, or any other customer, later claim that she gave you information that you forgot to include on the forms. In the bankruptcy area, where all debts must be listed to be discharged and customers sometimes fail to provide a complete list, keeping a signed copy of the customer's worksheet or questionnaire is particularly important. Second, if a prosecutor or other attorney organization ever questions whether or not you are practicing law, you'll want to produce the worksheet, complete with the customer's signed statement that they (not you) provided the necessary information.

Step 7:   Prepare the Legal Paperwork

Your next task is to prepare the necessary paperwork. For incorporation papers, which can run 60 or 70 pages, the only practical way to do this is by use of a computer or typewriter with considerable memory capacity. Since most needed language is standard legal boilerplate, it's a waste of time, and hence money, to type them from scratch. In other areas of the law, such as filling out preprinted divorce forms, it is practical to either use a typewriter or, in many states, to purchase a computer form-generation package designed for use in law offices. If you begin with the typewritten approach, there is no reason you must bang all the keys yourself. With a good information sheet keyed directly to necessary legal forms, any competent typist should be able to prepare the forms quickly. Especially after your business becomes established, your time will be better spent dealing with customers or marketing your business.

Step 8:   Review the Legal Paperwork With
Your Customer

Review the completed paperwork with Elmore carefully. This will normally be done at a second or third appointment. When your joint review is complete, have Elmore sign a brief statement such as this:

I have carefully reviewed all forms prepared by the Pacific Rim Self-Help Incorporation Service according to my instruction and find them to be accurate and complete.

_____   _____

Date   Signature

When paperwork is complete and ready for filing, it's appropriate to ask for final payment. Most typing services prefer to be paid the balance on the spot to save the trouble of billing and collecting from slow payers. I think this approach makes sense.

Step 9:   Tell Your Customer What To Do Next

Finally, you need to either file the paperwork for Elmore or give her a detailed instruction sheet telling her how to accomplish this. There is no legal reason why you can't file the papers, either in person or by mail. (Filing forms is not considered to be the practice of law.) However, I think it often makes sense to have your customer do the filing, to emphasize that it's her legal action and your role is simply that of a form preparer. Also, if your customer will have to make a court appearance, it makes sense for her to visit the courthouse first, to check out where and how this will occur. In any case, be absolutely certain that any filing information (including fees) you provide is accurate, complete and up-to-date.

In legal areas such as divorce, where a court appearance is often required, many customers will want you to coach them as to what to say and when to say it. Doing anything more than explaining how the particular procedure is normally structured comes perilously close to practicing law, unless your local court supports the idea of nonlawyers providing more extensive help (see the interview with Virginia Simons in the Appendix). Normally, your best bet is to refer them to the relevant parts of any self-help resource that discusses how to present a court case. Another good approach is to suggest that your customer stop by the court and watch how similar cases are presented.

Step 10: Maintain Accurate Records

Keep neat records of all work done. All information you get from Elmore or any other customer, particularly the signed statement that she recog nizes you are not a lawyer, the signed customer information sheet, and the signed statement that she has read all completed paperwork and finds it to be accurate, should be kept indefinitely in a well-organized file system. In addition, all information maintained in your computer, such as mailing lists, agency referral sources and customer demographic information, should be both impeccably maintained and regularly backed up.

How Much to Charge

I f you are planning to go into business to help nonlawyers prepare legal forms, you probably already have some idea as to how much is reasonable to charge in your community. This usually depends on a number of factors, including:

- How much lawyers charge to do the same task;
- How much other independent paralegals in your area charge for the task;
- How many hours it will take you on average to complete the legal pa perwork;
- How much your overhead is, over and above paying yourself a reasonable salary. If you rent a nice office, hire an employee and buy equipment such as a computer, this will be a significant amount;
- How much your customers are willing to pay;
- Whether some or all of your motive to work as an independent paralegal is to further a cause you are personally involved in, such as men's, women's or tenants' rights. If so, you may be willing to charge less than the market value for your services. This is especially likely to be true if you get support in the form of a grant from a foundation or other non-profit source.

A. Establish How Much Money You and Your Business Need

One sensible approach to setting a price for typing a divorce or bankruptcy, or any other form preparation task is to work backwards—to first decide on the total amount you need to take in to run your business and pay yourself a decent wage, and then determine how much you must charge per form preparation job to meet this goal. As part of doing this, you will want to budget carefully, making sure to add in all your costs, from the telephone bill and office rent to computer paper, brochure printing, phone book ads and office supplies. Also remember that if you will need to buy office equipment from your savings to get your business started, you should include in your budget an item to cover gradually reimbursing yourself before the equipment wears out. And if you plan to hire part-time office help, don't forget to include these costs.

Once you arrive at a final overhead figure, I recommend that you increase it by at least 20% to cover things you haven't thought of. If you have never previously been in business for yourself, increase your estimate by 30%.

Your next step is to realistically decide how much you need to live on. Again, I would budget a little on the high side so that even if the business doesn't initially produce enough income to meet your goal, you won't starve.

TAKE TIME TO PREPARE A PROFIT AND LOSS FORECAST

To really see if your proposed business will make money, given your assumptions as to your costs and the number of customers you can realistically expect, it's wise to prepare a detailed profit-and-loss statement and cash flow forecast. It is particularly important to accurately estimate cash flow to determine whether money coming in will be adequate to cover your expenses. Remember, most of your expenses will be immediate, but a least some of your income will be delayed because customers will pay late. Fortunately, it is easy to create both a profit-and-loss forecast and a cash flow analysis following the detailed instructions in *How To Write a Business Plan,* by Mike McKeever (Nolo Press).

Now add the amount you'll need for personal living expense to your estimate of the amount needed to cover business overhead. This is the grand total you'll need in order to prosper. For example, you might conclude that you and your business can both get by comfortably on a total income of $6,500 a month.

Your next task is to estimate how many customers you can realistically hope to attract in a month. If, for example, you decide to type divorces, and decide that, given a little time to develop your business, you should be able to attract and handle 50 per month, you must charge an average of $130 per customer to meet your $6,500 goal.

B. Find Out What Competitors Charge

Let's continue to assume that, like most IPs, you plan to type divorces. If so, you'll want to determine what lawyers, including any large, heavily-advertised legal clinics, charge for preparing divorce forms. In doing this, however, don't necessarily believe the lowest price quoted in ads; this is often a price for a bare bones service that very few customers qualify for. For example, if a customer asks a legal clinic for a widely-advertised $700 divorce, she is likely to be told that if she owns property or has children, she must pay extra, usually a lot extra. This sort of "bait and switch" approach is the reason why many customers find that heavily-advertised legal clinics usually end up being no cheaper than your typical run of the courthouse lawyer. In the divorce area, you will probably find that no matter what other legal clinics advertise, $750-$1500 is the usual low-end lawyer rate for uncontested divorces. If so, you will be extremely competitive if you charge in the range of $150-$300.

You should also check what existing independent paralegals charge for the same services you plan to provide. For example, if there are already several independent paralegals in your city who type divorces for $175-$225, you will probably want to charge about the same, or perhaps a bit less, until you get established. As you gain experience, you will want to adjust those amounts up or down based on the average amount of time it takes you to prepare a divorce.

C. Estimate How Long Form Preparation Will Take

If you're operating efficiently, you will probably find that a divorce takes you about two to four hours to prepare, depending mostly on how efficient your intake (fact gathering) procedures are and whether you use a computerized legal form generation package.[1] The time it takes to type other legal forms varies greatly, depending on state law and the particular fact situation. For example, a bankruptcy often takes one-and-one-half to two-and-one-half hours to prepare, including meeting with the customer. An uncontested guardianship petition involving custody of minor children might typically take two to three hours of independent paralegal time in most states. Small business incorporations can be done very quickly if you have all the repetitive boilerplate information stored on a computer, or a typewriter with adequate memory.

---

[1]In some states, very simple divorces that qualify to be done by mail can often be prepared in about one hour.

Preparing a living trust or a will using a form on a disk program, such as those available from the National Association for Independent Paralegals, should take no more than 90 minutes, including the time it takes to interview the customer and show her how to use the computer.

D. Draw Up a Price List

Once you have canvassed what the competition charges and considered this in light of how much you need to make and how many customers you believe you can attract, it's time to set your prices. To give you some idea of what one experienced paralegal charges for a variety of typing services, I asked Robin Smith, of People's Paralegal Service in Beaverton, Oregon, for permission to print her price list (exclusive of filing fees) as of mid-1991. Here it is:

- Divorce (co-petition) $175
- Bankruptcy (up to 35 creditors) 165
- Custody, visitation and support
  (unmarried couple) 175
- Stepparent adoption (with consent) 225
- Incorporation 195
- Guardianship 165

Commonly, some types of form preparation involve extra paperwork (for example, some divorces require a formal property settlement agreement), for which you will wish to charge extra. Doing this is fine, as long as you clearly state this in your ads and flyers. In addition, be sure you indicate that your fees do not include court filing fees, fees for service of papers, etc., unless, of course, they do. The point is to fully disclose all of your prices from the beginning. This honest business practice will be appreciated by your customers and will set you apart from other independent paralegal offices and especially lawyer-run legal clinics, which commonly use deceptive bait and switch advertising techniques.

In talking to a number of independent paralegals who face competition from other IP's, several have noted that they believe price is a major factor when customers choose one paralegal service over another. For example, Robin Smith notes that the existence of several competing independent paralegals who list prices in the paper makes her think twice before raising prices and can even mean that a price may occasionally have to be lowered. However, she adds that as long as an independent paralegal offers a good service at a fair price, and is known in the community, he or she doesn't have to meet the price of every low-end competitor. Perhaps even a better illustration of this point can be found in the San Francisco Bay Area, where the divorce form typing business has expanded to the extent that over 60% of divorces are now handled without a lawyer. This has meant that a constant stream of new independent paralegals has been attracted to the business, often advertising low prices in an effort to build up volume. Jolene Jacobs, former owner of the Divorce Centers of California office in San Francisco, made these comments about pricing:

> *A lot of people just starting out are able to set a low price because they have another job, or other means of support, and they operate out of a house or very inexpensive office. Eventually, as they build a clientele and move out of the house, they are likely to conclude that it makes sense to raise their prices somewhat. For the most part, established typing services with reasonably competitive prices do not have to lower prices to meet every lowballer. As in lots of other businesses, consumers choose a typing service based both on price and their perception of the quality of the service offered, which often comes down to preferring an experienced over an inexperienced provider. In short, establishing a competitive price will be a*

factor in a typing service's success, but if you have a good reputation and sound marketing, you don't have to offer the lowest price in town.

(See Jolene Jacob's interview in the Appendix for more about how this pioneer independent paralegal operated her business.)

Once you establish your prices, you should include them in your printed material for all to see and rely on. Here is a sample flyer:

Hours: 9:00-6:00: Mon-Sat   Phone: 416-555-1111

(evening appointments available)   Call for Appointment

QUALITY
SELF-HELP BANKRUPTCY CENTER

A Nonlawyer Typing Service

We type:

- Bankruptcy forms for Chapter 7 bankruptcy

- Our fee is $200 (this does not include the court filing fee of $120)

- We provide all customers with a copy of *How To File For Bankruptcy* and *Money Troubles,* published by Nolo Press. These excellent books provide comprehensive information about debt problems generally and bankruptcy specifically.

- All bankruptcy forms are prepared under the customer's direct supervision—we provide no legal advice.

- Our services are unconditionally guaranteed. If you are not satisfied, we will return your money immediately, with no ifs, ands or buts.

950 Pelham Road (at 45th). Park at Racafrax Parking, Pelham and 44th

Parking validated

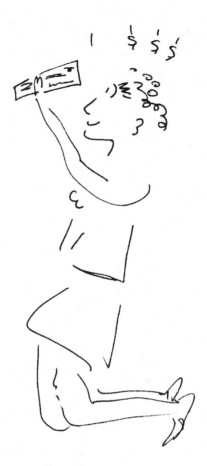

E. Fees For Preparing Bankruptcy Petitions

Unlike other legal areas, fees charged to help people file bankruptcy are sub-ject to review by the bankruptcy judge. The original purpose of this review was to prevent attorneys from ripping off both the debtor and the unsecured creditors—who might otherwise be entitled to the money used to pay the fees. In practice, few bankruptcy courts care how much lawyers charge. But an in-creasing number of bankruptcy judges are using their authority over fees to push down the prices charged by independent paralegals who help people do their own bankruptcies.

Now you can use a Nolo software program to help your clients prepare their legal paperwork quickly and accurately.

Nolo offers individual commercial licenses for the following programs:

WillMaker
- Windows
- DOS
- Macintosh

Living Trust Maker
- Windows
- Macintosh

Nolo's Personal RecordKeeper
- DOS
- Macintosh

Nolo's Partnership Maker
- DOS

California Incorporator
- DOS

With a commercial license, you are entitled to unlimited use of the program you choose. You will also receive all upgrades at our special registered owner price.

Commercial Licenses:

$299 per program

$200 per program when you buy three or more

For a complete information package on how our Commercial License Program can help you in your business call us at:

1-800-992-6656 (or in 510 area, 549-4648) or write to:

Commercial License Department, Nolo Press, 950 Parker St, Berkeley, CA 94710

Here is how this happens. Every bankruptcy filing includes a document, called a Statement of Affairs, that discloses the debtor's recent economic history. Among the items that must be disclosed is any money paid for help filing for bankruptcy. In addition, all attorneys must file a special form that discloses their fees, and most bankruptcy courts require IPs to complete this form as well. The bankruptcy trustee then reviews these forms and if it appears that a typing service is charging more than what the trustee thinks is acceptable for typing, the IP is sued for the balance. For instance, if the trustee thinks that the typing aspect of the bankruptcy would only cost $150 at a regular secretarial service, but the fees charged by the IP were $250, the trustee might sue the IP in bankruptcy court to recover $100.

If typing is all that is being done, this might be a reasonable approach by the trustee. But IP bankruptcy services often do a lot more than typing. Depending on the IP, additional activities and costs might include:

- conducting an extensive customer interview using a questionnaire;
- sorting debts into the proper categories;
- alphabetizing the customer's list of creditors;
- negotiating with creditors;
- providing the customer with adequate written materials to explain how to make their own legal decisions;
- helping the customer to use and understand whichever written materials are being used;
- preparing the customer to understand what will happen at the creditors' meeting;
- making photocopies and filing the forms with the court.

While many courts and trustees approve all of these activities by independent paralegals, others wrongly believe that any activity other than typing constitutes the unauthorized practice of law and that no fees can be charged for illegal services. Often, however, when IPs have carefully informed courts about how they conduct their business, pointing out that they offer a range of valuable services as part of helping people to help themselves, these courts are willing allow a reasonable fee.

If you are new to the bankruptcy typing area, start by finding out what your local bankruptcy court permits typing services to charge—many courts have reasonable limits—and stay within this limit. If there is no rule on fees, or you find the court has imposed a limit that is unfairly low, take the following steps:

- carefully itemize your activities (see above list) and costs;
- make these costs consistent with your overall business plan;
- restrict your activities to apparent clerical tasks;
- make sure that your customer gets all their basic bankruptcy legal expertise from publications or outside resources and not from you; and
- be prepared to present this information to any judge or trustee who inquires about how you set your fees.

F. Grant Credit Conservatively

Another issue that always comes up when you run a small business is credit. Should you allow your customers to pay you in installments? Despite the fact that I know several IP's who manage to do this successfully, my advice is not to give credit. Assuming your prices are primarily in the rock bottom $150-$350 range, depending on the type of forms you type, it is reasonable to ask customers to pay your entire fee at your first meeting. It usually makes sense to charge low prices and collect all your fees right away, or to charge higher prices and bill people, but not to attempt both ways.

By not advancing credit, you may lose a little business to the competition, but in my opinion, in the long run you will come out far ahead both economically and psychologically. Why? Because the fact that you will always be paid up front will mean minimal bookkeeping and no need to send bills. And of intangible, but no less real, value, your peace of mind will never be disturbed by all those folks who promise to pay you later for typing their divorce and then patronize another typing service to get a bankruptcy, listing you as a creditor. Of course, one good way to allow people to be served now and pay later is to take credit cards. A number of IP's do this very successfully for all types of legal actions, except bankruptcies. If you have a good relationship with a bank, establishing a Master Card/Visa account should not be difficult.

In fairness, I should add that, in discussing my position on credit with a number of IP's, many, although generally agreeing, find it a bit too strict. As an alternative, a number ask for full payment up front but are willing to take half when the customer comes in for the initial interview and the other half when the papers are picked up for filing. If the second half isn't forthcoming, neither are the papers.

G. Establish a Money Back Guarantee

As noted in Chapter 12, "Customer Recourse," it is wise to establish a fast and generous recourse policy and to disclose it in advance. Obviously, you can't afford to include details in a small "penny saver" or phone book type listing, but you can and should put it in your general information sheet or brochure. This should be given to all customers, available in your waiting room, and generally circulated in your community as part of your marketing efforts.

Marketing Your Services

Suppose now that you have done everything from getting skills training, to choosing a name, to printing disclaimers and have opened the doors on your own shiny new paralegal typing service. Congratulations—but what next? If you wish to avoid quick starvation, you had better round up some customers. Let's look at the best, and a few of the worst, ways to do this.

A. Conventional Advertising Is Usually A Waste of Time

For a lot of people who are not experienced in small business economics, letting the general public know about your service means advertising. Indeed, if you are new to the independent paralegal business, you may have already considered getting as much money as you can together and running a series of splashy ads in local newspapers and perhaps even on radio or Cable TV.

If I do nothing else in this whole book but convince you of one thing, I hope it's that spending a lot of money on advertising your services in conventional ways such as these is unlikely to produce a profitable return. Or, put more directly, major advertising expenditures just plain will not work. There are two reasons for my dogmatism. The first is economic—the amount of business that conventional advertising will produce will not pay for its cost if you charge a reasonable amount for your services. How do I know this? The same way a jockey knows the ground is hard when he falls off a horse—I've tried it.

The second reason that a major advertising campaign isn't a good idea for the independent paralegal is that it is almost sure to produce a negative reaction from the bar. As mentioned throughout this book, especially when your business is new, you are far better off maintaining a reasonably low profile. Of course, this may change in the years to come (and indeed, has already done so in parts of California, Oregon and Arizona) but in most places, it's unwise to run a lot of ads that will remind the slightly tottering, but still powerful, legal establishment of your existence.

Before I discuss several cost-effective ways to market your paralegal services, here is a cogent excerpt from *Marketing Without Advertising,* by Michael Phillips and Salli Rasberry (Nolo Press):

> *A large and growing number of business people have become vividly aware that if they are to succeed in the long run, it is essential that they*

attract more loyal customers. Unfortunately, the mechanics of doing this are less obvious. After all, if you are already working eleven hours a day, you have no time to join a self-improvement club for the self-employed, no money to compete with major advertisers and probably no desire to turn yourself into a super salesperson.

•   •   •   •   •

And even if you can afford more advertising, many of you have probably begun to form the sneaking suspicion that despite conventional wisdom that dictates that advertising is essential, it is not cost effective in your business.

•   •   •   •   •

The truth, of course, is that very few of the 1600 advertising messages we experience each day are effective in influencing our shopping or buying behavior and an even smaller amount of it is cost effective for the advertiser. When it comes to a small business trying to get its message heard against the babble of corporate America, the chances of people you want to reach really hearing or seeing your message is miniscule. And even worse than the cost involved, relying on advertising to improve your sales often stonewalls your imagination, keeping you from exploring the many superior methods available for promoting your business.

•   •   •   •   •

In fact, the best and most economical way to attract and hold customers is through personal recommendation. A customer who is prescreened and prepared for what you have to offer is far more likely to appreciate you and use your business than is someone responding to an ad offering a low price. The essence of marketing without advertising then is to encourage "personal recommendation." How do you do this? Lots of ways, all of which start with creating an atmosphere of trust. Central to doing this is to run an honest business."

B. Getting Recommendations And Referrals

Okay, assuming that positive personal recommendations of your business are better, and certainly cheaper, approach than advertising, how do you encourage them? There are two ways. The first is to provide an excellent service and to let your satisfied customers spread the word for you. This will work, but it will take time to build to a level that will support you. In the meantime, you should make your services widely known to the people who are most likely to refer you customers. Ask yourself, who are the people who need the types of services you offer likely to be in contact with? For example, people in the armed services who need a divorce are likely to contact a military legal office (Judge Advocate General). Military lawyers don't handle divorce, but they can refer enlisted men and women to you if they know about your service. Similarly, lots of people who consider incorporating a small business talk to accountants or small business financial planners, both of whom are a good source of referrals if you prepare incorporation papers.

To tell referral sources about your business so they can tell others, you'll need good promotional material. Here is an sample:

Once you have designed a good packet of information, including listing your prices, location, general philosophy, disclaimer that you are not a lawyer, etc., make it available to as many referral sources as possible. Depending on the type of forms you prepare, you will want to communicate with some or all of the following:

- Accountants and tax preparers (especially if you type bankruptcies)
- Legal services offices (legal aid)
- Battered women's shelters (especially if you handle restraining orders and divorces)
- Immigrants' help organizations
- Public library reference librarians
- Law school *"pro per"* assistance centers
- Law librarians (at courthouses and law school libraries)
- Community services referral agencies and directories
- Drug treatment centers
- Marriage counselors and family therapists
- Court clerks (this only works in areas where courts are open-minded about IPs)
- Mediation professionals (especially if you type divorces and other family law paperwork)
- Social services
- University and college student assistance offices
- Grey Panthers and other senior advocacy organizations (especially if you handle Social Security disability appeals)
- Local corporation personnel departments
- Parents Without Partners and other singles groups
- Law enforcement (including the Sheriff's Office, Probation Department, Parole Officers and the County Jail)
- Consumer organizations
- The State Employment Office
- Women's organizations
- Collection agencies
- Child care centers
- Military bases, including all Judge Advocate General military law offices
- Law bookstores (many stores featuring self-help law books are springing up and they are a great source of referrals)

- Local media (send it to reporters who care about consumer, legal or family issues)
- Foreign language media and support groups (but only if you or an employee can speak the language)
- Any community group directly interested in your activity. (For example, if you do small business incorporations, you will want to contact a wide range of small business groups, accountants and bookkeepers who work in this area, as well as the reference librarian at any public library with a large collection of business materials. Similarly, if you do evictions, you should work as closely as you can with the local apartment house owners' association, as well as real estate management groups and any other community organizations of interest to landlords.)

Sample Cover Letter to Referral Agencies

Here is a cover letter appropriate for communicating with guidance counselors. Modified slightly, it will also work well as a cover letter when you send marketing material to other groups.

Date _____

Dear _____ :

As a guidance counselor, we know you deal with difficult family concerns every day. Some of these involve counseling people who need basic legal services in areas such as divorce, child support modification, bankruptcy, step-parent adoption and guardianship.

At Legal Form, Inc., we offer high quality, low-cost legal form preparation in all these areas. We strive to create a relaxed, non-adversarial atmosphere in which our customers feel comfortable.

We are not attorneys and cannot give legal advice. But as part of our highly efficient legal form typing service, we can, and do, stock a large selection of quality self-help law materials designed to help our customers inform themselves about the legal issues they face. These materials may be used free of charge at our office library and are also available for purchase.

As you can see from our enclosed pamphlet, we also offer a fairly wide array of other legal form preparation services, including conservatorships, wills, living trusts and small business incorporations. If you have any questions, please feel free to call me at any time.

Sincerely,

John Kennedy

John Kennedy
Owner, Legal Forms, Inc.

Bob Mission of the Sacramento, California Superior California Legal Clinic, reports that about fifty percent of his total referrals come from community agencies such as these. Robin Smith, of Oregon's People's Paralegal Service puts her estimate slightly higher. Glenda Mathewson, former owner of the Divorce Center in Oakland, California, emphasizes that you should not only just send groups a flyer, but if possible, "follow up personally to see that it got to the right person and to convince them that you know your business and aren't a dingbat." For example, she occasionally spoke at luncheon meetings of groups interested in family matters and kept in close touch with a number of attorney mediators who work in the domestic law area, because she believed it was her responsibility to convince people who can refer customers that her office provided a really good service.

POST YOUR FLYER ON COMMUNITY BULLETIN BOARDS

Another cost-effective way to get the word out is by the use of flyers. Design an eye-catching informative one, clearly stating your services and prices. Post it at appropriate places around town. Good locations include laundromats, food stores (including natural food stores), factory, military and graduate school bulletin boards.

As a general rule, the closer to the courthouse you can get your material, the better, unless of course you are in an area where extreme hostility to IPs (on the part of organized lawyerdom) means you want to keep a low profile. Sharon Goetting of Self-Help Paralegal Services in Napa, California, is one person who has successfully learned how to work with court clerks and judges to get the word out. Sharon explains:

As part of starting my business, I went directly to the presiding judge and talked to him about the fact that over half the people who were trying to file papers were doing it without a lawyer and often experiencing great difficulty. I explained that I could help fix the problem by running a first-class form typing service. The judge said "Go for it" and allowed me to put my flyer right on the bulletin board in the Court lobby. The clerks aren't allowed to refer directly to a private business, but can and regularly do point out my flyer to frustrated pro pers. As a result, I get a steady stream of customers.

Especially in coastal states, such as New York, California and Texas, where there are significant concentrations of non-English speakers, targeting your services to people who speak a language such as Spanish, Chinese or Vietnamese can also make sense. To do this effectively, you will need to have all the promotional materials translated into the particular language. In addition, someone who is fluent in the language in question will need to be regularly available to handle your non-English speaking business. This will include telephone screening as well as customer interviews.

GETTING HELP DESIGNING ADS AND FLYERS

In 20 years of working with IP's, I have yet to see a truly well-written, well-designed ad or flyer. Some are mediocre; most are terrible. So here is the truth, whether you want to hear it or not. Unless you are a trained writer or graphic artist, you are not competent to write and paste-up a flyer that will make the best possible presentation of your business. To accomplish this, you need skilled, cost-efficient help. Here is how to find it:

- Contact a small, local, reasonably-priced ad agency or, better yet, an independent reporter, freelance writer, English teacher or someone else with truly excellent language skills. With their help, write, re-write and proofread every word of every flyer, pamphlet and other promotion piece you distribute at least five times;
- Find a reasonably-priced graphic artist. Usually you can get a referral from a local "instant printing" shop. Work with her, incorporating your written material into well-designed promotional material. And don't let her talk you into ultra-slick designs—instead, your materials should be a little on the conservative side, to reassure customers that your business is reliable and trustworthy.

C. Open Your Own Self-Help Law Store

A few years ago there were only a few self-help law books. Now there are hundreds of books and dozens of software programs. Enough that in a number of places small business people are opening small self-help law book and software stores which occasionally also stock small business and consumer titles. For the IP, a small store can be a perfect sideline, since a significant percentage of the people who come to buy self-help materials will also need help preparing legal paperwork. And a store can also be a good place to run the occasional class or workshop, thus generating the possibility of even more business.

D. Keep a Good Mailing List

As part of contacting likely referral sources and your satisfied customers, it is essential that you collect, maintain, and regularly use a good mailing list. Keeping in touch with former customers, supporters and others interested in your work provides these people with the necessary information to tell others about you. If you store your list on a microcomputer and request the post office to supply you with all address changes (there is a small fee), you can easily and cheaply maintain and expand this marvelously effective, relatively low-cost marketing tool.

You will want to use your mailing list in all sorts of contexts, including:

- To inform customers if you offer new services;
- To let people know about significant law changes that could affect them;
- To help organize potential supporters should you face a political fight, as will be the case if you introduce legislation (as discussed in Chapter 15) or are sued by organized lawyerdom;
- To remind customers to refer friends (a coupon offering a small discount often helps);
- To invite everyone to a party. Try this a couple of times a year—it allows you to market your services and have fun too.

E. Listing the Availability of Your Services

In addition to talking to community services organizations, it is essential to widely list the availability of your services in places where people are predisposed to look for them, such as the yellow pages. Some types of listings are free, such as those maintained by public service organizations and agencies. More typically, you must pay a small fee to list, as is the case for business directories and phone books. But even where a fee is involved, costs are usually very reasonable when compared to your likely return. This is because unlike display ads or electronic media spots, where you pay fairly large sums to aim your message at a very broad and mostly uninterested audience, listings are targeted at people who are looking for the particular service you offer. In addition, business listings have the advantage of being fairly inconspicuous and thus are far less likely to come to the attention of organized lawyerdom than is a real advertising campaign. Here are a number of good places to list:

- Phone book yellow pages—you can't list under "Attorneys," but probably can list under headings such as "Document Preparation," "Divorce," "Legal Form Preparation," "Typing Services," and so on. The phone company makes up the headings; the best you can do is pick the available one that comes closest to describing what you do;
- Local business and community service directories, such as those put out by the Better Business Bureau and local trade groups;
- Self-help law books—Several publishers of divorce, and other self-help law books charge IPs a modest fee to list right in the book. This, of

course, is a great opportunity for IPs, as many book purchasers get disgusted in the middle of doing all their own paperwork and are likely to turn the whole thing over to an IP. One book that does this is *How To Do Your Own Divorce in California,* by Ed Sherman;

- Classified ads in newspapers. Most newspapers place these ads under "Business Personals." You need to leave the ad in for a month or two to begin to see results, since people will often find out about it when a friend says something like, "You know, I saw an ad for low-cost patent drafting services in the back of *Popular Invention* magazine;"

- Classified or display ads that list your services in low cost "penny saver" or "classified flea market" type papers. This, of course, is advertising of a sort, but is far different in general approach and cost than are large display ads. People who pick up classified ads are often looking for a specific service at a reasonable price. Again, these ads work best if you keep them in the publication over a long period of time in the same place;

- Directories and business listings aimed at people who don't speak English. In many communities, there is a large and growing need for IPs who work with Spanish and Chinese speakers, as well as those who know Southeast Asian languages.

Here is a small ad—essentially a listing of services—that would be appropriate for a free classified ad paper:

OREGON DIVORCE TYPING, INC.

Since 1978

UNCONTESTED DIVORCE........ $125-$250

We help you prepare your own divorce without an attorney.

1113 Melrose Street, Pullman, Oregon   441-5157

Monday - Saturday 10-6

And here is an ad that appeared in a classified ad publication in Portland, Oregon, called "Nickel Ads":

F. Prepare Factual Information About the Areas You Specialize In

When telling people about the existence of your service, you usually want to keep your message short and to the point. After all, most people have more important things to think about than the details of your business. However, for those who ask for more information (and for helping agencies and others who are genuinely interested in your service) you'll want to develop material that goes into more detail. In Section B, above, I present a general flyer designed to accomplish this. In addition, you will want to prepare more in-depth material about each of the form typing areas you specialize in. Your goal in doing this is to simultaneously accomplish these few objectives:

• explain what you do in detail
• educate the potential customer or referral source about the particular legal task
• convince the reader that you offer a high quality, reliable service
• present your message in a way that does not give organized lawyerdom an opportunity to charge you with unauthorized practice of law

Here, by way of example, is a very informative flyer used by a Divorce Center of California Office:

DIVORCE
CENTERS OF CALIFORNIA

870 Market Street #7   (415) 434-4485
San Francisco, CA 94102   (415) 956-5757

Information About Uncontested Divorce

There are now two kinds of uncontested divorce procedures in California. The first and most widely-used is the "**standard dissolution**," which usually requires a court appearance and the preparation of a good-sized packet of forms. The second, for those who meet its requirements, is a "summary dissolution," which has fewer forms and no court appearance. Both divorces take 6-1/2 months to complete.

Who Qualifies for a "Summary Dissolution"

1. One spouse has lived in California for six months and in the county of filing for three months just before the date of filing.

2. The Petition for the divorce is filed before the fifth wedding anniversary.

3. There are no minor children of the marriage (or of this relationship), and the wife is not pregnant.

4. Neither spouse has any interest in real property (houses, land, etc.)

5. There is less than $4,000 in community obligations, not including car loans.

6. There is less than $25,000 in community property, not including cars.

7. Neither spouse owns more than $25,000 separately, not including cars.

8. Both spouses must sign the first papers.

9. Both spouses must read and understand the Summary Dissolution Booklet published by the State of California.

DIVORCE

CENTERS OF CALIFORNIA

870 Market Street #7   (415) 434-4485
San Francisco, CA 94102   (415) 956-5757

If for any reason you don't qualify for the Summary Dissolution, you must use the Standard Dissolution.

What Does it Cost?:

	Our Fee	Court Filing Fee
Summary Dissolution	$120	About $140 in many counties (it varies slightly)
Standard Dissolution	$220	About $170 in many counties (it varies slightly)

Please call for an appointment:
Monday-Friday, 9:00 a.m. to 5:30 p.m.
Telephone: 555-5757 or 555-4485

Thank you for your inquiry.

Jolene Jacobs
Jolene Jacobs

G. Longer-Term Marketing Strategies

So far we have discussed several things you can do to get the word out about your business fairly quickly. This is crucial to the survival of a new business, of course. But taking a slightly longer view, it's also important that you plan now for the growth and expansion of your business in the years ahead. Again, to emphasize the point I made at the beginning of this chapter, the best way to do this is through the positive personal recommendations of satisfied customers. To encourage people to be enthusiastic about your business and tell others about you (and to report back favorably to referring agencies), it's essential that you do an excellent job. If your customers come to respect you and the service you offer, they will send others. If they don't, negative word will spread just as fast. To fully understand this point, ask yourself this: How often do you patronize a restaurant, service provider (carpenter, plumber, shoe repair shop) or buy a particular product or go to a movie because someone you know recommended it? Now ask yourself how often you engage in any of these transactions after a friend tells you the service or product is poor?

In *Marketing Without Advertising,* which I again heartily recommend (you can order it from Nolo—see ad pages at back of book), Phillips and Rasberry state that there are three essential elements to building the trust necessary to get the personal recommendation process going. They are:

- Providing a good service at a good price. (See Chapter 9 for a discussion on price.);

- Giving your customers a way to measure the quality of your service and reasonableness of your prices. Phillips and Rasberry discuss the general principles of how to do this. For independent paralegals, one good approach is to create office and waiting room displays and written material indicating exactly the services you perform, how much time it takes, how much the competition charges, etc.; and

- Providing your customers a money-back guarantee if they are unhappy with your service for any reason should be an essential part of your marketing strategy. Many public agencies and others may be reluctant to refer people to your somewhat controversial business unless they have confidence that any problems will be taken care of.

One good way to allow the community to see for itself that you are competent is to teach a course in your specialty. A number of legal typing service owners have done this. To reduce chances of being hassled for practicing law without a license, many charge no fee. Others charge a modest fee for the course but require students to own and read a good self-help law text and limit their oral presentation to the material in the book. The approach of reaching potential customers through courses works particularly well for typing service owners in specialized fields, such as those who prepare forms for landlords, nonprofit corporations or people who want living trusts—areas where customers typically want a good deal of information about the subject before committing themselves.

Another good approach is to occasionally publish and distribute good consumer information about the subject areas in which you work. For example, if your state changes any aspect of its divorce, adoption or landlord-tenant law and you type papers in any of these areas, you might prepare a flyer describing the details. Of course, the circular should also remind people of how your business works. Do a nice job on the graphics (again, it often it pays to work with a graphic artist) and make sure you proofread it at least three times to catch all errors in spelling and grammar. When you're satisfied, mail the flyer to all interested individuals, consumer groups, media organizations, former customers and referral agencies.

H. Where to Get Marketing Training

Throughout this book, I highly recommend the services offered by the California Association of Independent Paralegals (CAIP). Although CAIP is California-based, it offers out-of-state memberships. CAIP sponsors occasional training courses on marketing and market research techniques for independent paralegals, as well as publishing an informative newsletter and sponsoring skills-based workshops. I also recommend the classes and workshops offered by Independent Paralegal Workshops. This organization is run by Lois Isenberg (see interview in Appendix), an IP with over 20 years experience in the field and a proven record of running a high quality business. For information, call 213-655-6141.

I. Summing Up

To put the marketing suggestions made in this chapter in the context of the independent paralegal business, I recently discussed marketing strategy with

Robin Smith, of People's Paralegal Service, in Beaverton, Oregon. Here is an excerpt of our discussion (see Appendix for a longer discussion with Robin):

Ralph Warner (RW): *How important are referrals to People's Paralegal Service?*

Robin Smith (RS): Crucial. It takes time and patience to develop a positive reputation with lots of community agencies. But once you do, and they trust you, they can really make a big difference. The power of 50 to 100 groups all occasionally referring you customers is amazing.

RW: *How do you develop good contacts at places that are likely to send you customers?*

RS: Slowly. People at legal aid, or the Sheriff's Office, or the Army (which, incidentally, is a great source of referrals), aren't going to plug your business unless they truly believe in it. It's up to you to prove that you are worthy of their trust.

RW: *And how do you accomplish that?*

RS: As I've said, offering good service is essential, but you also have to make sure the key people who make the referrals know who you are. One excellent way to do that is to send good solid information to them on a regular basis. Your best bet is to adopt many of the strategies followed by non-profit consumer organizations. In other words, draft informative newsletters, contact the media when you have something to say, and generally tell the world what a truly good, innovative and cost-effective job you are doing.

RW: *What about talking to people at public agencies, courts and law libraries directly?*

RS: Yes, sure, but a hard sell won't work. Remember, these people are motivated to help the people they deal with on a daily basis, not to help your business. You have to convince them that when a person is referred to your typing service, you will really provide a great service. This takes time.

RW: *What about the media? Does People's Paralegal get much free coverage?*

RS: Definitely. The lack of access the average person has to the legal system is a story of continuing media interest, which means our business is newsworthy. I've been providing consumer help and information for over ten years now, which means I know a number of local news, feature and consumer reporters.

RW: *How often are they interested in hearing from you?*

RS: It's a fine line. If you self-promote too much, too often, you'll turn people off. Reporters are interested when there is something new, as would be the case if your business changes significantly.

RW: *What about the bar association? Does their hostility to the self-help law movement help you?*

RS: Absolutely. Whenever the bar makes a negative statement about non-lawyer legal form preparation, two things happen. First, the press needs to get the other side of the story, which means they are likely to call an IP they know and trust. Once the article is printed, many people who need help with legal paperwork and can't afford a lawyer will find out that alternatives exist and are likely to call the IP who is quoted in the article.

RW: *What else does an IP need to know to deal with the media effectively?*

RS: Tell the truth, and if you make any promises, keep them. For example, if you send out a press release about a protest event that doesn't happen, or promise exciting news you can't deliver, your credibility will be shot. Finally, let me make one more point. No matter how clever your promotional efforts, they will avail you little in the long run unless your business really delivers what it says it will. In this age in which all sorts of mediocre products and services are vastly over-hyped, people are looking for performance, not promises.

Computers and the Independent Paralegal

efore I discuss how independent paralegals can best work with computers, a few introductory words are in order. Computers have come to the law relatively late. More than most groups, lawyers have resisted storing and massaging information electronically. More recently, however, there has been an explosion in the availability of legal software. Some is designed to help manage law office tasks, such as word processing, billing and case management. Others provide "expert systems" that help lawyers do research and make choices in complicated legal areas. And increasingly, legal applications software is becoming available—software designed to accomplish a particular legal task, such as preparing the paperwork necessary to probate an estate, file for bankruptcy or divorce, compute child support levels or incorporate a business.

While most of this task-oriented software is designed for use by lawyers, some, such as *WillMaker, Partnership Maker, Living Trust Maker, California Incorporator,* and *Patent It Yourself,* all published by Nolo Press, and *It's Legal,* published by Parson's Technology, and *Home Lawyer,* published by Mecca Ventures, are designed to be used directly by the consumer. Indeed, consumer legal software has become such a good-sized business that in the late 1990's, it's likely that more wills will be prepared on a self-help basis using a personal computer than will be written by lawyers. Against this background, it's appropriate to ask why legal software is so attractive to nonlawyers. After all, printed self-help law materials designed to help people accomplish uncontested actions in a number of fields, such as divorce and bankruptcy, have been available for a number of years and have never achieved the same level of popularity.

The answer is that computers do three things better than books. First, computers are well-suited to printing out a fresh copy of legal forms such as wills, living trusts and small business incorporations after the user has entered the necessary data. By contrast, with a book you must tear out a form and try to print or type necessary data in the designated spaces.

Second, unlike a book, which is an excellent tool to provide access to a broad spectrum of information, computers can be programmed to be directly responsive to a particular need. Thus, a book may be the most efficient way to review the broad field of landlord-tenant law, but a good software program offers a far more efficient way to custom-tailor a lease form to fit a particular need. This is because the computer can store all common lease variables, allow the user to examine, edit and change them and then to print out the final product. To accomplish this using a self-help law book would commonly involve hours with scissors and a glue pot.

Finally, computers are better at guiding the user to the desired result than are printed materials. Correctly programmed, software can present the user many options, all of which have been error-checked in advance to almost guarantee a legally accurate result. Thus, in relying on good legal software, the user gains a justifiable sense that she is receiving guidance from an expert.

A. The Independent Paralegal and Legal Software

The fact that legal applications software is increasingly available on both the home and lawyer market raises an obvious question. How can the IP use it as part of his legal form preparation business?

Because of unauthorized practice laws, the answer is more complicated than you might guess. As I will develop further below, the problem is that using legal software necessarily involves making legal choices. If the IP makes these choices, she risks being charged with unauthorized practice. So the problem becomes how can the IP make sure the customer makes the legal decisions at the same time the computer is used efficiently?

One approach is for the IP to provide (rent) both a computer and the necessary legal software to the customer, letting the customer make her own choices. In my experience, this doesn't work for a very basic reason. Most people who come to typing services simply aren't familiar with computers. A better method is to provide the user with a self-help manual and questionnaire keyed to the program. If the user reads the manual and then completes the questionnaire, she, not the IP, makes the legal choices. Now, entering the information into the computer becomes a "word processing," as opposed to a "legal," function.

In Chapters 2 and 3, I thoroughly discuss UPL and how an IP who types legal paperwork can avoid it. This involves making sure the customer has the legal information necessary to make her own choices. The best way to insure this happens is to require the customer to purchase a good self-help law book. If you do not thoroughly understand this point, please go back and reread this material.

1. Forms on Disk

A number of programs are now available for lawyers that automate the process of filling out legal forms. For example, in California, where pre-printed state-mandated forms are in use for most routine actions, purchasers have a choice of competing programs for both IBM and Apple Macintosh computers. Bankruptcy forms on disk are also available from several publishers in both software formats. And Nolo Press publishes forms-on-disk software to incorporate small businesses in California, New York, Florida and Texas. To repeat the important point I discussed above, as long as the customer has access to a good self-help law book and completes a questionnaire based on the information provided in the book, use of this type of program is also pretty safe as far as UPL charges are concerned. After all, the IP is simply using this software as a sophisticated typewriter.

2. Clauses on Disk

Programs are also available both to lawyers and the general public that allow the user to assemble a document by selecting appropriate clauses from a large library of clauses. This approach is particularly useful in drafting documents such as leases and contracts, which do not readily lend themselves to the form-on-disk approach discussed above. For example, Nolo Press publishes *Nolo's Partnership Maker,* which fits the "clauses-on-disk" category since it allows the user to choose and assemble partnership clauses from a pre-selected menu.

3. Stand-Alone Programs

As mentioned early in this chapter, a number of stand-alone legal programs are now available. This software typically accomplishes one or more legal tasks by asking the user a series of questions and using the answers to create the necessary legal paperwork.

As an example, let's briefly examine *WillMaker* (Nolo Press), the all-time most successful self-help law program. *WillMaker,* a computer program designed to help the average nonlawyer make a will and prepare related documents, including a durable power of attorney for healthcare and a living will, operates by asking the user a number of questions. Depending on the answers, the program asks, or bypasses, other questions. It's a bit like climbing a tree. Based on your choice as to which way to proceed at the first major fork, you have an option to climb certain higher branches but not others. For example, *WillMaker* asks the user if she is married. If the "No" answer is entered, *WillMaker* skips to another area entirely. If the answer is "Yes," *WillMaker* provides the user with certain information about marital property rules as they affect wills and asks for the name of the spouse.

A little later, *WillMaker* asks the user if she has any children. If the user responds in the affirmative, *WillMaker* first asks for the children's names and then if any of the children are under 18 years of age. If the user answers "Yes" (meaning one or more children are minors), *WillMaker* asks if she wants to appoint a guardian to take over should the user and the other parent, if there is one, both die simultaneously. However, if the user responds that there are no minor children, *WillMaker* skips all questions about appointing a guardian.

Now, suppose a computer user becomes confused as to how to answer a question because he doesn't know the meaning of a technical word. How does *WillMaker* deal with this, or with a user's need for answers to general background questions of the type a lawyer would handle routinely? For example, suppose a user is faced with the question as to whether a child from a former marriage, or a child born while the user wasn't married, should be considered a "child" for purposes of the will. First, *WillMaker* contains an information screen that backs up every data entry screen. In this instance, the back-up screen tells the questioning user that it's best to list all possible children, including those born out of wedlock or in a former marriage. Second, as part of the *WillMaker* package, the user receives a manual that contains a thorough discussion of all major issues involving children and wills.

What do programs designed for home use offer to the IP? As mentioned, if an independent paralegal simply asks a customer a series of questions and then plugs the answers into a program, she risks being charged with the unauthorized practice of law. What's needed to avoid UPL is for the customer to have a copy of a self-help law manual that explains all of the legal decisions included in the program and then to complete a detailed questionnaire to supply the information to the IP for entry in the computer. Foreseeing this type use, Nolo licenses *WillMaker* and all of its other software to IPs for commercial use. (See back of the book for commercial license information.) In addition, Nolo sells extra copies of their manual for distribution to IP customers at a very reasonable price.

CALIFORNIA INCORPORATOR: A STAND-ALONE PROGRAM THAT AVOIDS UPL

California Incorporator is a stand-alone program that allows the user to form a privately-held California corporation. It comes with a comprehensive manual that contains detailed information necessary for the user to supply the relatively few bits of information necessary to incorporate. As long as every user has a copy of the manual and the IP follows the general approach to avoiding UPL discussed in Chapter 3 of this book, I believe using this package is relatively safe.

At this point, you may be wondering why publishers of all legal software programs sold for home use don't include more comprehensive legal help. The real reason is that most don't understand the needs of the IP market. As the legal typing service movement grows, this will surely change.

B. Software Designed or Customized by IPs

To solve the software shortage problem, some computer savvy paralegals have begun to design their own, based on the increasingly sophisticated word-processing technology now on the market. For example, one Oregon paralegal service has entered the language necessary to write a basic will, living trust or incorporation into its computer. Then, following the customers' instructions taken from the information sheet, they are able to use the word processing program Wordstar to create the finished document. While this process may sound difficult, it often isn't, because many common legal forms mostly consist of standard language, with a few blanks and boxes to complete. If the information sheet is well-designed, it should provide the information necessary to quickly complete the paperwork.

Three warnings are in order. First, the layout and design of legal forms such as leases, powers of attorney and wills published by commercial printers and publishers are protected by copyright. If you wish to enter these forms in your computer and use them as part of your business, you must get permission. Some form publishers won't license their forms to paralegals at all, while others, such as Nolo Press, do so if you pay a commercial license fee.

Another alternative is to create your own form and enter it into your word processing package. For example, there are dozens of lease forms in print, and most of the language is fairly standard. It shouldn't be hard to study these and rewrite the language and reorganize the presentation with the result that you create a form of your own that doesn't violate anyone's copyright. If you follow this approach, however, be sure that you really do create a new lease and that you have your work checked by a knowledgeable expert in your state to be sure it's accurate and up-to-date.

Second, if the finished form must be filed with a court or agency, it must be acceptable in both content and lay-out. This means you will need to pay close attention to all relevant rules before you design your own form.

The third, and more serious, problem of following this approach is UPL. As discussed above, unless your customers have access to the information necessary to make their own legal choices, you risk being charged with supplying it, which is the same thing as saying you are practicing law without a license. Specifically, the customer would need a manual or other published legal information containing a thorough discussion of the legal forms and documents to be completed. And the independent paralegal would need a well-designed questionnaire to record the user's legal choices for later entry into the computer. So, once again, the IP's objective must be to supply customers with enough self-help information that they, not the IP or the computer, is calling the legal shots.

C. Computer Databases

As discussed near the beginning of this chapter, a computer database typically consists of a great deal of information on a particular subject available to the user according to a broad range of selections or indexing criteria. A computer programmed to contain fairly comprehensive information dealing with the legal concerns of the average person (debt problems, divorce, landlord-tenant, real property ownership, wills) could be operational now. Housed at the same location with a small printed library of good self-help law books and other resources, and staffed by knowledgeable paralegals, this would allow a great deal of legal information to be brought to the street corner at a very reasonable price.

TELE-LAWYER:
A FIRST STEP TOWARDS A PEOPLE-FRIENDLY LEGAL DATABASE

In Chapter 3, I mention Tele-lawyer, a service that allows nonlawyers to pay a small per-minute charge to get legal questions answered by phone. It is interesting to note that while callers talk to a lawyer, these people in turn can pull needed information from a computer database. Growing all the time, this specialized information retrieval system allows Tele-lawyer lawyers to have an incredible array of consumer legal information at their fingertips.

Are such interactive people's law databases likely to be operational soon? In fairly primitive form, they already exist in the form of divorce kiosks, which are now available at some courthouses in Arizona and Colorado. Consumers can use these kiosks to get basic information about divorce as they prepare their own self-help divorce paperwork. But what about data-rich programs in more complicated areas of the law? With the 1994 publication of *Patent It Yourself,* by David Pressman, this, too, is now available. *Patent It*

Yourself not only allows you to prepare your own patent application, but contains voluminous information about the patent process, carefully linked to each procedural step. For example, if you are drafting your patent claim and want to see how others have done it, you can quickly access the text of a collection of real patents. Or, if you are ready to conduct your search for any existing patents that are similar to yours (searching for prior art), you'll find the program contains lots of helpful information about how to do it.

Legal databases have also been developed for lawyers. Some, such as Westlaw and Lexis, are sophisticated and expensive on-line legal research tools used by both lawyers and paralegals, including freelancers who establish their own legal research business. Others, such as Dialog's TRADEMARKSCAN, are very specialized databases used for a particular purpose, in this case to check business and product names to see if they have already been reserved for use. Mostly because of the expense, few independent paralegals currently use these tools. But as a result of many new sources of legal information, IPs are now able to access a great deal of good legal information at a low cost. For example, many Nolo Press materials are available through the Internet by using World Wide Web (www) to connect to O'Reilly and Associates Global Network Navigator (GNN). Nolo Press can be found within GNN's Legal Metacenter. Users of Apple Computer's eWorld service can find the Nolo Press Self-Help Law Center in the Business and Finance building in the Resources and Reference wing. It is beyond the scope of this book to provide a comprehensive list of all legal information available via computer access. However, in 1995 Nolo will publish a book listing this information and telling readers exactly how to access it.

D. Computers As Office Efficiency Tools

Up to this point, I have stressed how computers can help independent paralegals generate legal forms. However, computers are also wonderful office automation tools, and the reasons most businesses eventually decide to computerize are also applicable to independent paralegals. Here is a brief review of some of these:

Word Processing: Good word processing software, and a knowledgeable person to use it, is essential in any modern office. Whether you are creating a form, writing a letter or customizing a document, the power of this type of software to quickly and efficiently create the format you want is wonderful. Because much legal software is designed to work with it, WordPerfect on the IBM (DOS) style personal computer is the software program of choice for legal applications.

Accounting: There are many good office accounting programs which, especially if set up at the beginning, can make basic business accounting chores a lot more efficient. You will want a program that does accounts payable, accounts receivable and maintains a general ledger. If you're a novice, one good way to choose one is with the advice of an experienced small business accountant or tax preparer. You will want the system you choose to generate the information you'll need for your tax return without much additional labor. *Small Time Operator,* by Bernard Kamoroff, is a good introductory source of information about small business accounting.

Pricing: Spreadsheet programs can be very useful for predicting the effect that changes in such variables as fees, costs, and client volume will have on your bottom line. For example, if you're trying to figure out whether you'll gross more income by charging $150, $160, $170 or $180 to prepare a bankruptcy, assuming customer volume drops 5% with each incrementally higher price, a spreadsheet will accomplish it in a wink.

There are a number of excellent ones on the market, such as Lotus 1, 2, 3 and Excel.

Office Management: There are a number of programs designed to help law offices manage their cases. These keep client information, list crucial filing and notice dates, organize follow-up tasks, and generally act as a storehouse for other data related to individual cases. They then can produce daily, weekly and monthly reports showing what activity is required on all open cases. The degree to which this type of information is useful to independent paralegals clearly depends on the scope and variety of services being offered. If you have a significant volume of customers, or type forms in several legal areas, or have several offices, a management program can be a big help.

Mailing Lists: As I discuss in Chapter 10, "Marketing Your Services," it's essential that you maintain up-to-date lists of all former customers, agency people who make referrals to you, media contacts, etc. Names on your list should be easily recoverable by category. For example, if you want to send a flyer to reporters but not former customers, your mailing list should be coded to allow you to do this. A computer is the only sensible way to maintain this information. Mailing list programs are available for all microcomputers. Make sure you buy a printer that will print on mailing labels at high speed.

Database: Finally, a number of popular database-management programs can be used to collect and store information in an organized form about the unique characteristics of each customer. It thus becomes possible to build an intra-office database that allows quick retrieval of materials from an earlier case that can help solve a current problem. For example, if a question comes up about how to serve a divorce complaint on someone living in Canada, it would help to be able to punch up a list of any previous customers who had the same problem.

E. Getting Started With Computers

Of course, all the wonderful uses of computers discussed here may seem like a distant dream to a person with no computer experience who is new to the independent paralegal business and worried about how to afford a good secondhand typewriter. Indeed, even those readers who own a personal computer may not have the experience necessary to effectively use it in the ways suggested here. If you are one of them, it's past time you bootstrapped yourself into the computer age.

If you have no computer experience at all, your first step is to become at least somewhat computer literate. When you set out to explore which hardware and software are most appropriate to your needs, this sort of basic understanding will be absolutely essential if you don't wish to waste a small fortune. Many community colleges and adult education programs have beginning computer courses. Take one of these and read a few introductory self-help books, which are available in virtually all bookstores.

Once you can tell a hard disk from a floppy, and don't hide the cheese every time someone mentions a mouse, your next step is to figure out which type of computer and software you require for your tasks. Your choice is basically between the Apple Macintosh and a personal computer using a DOS operating system. The latter are made by IBM, Tandy, Compac and dozens of other companies who manufacture IBM clones.

The Macintosh is easier to learn and more fun to use. In my opinion, it's the best choice if you plan to use your computer as an office efficiency tool, not to run legal applications programs. However, if you want to experiment with legal document and form completion programs such as those discussed above, you will probably want to buy an IBM (DOS) type computer, because a good deal of law office-oriented software is available in this format only. And, as mentioned above, when you check out word processing software, take a close look at WordPerfect.

Customer Recourse

T his is one of the shortest and most important chapters in this book. It deals with what to do if a customer is not satisfied with your work. I refer to this process as providing customer recourse.

A. The Importance of Satisfying Unhappy Customers

The willingness to provide the dissatisfied customer with an efficient way to gain recourse is important to all businesses. Huge and successful companies, such as the mail order high flyers Land's End and L.L. Bean, have been built to a substantial degree on their commitment to promptly taking care of all customer complaints. In the retail area, Nordstrom's bases much of its marketing effort on convincing customers that it provides excellent recourse should any of its merchandise fail to live up to a customer's expectations.

Providing a quick, fair way to resolve customer complaints is even more crucial to small business success, because it's an essential element of establishing a good "word-of-mouth" marketing plan. (I discussed how to do this in Chapter 10.) If you doubt the strong link between taking care of the occasional customer complaint and generating positive recommendations about a business, ask yourself this: If you hear about a skilled carpenter who does spectacular work, but also hear that he is temperamental and has a reputation for not taking care of problems, would you hire him? And if you did, and were upset by his refusal to take care of several loose ends as part of an otherwise competent job, would you recommend him to your friends? Despite his skill, probably not.

And it isn't only carpenters whose business will suffer if they don't satisfy customer complaints. The same is true of a dentist, plumber, computer programmer and, as you have no doubt guessed, an independent paralegal. If word gets out that you aren't reliable and don't take care of complaints, your business will not grow.

And don't think it's adequate to simply work out solutions to the occasional customer complaint as they come up. This is a rotten business practice for several reasons. First, you are likely to be emotionally involved with the particular complaint and thus may not be objective enough to look at the situation from your customer's perspective.

Second, and more important, your failure to establish a complaint resolution procedure in advance and announce it early and often means that your customers, and the agencies and other people who refer your customers, won't know what to expect if something goes wrong and therefore may not patronize you in the first place. Think about how many times you have patronized one store or service provider (again, L.L. Bean, Land's End and Nordstrom's are excellent examples) instead of another because you know you'll be in good hands if a problem develops.

Third, if you fail to reassure all customers that you will promptly take care of any problems, you risk a dissatisfied customer complaining to the Bar or a public agency such as the district attorney or State Department of Consumer Affairs instead of to you. This reason for adopting a good recourse policy deserves emphasis. Never forget that you are working under the always mistrustful, and often hostile, eye of organized lawyerdom and that the majority of prosecutions for unauthorized practice that are not initiated by lawyers or judges themselves, result from complaints from members of the public who feel ripped off by an independent paralegal.

Here are the key elements of any good customer recourse policy:

- The customer should be encouraged to tell you about any problems;
- The customer should know her rights (and responsibilities) from the beginning;
- The customer should be able to ask for her money back at any time, with no need to give a reason;
- The customer—not you—should feel in control. Again, it's far better to provide a full refund if the customer is dissatisfied with your service for any reason than it is to demand that the customer come up with a "good reason" why she is dissatisfied;
- The customer should know exactly what to do to take advantage of her rights;
- Once a customer asks for her money back (or any other recourse you offer), it should be provided promptly.

One more important point. When you're deciding whether it's worth the trouble to develop a bullet proof recourse policy, consider and learn from the current plight of lawyers. Because bar associations and other lawyer-controlled professional regulatory groups provide such a poor system to handle and resolve complaints about lawyers who are corrupt, incompetent and price-gouging, the entire legal profession's reputation isn't much higher than the

Moscow subway. This is evidenced by the fact that in many states we are now witnessing a ground swell of public demands to take away the bar's historical power to police its own members and, instead, give this responsibility to nonlawyer-controlled public agencies.

The reason I belabor the point that establishing a good recourse policy in advance is essential is based on my finding that many independent paralegals haven't done so. A few have even told me proudly that they never give a refund. Clearly, no matter how good a legal form typing service some of these independent paralegals offer, they have not learned the basics of running a successful small business. It's as if Macy's advertised "The customer is always wrong."

I have found the intransigence of a number of paralegals on this issue to be particularly surprising in light of the fact that many do excellent work and, as a result, receive only a couple of complaints a year. The idea that these IPs are willing to fight with customers (even if the customer is being unreasonable) over the return of a few hundred dollars at the risk of having these people badmouth them to the public at large, or to the bar in particular, is appalling.

B. The No "Ifs, Ands or Buts" Recourse Policy

I recommend that you establish a "no ifs, ands or buts" money-back recourse policy. Not only is doing this a good deal for your customers, it is also a good deal for you. Why? Because assuming you sensibly screen your customers in the first place to eliminate inappropriate people, and you do a good form preparation job, experience indicates that less than 5% of your customers will be dissatisfied. (This percentage may be a little higher for divorces and lower in many other types of form preparation, such as small business incorporations.) The reason divorce seekers are more likely to complain is explained by the fact that these people are often under considerable emotional stress, and occasionally some of this is bound to spill over to their relationship with you.

Here is a recourse policy that I believe makes sense:

The ABC Typing Service is dedicated to providing quality legal typing services under the direction of its consumers for a fair price. If at any time you believe we have not fully met this goal, please ask for your money back. It will be provided promptly, no questions asked.

C. How To Deal With Predictable Customer Complaints

Enough lecturing! Let's assume you are convinced that it is wise to make sure that you don't have unsatisfied former customers wandering about maligning your reputation and you have adopted the policies listed above.

Let's now look at how to handle several predictable situations in which at least a few customers are likely to be unhappy. The first involves what to do when the customer simply changes his mind about pursuing the legal action and asks for his money back after you have competently completed the work. (IP's who type marriage dissolution forms call this "divorce remorse.") Some independent paralegals provide no refund, or only a partial one, reasoning that since their work was done before the customer changed his mind, it's the customer's problem. While this policy is logically defensible, I believe it's nevertheless mistaken. As mentioned above, it's far, far easier, and in the long run far less trouble, to simply state a policy that if a customer is dissatisfied for any reason, you'll give a full refund—no "ifs, ands or buts."

Another fairly common refund situation can occur when a legal action that starts out to be uncontested becomes contested while you are typing paperwork. If, as is likely, a lawyer ends up taking over the case, and you do not complete the paperwork, your customer may feel ripped off by having to pay an attorney in addition to having already paid you. Again, the best way to deal with this problem, which probably won't happen more than a few times a year, is to simply refund all, or at least a substantial part, of the customer's money.

Here is some language you may wish to include in your printed material to deal with this problem:

Any uncontested legal action has the potential to become contested, often resulting in both parties hiring a lawyer.[1] If this occurs during the course of any legal procedure for which ABC typing service is helping prepare paperwork, all fees and charges will promptly be refunded.

Customer unhappiness can also occasionally develop if, as part of working with your typing service, the customer needs legal information or advice not available from a self-help law book. As discussed above, it's best to cover this possibility in your original information sheet, indicating that the fee for your service does not cover any necessary lawyers' consultation fees. Assuming your customer simply confers with a lawyer (or calls a legal information phone service) who charges a reasonable fee, and comes back to you to complete the paperwork, there should be no problem, since the customer will almost surely understand that your typing fee has been fairly earned.

As part of working with ABC Typing Service to prepare your own legal paperwork, you may need to obtain legal advice or information from a lawyer or legal information telephone service. It is understood that you are responsible for paying for this legal advice separately and that it is not included in the fee paid the ABC Typing Service to prepare your legal paperwork.

---

[1] In a few areas of the country, IPs now handle contested actions with the approval and often support of local courts (see interview with Virginia Simons in the Appendix.) If you work in this favorable type environment, you obviously do not need to include this statement in your printed materials.

D. What To Do If You Make a Serious Mistake

Finally, we come to the sticky question of what to do if a customer feels that your negligence or lack of knowledge resulted in loss of a substantial right and is not satisfied with a refund. Many IPs I have talked to state that, over the many years of preparing legal forms, this has never occurred. Others say that they have made mistakes that have caused consumers problems, but it's always been possible to fix them at a reasonable cost, usually by redoing the paperwork.

Fortunately, in most situations, the economic harm that an IP's mistake causes is fairly modest. For example, one IP who has been in business for a decade can remember a situation in which she filed a final decree of divorce before the end of the year, forgetting that the customer had asked her to wait until January 2, for tax reasons. The IP immediately asked a trusted tax preparer to compute the extra tax liability and reimbursed the customer. The amount was only a few hundred dollars.

Even though IPs who know their field and keep good records don't often experience customers who claim that their lack of care resulted in a substantial loss, it can happen. For example, let's say you type divorce papers for Mary C. A year later, she claims you neglected to include several valuable assets that she told you about and blames you for the fact that she wasn't awarded this property in the court divorce decree. Assuming you did all the things I discussed in Chapter 3 to establish that you are only a typing service, do not provide legal advice, and it's up to your customers to understand the laws that affect the particular legal area, you are off to a pretty good start. In addition, however, it's essential that you keep a written record of all information provided by your customer (preferably in her own handwriting), and have her sign a clear statement that the information provided is accurate and complete. (I discuss this in detail in Chapter 8.) In addition, after you type the necessary court or agency forms, your customer should read them carefully (or if necessary, have them read to her) and again sign a statement that they are complete.

Assuming your divorce customer did all this, and the missing property wasn't listed, you are in an excellent legal position. Assuming property existed in the first place, it's your customer's responsibility, not yours.

E. Malpractice and Business Liability Insurance

Although most mistakes can be corrected and real harm avoided, it is theoretically possible for a mistake to expose you to serious liability (although I personally am unaware of such an instance). Until very recently, errors and omissions insurance was unavailable for independent and freelance paralegals. This has led some paralegals to work with a lawyer solely for the purpose of gaining coverage provided by the lawyer's malpractice policy.

In keeping with the growth of the paralegal movement, however, at least one insurance company has begun to underwrite errors and omissions insurance for limited paralegal practice. This insurance is available through a national paralegal association known as NFPA (National Federation of Paralegal Associations). To apply for this insurance, you need to join a local paralegal or legal assistant association that itself is a member of NFPA. Most states have at least one such association and the larger states have many.

The insurance is reasonably priced as of the writing of this book (about $500 per annum per paralegal covering liability up to $100,000 per incident and up to $300,000 for a year).

In addition to covering liability for errors and omissions, the policy may also provide a legal defense against charges that you have engaged in the unauthorized practice of law. However, the decision of your carrier to provide this defense may not be automatic, given the relatively new nature of the underlying insurance and the relative inexperience of the insurance company in dealing with independent paralegals.

⚠ It is possible that the insurance company does not underwrite insurance for paralegals in your state, due to a number of factors. So, before you join an organization just to get insurance, do some checking first.

BUY INSURANCE TO COVER NORMAL BUSINESS RISKS

In addition to providing recourse to customers who complain about your service for any reason, you should purchase normal types of business insurance to protect your business and, especially if you are not incorporated, your personal assets, should customers be hurt in or outside your premises. This liability insurance is often sold as part of a package with fire and theft coverage, which is also a good idea to cover your business equipment. In addition, if your car, or a car of any employee, is ever used to do errands for the business, be sure your auto insurance policy covers you for any liability incurred. (This usually involves paying extra for business coverage.) If an accident occurs while you are or an employee is on a business errand, even if the employee is driving his or her own car, your business is likely to be sued.

But suppose now that you are faced with a large financial claim by a customer in a situation where you may be at fault (for example, as part of a divorce or bankruptcy you didn't include property your customer listed). After you recover from the urge to run and hide, what should you do? Instead of arguing with the customer over who is at fault, your first job is to see if anything can be done to salvage the situation. Because lawyers themselves make a great many mistakes, the legal system is often very forgiving of errors, especially if prompt action is taken to fix them. In this context, you may want to check with a friendly lawyer to see if corrective action can be taken. Be ready to move fast and be willing to pay for the lawyer's services, even if you still aren't convinced you caused the problem.

Now suppose you establish that it's too late to take corrective action, but you believe your work didn't cause the problem (for example, your customer supplied you with a signed property list that didn't include the disputed property). Your best bet is to suggest mediation. This involves both of you sitting down with a trained mediator to try and work out your own settlement of the dispute. Since the mediator has no power to impose a decision that you don't agree to, there is no risk that the process will result in financial liability on your part, unless, of course, you voluntarily accept it. One of the best aspects of mediation is that it allows your customers (and you, too, for that matter) to air all grievances, not just the one that directly caused the dispute. Once everything is out in the open, a surprising number of supposedly intractable disputes are settled.

Finally, a note on malpractice insurance. One good reason to work with a lawyer is to gain the coverage provided by the lawyer's malpractice insurance. At this point, I know of no insurance company that writes insurance coverage for errors and mistakes made by IPs. Given the fact that I have rarely heard of a substantial monetary claim being made against an IP, I don't think that gaining insurance coverage is so important that it mandates that you work with a lawyer, but it is something to consider.

Working for Lawyers: The Freelance Paralegal

The fastest growing area of business opportunity for paralegals isn't helping nonlawyers prepare legal forms. Instead, it's doing work for lawyers as an independent contractor. This takes many forms. In some instances, this means establishing an independent business to prepare legal documents that have traditionally been prepared in-house by a legal secretary. Other times, it means collecting evidence, preparing exhibits (often involving visuals), and lining up witnesses for personal injury cases. In still others, it means helping lawyers manage the information that must be gathered as part of any major case.

In this age of specialization, many lawyers have learned that by contracting with freelance paralegals to handle specialized work in a particular legal area, such as divorce, personal injury, probate, or incorporation, the work is accomplished faster, more accurately and, best of all, substantially more cheaply than they could do it in their own offices. A few lawyers have taken this principle so far, they don't really have an office in the traditional sense. Instead, they rent an "executive suite" which comes with a receptionist, and contract out all their form preparation.

A. The Pros and Cons of Being a Freelance Paralegal

Lawyers, like everyone else in society, have trouble affording to hire other lawyers to get necessary work done. This economic fact of life has created a unique opportunity for freelance paralegals with an entrepreneurial bent to sell their competitively-priced services to a number of different lawyers and make a good living doing it. In addition to being able to run their own business, however, there is another big advantage enjoyed by paralegals who work for lawyers on a contract basis. Since lawyers profit from the relationship, you rarely hear organized lawyerdom complain that freelance paralegals are guilty of unauthorized practice.

THE FREELANCE PARALEGAL:
EMPLOYEE OR INDEPENDENT CONTRACTOR?

The Internal Revenue Service and other federal and state agencies have established criteria to decide if a business person is truly an independent contractor or has the legal status of part-time employee. This is a crucial distinction for both you and the lawyers you work with, as tax withholding and employee contribution rules are far different for employees than they are for independent business people. Very generally speaking, an employer/employee relationship exists when the business for whom the services are performed has the right to control and direct the person who carries out the services—both as to the result of the work and to the detail of how it is carried out.

If you only work for one or two lawyers, do much of your form preparation in their offices, and operate under their direct supervision, your legal status is that of a temporary employee.

If you work with lots of lawyers, spend most of your time in your own office, have a local business license, establish your own hours and working conditions, join professional associations, own your own sophisticated equipment, occasionally hire people to work for you (don't forget to get Federal tax I.D. numbers) and make many of the decisions necessary to accomplish your work, chances are you are a legitimate independent contractor.

For a few readers of this book, the idea of working with lawyers, even as an independent businessperson, will be an anathema. After all, if a significant part of the reason you want to be an independent paralegal in the first place is your conviction that the self-help law movement is a wholesome development as compared to lawyers' monopolistic approach to legal information, you will undoubtedly want to open your own business to work directly with the public.

For other freelancers, working with lawyers and their clients is a positive experience. In fact, many freelance paralegals report that once they establish their own businesses and contract to provide specialized services to lawyers, they do interesting and challenging work and are treated with far more collegial respect than they were when they worked as law firm employees. For example, freelance paralegal Afroditi Price states:

I never work for lawyers who treat me in a condescending manner. In most cases, they respect me more than their in-house staff, because they know I am not a "yes person." In fact, because I walk in with a contract and act like a businessperson, like their own clients, they have a lot of respect for me.

There are some other good reasons why an independent paralegal might consider working for lawyers rather than the public:

- As opposed to preparing paperwork for nonlawyer customers, you need relatively fewer lawyer customers, because they will often supply repeat business. This doesn't free you from the need to market your services, but it does allow you to concentrate on a much smaller group of potential customers;

- Your income will often be better, at least at the beginning, as it's commonly easier to line up a few lawyers than it is to become known to the general public;

- The work you handle may be more complicated and challenging than if you prepare routine paperwork for consumers;

- As an independent business person providing valuable, cost-effective service, you may be accorded more respect than you would be if you were an employee of a law firm;

- There is no paranoia that you will be arrested for practicing law without a license. As I mentioned above, as long as you are economically benefiting lawyers, few will challenge your right to do legal work;

- You will have the opportunity to work with new and sophisticated technology. For many, this will mean using computers and specialized software to produce legal documents, create databases or do legal research. For others, it may mean supervising the creation of visual presentations for use at settlement conferences or trials.

B. What Services Do Freelance Paralegals Offer?

Okay, suppose now that you are interested in setting up your own independent business to do subcontracting work for attorneys. How do you begin? First, it helps if you have a specialty.

An independent paralegal who works directly for an attorney usually makes herself extremely knowledgeable about a particular, often narrow, legal area that requires the preparation of routine, labor-intensive paperwork. Probate is a good example. Security regulation filings necessary to establish a public corporation, preparing evidence and witnesses for personal injury cases, tax form preparation, bankruptcy, evictions, and family law are other good examples. As a general rule, the more you specialize in a narrow area, such as doing trademark searches or preparing patent applications, the more you will end up dealing with the relatively few lawyers in your area who handle that specialty.

LAWSUIT MANAGEMENT

Today, major court cases quickly produce massive amounts of information. This means sophisticated information and paper tracking systems must be implemented to catalogue, store and retrieve it. To accomplish this, lawyers often hire freelance paralegals who specialize in case management to work with in-house staff. In most urban areas, groups of freelance paralegals have set up small businesses to provide these services.

Don't assume that because I have not mentioned a particular area here that it isn't a suitable one. Freelance paralegals are currently working with lawyers on a freelance basis in dozens of form preparation areas. The trick to analyzing whether a particular legal field is a good one for an independent paralegal to work in is to ask yourself the following: Does the particular legal area involve picky, time-consuming, repetitive form or evidence preparation work? If so, lawyers are likely to want to farm it out to a freelancer, who, in turn, can often apply efficient computer techniques to accurately and efficiently accomplish the necessary work at a far lower cost.

By contrast, legal areas that principally rely on the personalized advice or skills of a lawyer, such as negotiating contracts or settlement agreements, are not good candidates for freelance paralegals. Remember, since freelancers don't have a law license, they risk being charged with unauthorized practice if they transfer legal information or expertise directly to a customer.

In the probate area, particularly, where in many states fees are set by statute or court custom as a percentage of the gross value of the estate, freelance paralegal/lawyer relationships often work beautifully. In part, this is because attorney fees are high enough that the lawyer can afford to pay the freelance paralegal well for processing the paperwork and still make a bundle himself. For example, in many states, a $12,000–$15,000 attorney fee is typical to probate an uncomplicated estate with a gross value of $500,000.[1] In short, there is plenty of money to pay a freelancer to do the form preparation, while the lawyer still collects a big pay check. (Incidentally, when you realize that most of the work involves completing 10-25 pages of routine—albeit picky—paperwork and filing it with the probate clerk, it's easy to see why lawyers are so opposed to legal reformers' proposals to eliminate probate.)

In more populous states, one way to get an indication of whether a particular legal specialty will work for a freelance paralegal is by checking out whether form preparation computer software is available. If the answer is yes, it means that a legal publisher has done market research that indicates that the particular form preparation niche is large enough to be profitable. For example, in several states, you can purchase one of several legal form packages designed to produce family law forms or incorporations on a personal computer.

It is also important to recognize that the existence of state specific computer packages designed for, and marketed to, lawyers, presents the freelance paralegal with a great business opportunity. Because these programs are relatively expensive (often $500 or more), it means that many small general practice law offices do not find that purchasing them is cost-effective. However, a freelance paralegal who works with a number of law firms, will often have the volume to justify the purchase. And once she does, the fact that she has the state-of-the-art software will be a good selling point as part of recruiting new lawyer customers. To learn about software packages available in your community, read the ads in your state bar publication and in local newspapers. Also, Julius Blumberg, Inc. publishes and distributes useful software. You can get their catalogue by writing them at 62 White St., New York, NY 10013.

---

[1] If the lawyer is both the executor and the lawyer for the estate (a practice known as "double dipping"), the lawyer will get twice as much for the same work.

C. How To Get the Necessary Skills

There are two principal routes to gain the skills necessary to open your own freelance business that are often used in tandem. One is to work in a law firm or court clerk's office. In a sense, the paralegal serves an apprenticeship to learn how to perform particular tasks.

The other main approach is to attend a paralegal school where the relevant skills are taught. But if you consider the school route, be sure you pick one that emphasizes hands-on training as opposed to lots of legal theory. It is beyond the scope of this book to discuss paralegal schools in detail; your best bet will be to talk to local freelancers and get their recommendation.

Once you are established as a freelancer, you'll want to further develop your skills. One way to do this is to join a paralegal organization, most of which sponsor training sessions and/or work with bar associations to allow paralegal members to attend lawyer training sessions.

D. How to Get Freelance Work

Once a freelance paralegal develops the skills to handle legal paperwork in a particular legal area, she often gets her business started by quietly and privately letting local lawyers know about her specialty. For example, many lawyers, especially those who only have part-time secretarial help or who employ a typist with little legal form preparation experience, have a need for help in specialized areas such as probate, non-profit corporations, guardianships or adoptions, especially if they only handle a few per year. In this situation, working with a highly skilled freelance paralegal is very attractive. After all, the lawyer only contracts with the paralegal service in a situation when he is assured of collecting a much greater fee. For example, Nancy Baird, an extremely successful paralegal whose office is in Alameda, California, works with about 25 lawyers and has 40 to 50 open probate files at one time.

Larger firms also work with freelancers, although here the freelancer is likely to function as a small cog in a big law machine. Big firms are especially likely to look for freelance help as a part of collecting, storing and managing evidence for complex major litigation, such as copyright and patent infringement, asbestos and toxic waste cases, construction defects, and all types of class actions. Freelancers also often work in personal injury cases, where their job is usually to work up a case (find expert witnesses, manage discovery, organize evidence and supervise videotaped testimony) as part of making a settlement offer.

Most freelance paralegals who set up a business to work with lawyers already have lawyer contacts. Typically, these are developed while working in a law office, for a court clerk, or in some other way that has brought them into close contact with lawyers.

If you don't choose to make your contacts via this traditional route, you will not only need to develop the necessary skills on your own, but you'll have to convince at least one lawyer to give you a chance. If you do well, and the lawyer is willing to put in a good word with others in your community, before long, lawyers will be calling you.

Another way freelancers find work is through employment agencies specializing in legal secretary and paralegal placement. Many of these businesses that started out as traditional employment agencies have more recently broadened their scope and also act as employment brokers for freelance paralegals.

Still another way to get the word out about your freelance paralegal business is to join a local paralegal association. These associations often promote the services of their members by circulating lists of freelancers and specialties to lawyers and other in-house paralegals. In some states, including California, freelancers have established their own membership organizations, which help freelancers develop focused marketing efforts. In an effort to better understand how the freelance paralegal movement is developing, I asked Afroditi Price, President of the California Association of Freelance Paralegals, a few questions:

Ralph Warner: Paralegals selling their services to lawyers on a contract basis is a recent development, is it not?

Afroditi Price: Not really. Some freelance paralegal specialists, such as those working in the probate area, have been running their own businesses for more than 15 years.

RW: *If that's true, why was it 1989 before CAFP was founded?*

AP: It was largely a question of critical mass. Until a few years ago, there were not enough freelancers in one geographical area to justify a separate paralegal group.

RW: *What changed?*

AP: Suddenly freelancers were being hired by law firms to do all sorts of things beyond the original freelance paralegal standby's probate, deposition summary work and computer litigation support. Let me back up a little. Over the years, law firms trained in-house paralegals to do all sorts of specialized tasks in areas such as worker's comp, family law, personal injury, environmental law, corporate securities litigation and regulation and ERISA, to mention a few. Once they had these valuable and highly specialized skills, paralegals began to leave the law firms and start their own businesses that, for the most part, consisted of selling their skills back to their former employers and other law firms on a contract basis. In a sense, it was the birth of new service industry.

RW: *So most CAFP members have a high level of skill. Do your membership rules require a lot of paralegal experience or training?*

AP: Yes, to be a regular CAFP member, paralegals must provide services exclusively to attorneys on a freelance basis, and must have had two years experience as a paralegal providing services to attorneys.

RW: *That amounts to saying a new CAFP member has to work for a lawyer to meet your experience rule.*

AP: Right. The reason for this requirement is CAFP does not want a recent paralegal school graduate with no real world experience claiming CAFP membership as part of marketing their services to law firms. Very few businesses hire other professionals who have zero year's experience.

RW: *You obviously believe freelancers should have a track record?*

AP: You bet. A paralegal school gives exposure to what a job may be like— but until the job is successfully completed, you will never understand what is really involved. And I don't just mean skills—you need to learn about taking responsibility to get a job done, have a good handle on practical legal ethics, and manage deadlines and stress.

RW: *CAFP doesn't accept members who also sell their services to both lawyers and directly to the public. How come?*

AP: Because our job is primarily to help members with marketing. To do that in a focused way, we want to concentrate on the attorney/law firm market.

RW: *Is there some other reason? Do you look down on people who market their services both to lawyers and directly to the consumers?*

AP: No. My parents taught me the value of an honest day's work, regardless of the type of work. If individuals have the chutzpah to sell information directly to nonlawyers without giving legal advice, more power to them.

RW: *Over the long term, do you see a trend towards paralegals selling legal information directly to the end user, bypassing lawyers?*

AP: I don't advocate violating current unauthorized practice of law rules, but taking a longer view, information is just that—information. If a legal tech steers clear of giving legal advice, there should be no barrier preventing marketing it to anyone. And yes, this probably qualifies as a trend. Lawyers will not be able to artificially restrict the flow of information just because they find it profitable to do so. And as I said earlier, legal advice and information are two different things.

E. Combining Freelance and Independent Paralegal Work

It's possible to combine doing work for lawyers with providing services for the general public. I know several paralegals who do this successfully. Obviously, this can be a difficult career path if the lawyers you work with are hostile to the self-help law movement. However, if they are supportive of your efforts to help nonlawyers, combining both types of customers can have several advantages. The most obvious of these is that you get referrals from two different sources. Another is that from a self-protection point of view, it will be much harder for organized lawyerdom to attempt to have you prosecuted for unauthorized practice if you are doing much the same form preparation work for both lawyers and the public.

Evelyn Rinzler of Oakland, California, is a good example of a freelance paralegal who works directly for lawyers as an employee, freelances for other lawyers, and runs her own independent paralegal business. Evelyn's expertise is in the field of Medicare and Medi-Cal (California's medical plan for low-income people) appeals—a legal area that is not prohibited to nonlawyers by UPL rules. She does this work at her part-time job at a local legal aid program. In addition, one day a week she handles the same tasks on a freelance basis for a legal aid program in another county. And recently, she has begun to offer her services directly to individuals as an independent paralegal.

One way she recruits customers for her independent business is to contact lawyers to tell them about her cost-efficient service. Because the amounts of money involved are usually in the range of $500-$2,500 (rarely more than $5,000), lawyers can't handle these appeals in a cost-effective way. In addition, most don't have the specialized expertise necessary to do a good job. The result is that many are happy to send business to Evelyn.

Working for Volunteer, Community or Social Change Organizations

The Pittsburg, Pennsylvania bar association charged "Legal Advocacy for Women," a nonprofit center that helps mothers get child support they are legally entitled to, with unauthorized practice of law. (See interview with Rose Palmer in Appendix.) In Lackawanna, N.Y, the Erie County Bar association called Judy Lamb on the carpet for similar activities. In other areas of the country, similar types of bar harassment have occasionally been directed against nonprofit groups involved in environmental, consumer and tenants' rights activities. So the question arises, if you work with a good cause and, as part of doing so, help people understand their legal rights and formally deal with the legal system by filing papers and appearing in court, are you likely to become the target of organized lawyerdom's official ire?

The answer is a qualified "probably not," although, as the Pennsylvania and New York examples illustrate, IPs who work in a nonprofit context are not immune from being charged with the unauthorized practice of law. Why do I say that volunteer groups normally have less to fear? Because by definition these groups work in areas where people traditionally don't have the money to hire a lawyer. And despite lip service to the contrary, the American legal profession has traditionally had little interest in representing people who can't pay their stiff fees. What about all the free (pro bono) work lawyers claim they do? It's mostly public relations hooey designed to frustrate any serious reform of the legal system.

Put more directly, when all the professional hype is stripped away, the legal profession defines the practice of law to involve only legal disputes and procedures where there is money to be made. It follows then that since lawyers profit handsomely from business formation, probate, personal injury, domestic disputes (especially between affluent people), and estate planning, to name just a few, they are extremely interested in defending their monopoly power in these areas. This means they are quick to charge nonlawyer interlopers with the unauthorized practice of law.

In many other legal areas, however, lawyers have never found a way to collect what they view as decent fees. These include small consumer disputes, the collection of child support, arguments among neighbors, the right of a poor person to die with dignity, domestic violence, and dozens of other everyday hassles. So, even though working in these areas involves giving advice about legal procedures, completing legal forms, etc., lawyers are often willing to look the other way if nonlawyers do it.

You surely get the point. Because many nonprofit organizations work in areas of little or no lawyerly profit, lawyers normally do not initiate charges of unauthorized practice of law against them. This is true even though paralegals who work for these nonprofits often get far more involved in giving legal advice than do independent paralegals who sell form preparation services directly to the public. And once a particular nonprofit legal self-help group exists for several years (say an AIDS support group, where nonlawyers help dying people complete a living will or durable power of attorney), the very fact that lawyers haven't harassed it in the past often results in a politically convenient and widely-accepted fabrication that the organization in question doesn't really engage in the practice of law.

A good example of how this process works is the establishment of tenants' rights groups in the 1960s and 1970s in many areas of the country. At first, there was a great deal of nervousness about the reaction of organized lawyerdom. The fear was that since in most tenants' rights groups nonlawyers routinely counseled tenants as to their legal rights and helped them fill out court forms, such as answers to eviction suits, organized lawyerdom was sure to file unauthorized practice charges. Instead, of course, the bar's response in most places was to do nothing. Apparently, this was for two reasons. First, because lawyers never made much money defending tenants in the first place, no one cared enough to get involved in trying to suppress these activities. Second, lawyers were afraid if they put nonlawyer tenant-advocacy services out of business, they would have to do the work themselves, often on a pro bono (free) basis.

By contrast, organized lawyerdom has gone after a number of independent paralegals who offer services to landlords.[1] These for-profit landlord paralegal typing services are often charged with unauthorized practice, even though the work they do is the mirror image of what tenants groups do. There is, of course, one crucial difference between the two: When it comes to landlords, who have traditionally hired lawyers, an independent paralegal eviction service is seen as taking money out of lawyers' pockets rather than providing a community service.

---

[1] One of the leading cases in this field, which incidentally establishes rules for California IPs who wish to operate in this field, is *The People v. Landlords Professional Services*, 215 Cal.App.3d 1599 (4th Dist.,1989).

A. Appearing In Court

There is one legal area, besides representing paying clients, over which lawyers are extremely protective of their monopoly. This involves appearing in court on behalf of a client. As you'll see when you read Rose Palmer's interview in the Appendix, this is one of the things that got Legal Advocacy for Women in trouble in Pittsburgh, PA. Indeed, the first formal complaint against the group was filed by a lawyer who objected to volunteers from the group attending court sessions and whispering instructions to women trying to petition for adequate amounts of child support. And later, when Pittsburg lawyers accepted a settlement allowing nonlawyers to come to court to provide moral and legal support to women, one of the stipulations was that nonlawyer advisors not be allowed to touch, or put their belongings on, the lawyers' (counsel) table. Yes, it's sad that the once proud legal profession should stoop to measure its prerogatives in such petty ways, but petty or not, it's a good illustration of the overt lawyer hostility nonlawyers who try to help people who appear in court are sure to encounter.

No matter what the dispute, or how much or how little money is at stake, lawyers are absolutely bent upon defending their right to be the only people who can speak for others in court. The reasons for this probably have as much to do with concerns about loss of status as they do with economics, but it is also true that, traditionally, enforcement of this rule has done much to fatten lawyers' wallets. When faced with the need to file or defend a court action, even perennially cash-starved public interest groups such as environmentalists, advocates for the disabled, friends of animals and supporters of the homeless have often been able to raise money, often significant amounts of it, to pay a lawyer.

Lawyers, of course, argue that greed has nothing to do with their position that only they can speak on behalf of clients in court. They contend that only they are trained in, and tested on, courtroom skills and it would risk doing great consumer harm to allow others to represent people in court. Without boring you with many pages as to why this argument is a largely self-interested sophistry, let me simply point out that in the vast majority of American law schools, courtroom advocacy is not a required course, and that bar examinations do not test this skill. In short, lawyers normally pick up courtroom skills by working with more experienced colleagues and by practicing (literally) on clients. The fact that nonlawyer advocates who work in nonprofit organizations gain their skills in much the same way is, of course, ignored by lawyers.

In Chapter 2, Section C, I discuss how judges use the "inherent powers" doctrine to protect the legal profession's monopoly over the courtroom and in some instances even the preparation of routine legal paperwork.

B. Defending Yourself From Lawyer Attacks

But suppose you plan to work with a volunteer group in a situation where you will be routinely dispensing legal information and, despite my advice that you are unlikely to experience trouble with the bar, you are worried. After all, like the people who worked with Pittsburg's Legal Advocacy for Women, you might be targeted for an unauthorized practice of law enforcement action. Certainly it is appropriate to ask what is likely to happen to you personally if organized lawyerdom tries to suppress your group?

As long as you are working in the broad public interest sector, the answer is "little or nothing." I know of no current criminal prosecutions in this area. Instead, even when a complaint by organized lawyerdom is initiated, what almost always occurs is something like this:

1. The bar, district attorney, or state supreme court threatens to charge your group (let's assume you work at a center that helps with the legal problems of students) with unauthorized practice. Incidentally, this threat is almost always initiated because a local lawyer handles a dispute against someone who gets legal help from your organization, not because a consumer of your services complains;

2. The media gets involved on the side of your group, asking where else penniless students (or in other situations, mothers without child support, tenants, immigrants, etc.) can get affordable legal help;

3. Organized lawyerdom comes under general attack for not offering free *"pro bono"* help in the particular area, and for generally overcharging and not providing reasonable access to the legal system for the average student (and by extension, most Americans);

4. Meetings are held between the advocacy group and organized lawyerdom and a compromise is worked out. It typically allows the lawyers to

save face by getting the nonprofit group to agree to slightly modify its activities to avoid a charge of UPL (or, if a UPL action has already been filed, to have it dropped). Sometimes this "slap on the wrist" takes the form of limiting some inconsequential aspect of the non-profit's activities; other times it is accomplished by the nonprofit agreeing to token supervision by a lawyer who is personally interested in the particular activity or cause. Almost always, when you look beyond the surface, the advocacy group is allowed to keep operating much as before.

As Rose Palmer discusses in her interview, the Legal Advocacy for Women situation well illustrates how this usually works. The Bar and Legal Advocacy for Women settled their dispute as follows: In exchange for organized lawyerdom backing off, the organization agreed to change its name to "Support, Inc." and clarify a few of its procedures. This consisted of informing all clients that their paralegal helpers are not lawyers (something they knew already), agreeing not to whisper to clients in court and, as mentioned, agreeing not to touch the counsel table. In short, whispering excepted, Support, Inc. is free to do exactly the same work as Legal Advocacy for Women did. And while the group refused to accept any official supervision by a lawyer or bar association, they were canny enough to partially mollify the local legal establishment by 1) putting a few lawyers on their Board of Directors, 2) working closely with several local sympathetic lawyers and supportive judges, and 3) beginning a law student intern program under which students from two local law schools help out with Support, Inc. programs.

C. Paying the Bills

Unfortunately, paralegals who work with non-profits often face a larger problem than the threat of lawyer harassment. Their problem is economic. Most nonprofit groups, whether organized to help AIDS sufferers, artists, alcoholics, or animals, or any of thousands of other worthy endeavors, are severely under-funded. All too often they try to survive from one inadequate grant to the next, existing in large measure because of the personal economic sacrifices made by their own staff. Or put more bluntly, a paralegal who works in this setting is typically either unpaid or underpaid. For the rare persons with plenty of money in the bank, this may not be a problem. For everyone else, it is a severe one.

The result is that many nonprofit organizations that try to help their members, or the public generally, with legal problems usually experience rapid staff turnover. Often it seems that as soon as a competent paralegal is trained, she has moved on. Commonly, this isn't because the person wants to leave, but because the hard rock of their altruism has been ground into dust by the even harder economic reality of being poor in America. Obviously, rapid turnover is not only harmful to the paralegals involved, but also takes a severe toll on the quality of the legal services delivered by the group.

In my view, many of the problems non-profits have paying paralegals to deliver good legal services could be avoided. The key to doing this is understanding one of the great lessons of the independent paralegal movement— people are willing and able to pay for competent, reasonably-priced legal help if charged for it at paralegal, not lawyer, rates. In other words, the seeming conclusion of many nonprofit groups that there are only two alternatives to the delivery of legal services—hire a lawyer and pay the market rate, or provide free services—is just plain wrong.

PARALEGAL SERVICES AND NONPROFIT TAX LAW

Most nonprofit organizations are exempt from income taxation under Section 501(c)(3) of the Internal Revenue Code as educational or charitable organizations. Since education is defined by IRS regulations to include "instruction of the public on subjects useful to individuals and beneficial to the community," and since "charitable" generally means "promotion of the public good," nonprofits that provide paralegal services should fall well within the guidelines of their tax exemption requirements.

Can tax-exempt nonprofits charge hourly fees for paralegal services? Yes they can. (Just think of the substantial service fees collected by other nonprofit organizations, such as nonprofit colleges, trade schools, hospitals, medical clinics and the like.) As long as the services charged are reasonable, the IRS should not object. In fact, in Ruling 78-428, the IRS decided that a nonprofit group that operated a legal services clinic could charge a fee based upon the income of the client.

This is not the place for a detailed discussion about the mechanics of setting up an economically self-sufficient paralegal office as part of a nonprofit organization. However, it is appropriate to look at one example of how an independent paralegal could provide low-cost legal help at the same time he charges enough to support himself.

Artists of all stripes and spots (dancers, painters, sculptors, jugglers, to mention but a few) often form nonprofit corporations when they want to come together to further their activities, whether it be to establish a performance space, publish educational materials, or sponsor a performance or display. Like the rest of us, most can't afford to hire a lawyer to do this at $200 an hour. As a result, unless they know a lawyer interested in the arts who will volunteer her time, most end up either doing it themselves or knocking on the door of a local nonprofit artists' support group with the hope that someone there can provide free legal help. Because artists' groups are chronically underfunded, they are often unable to do this.

Now, as an alternative, let me propose a different solution. Have the arts support organization work with an independent paralegal, or a paralegal on its own staff, to provide low-cost nonprofit incorporation services to local artists. To establish a fair fee, the first step would be to determine exactly how long it takes to prepare the paperwork to establish a nonprofit corporation and apply for a federal tax exemption. *How To Form a Non-Profit Corporation,* by Anthony Mancuso (Nolo Press), provides instructions on how to do this in every state and contains the step-by-step instructions necessary to apply for a Section 501(c)(3) federal tax exemption. After reading this book and examining the specific forms and procedures necessary in your state, you are likely to conclude the answer is about four to five hours, assuming someone in the nonprofit group has read Mancuso's book and worked with other members to gather necessary information and make practical choices.

The next step is to figure out a fair hourly return for the person doing this work. Assume after taking overhead into consideration you decide this is $65 per hour. This means you will probably find that a paralegal can prepare a nonprofit corporation for less than $300. Most arts groups, no matter how struggling, can scrape together this amount, especially if they have already checked prices with local lawyers, which are likely to range from $1,000-$2,000.

15

Political Organizing for Change

Let's start this chapter by reviewing several points that have been discussed throughout this book.

1. The American civil legal system is slow, expensive and inaccessible. Too often, it's also unjust and corrupt. As a result, the monopoly power of lawyers to deliver legal services in the U.S. is under attack as, increasingly, people see that lawyers are primarily interested in protecting themselves, not the public.

2. The self-help legal movement (and public support for it), has grown immensely in the last twenty years. For example, in several states, including California and Arizona, almost two-thirds of divorces and related family law court actions are now done without a lawyer.

3. The number of people who are running independent paralegal businesses has grown dramatically in the last decade, especially in Florida, Texas, Arizona, California, Oregon, Washington, and Nevada which, taken together, now have thousands of independent paralegals.

4. Several studies,[1] as well as a good deal of practical experience with independent paralegal offices, support the proposition that nonlawyers are competent to handle routine legal paperwork.

5. Self-help law software, such as *WillMaker*, together have sold millions of copies. Ten years ago, these materials didn't exist.

6. The types of legal tasks that the general public is successfully accomplishing on its own using self-help law books and software (and often the help of independent paralegals), are expanding rapidly. In the 1980s, when people thought of self-help law they thought primarily of divorce; today, nonlawyers routinely prepare a wide variety of basic legal forms, including those for step-parent adoption, incorporation, probate and wills, living trusts and house purchases.

7. Consumers are increasingly objecting to organized lawyerdom's monopoly power over the legal system, and it is beginning to be reflected in judicial decisions. Specifically, several recent court decisions

---

[1] One of the best is Rhode, "Policing the Professional Monopoly: A Constitutional and Empirical Analysis of Unauthorized Practice Prohibitions," 34 *Stanford Law Rev.* 1 (1981).

(see Chapter 2) more narrowly define what constitutes the practice of law and allow the role of independent paralegals to expand.

This laundry list of trends adds up to the fact that America is in the midst of a period of fundamental and powerful change in the ways routine legal services are delivered to the middle class. This switch, which is of truly historic proportions, is clearly towards low-cost alternatives to the traditional ways lawyers deliver legal services. As one of these alternatives, the independent paralegal movement is in an excellent position to both help this trend along and to profit from it.

The fact that independent paralegals have made significant strides towards public acceptance in the last few years is not the same thing as saying this new profession is bound to succeed. As noted throughout this book, independent paralegals still face serious political and legal problems because of the hostility of organized lawyerdom. This brings me to the central question of this chapter—how can IPs best protect the advances their occupation has already made and take sensible steps to further expand their role in delivering routine legal services.

A. Paralegal Political Organizing

The best way to accomplish both of these goals is to organize politically. As long as the independent paralegal movement consists of isolated individuals and lawyers are organized through bar associations and judges' associations, the trend toward acceptance of paralegals can be slowed, if not contained, by lawyers. Once organized and politically active, however, independent paralegals obviously have a much better opportunity to get the message across to the public that they represent a low-cost, high-quality alternative to lawyers. (If you doubt this, see Virginia Simons' interview in the Appendix.)

There are several important elements to any successful political organizing effort. One of these involves establishing an efficient way for IPs to communicate with each other at both the state and national level. It is particularly essential that IPs in the same state be in close touch, as most unauthorized practice of law is regulated at the state level. It's important to realize that while IPs may all be competing with each other to some degree, the organized bar, with its dedication to putting everyone out of business, is the real adversary. Or, put more directly, it is essential that IPs avoid squabbles with each other at least long enough to present a united front to the bar. If you doubt this, think back to what it cost the Native American tribes to continue their inter-tribal spats after the Europeans arrived.

Jolene Jacobs, one of the first successful independent paralegals, advises:

> *Develop, if possible, good relationships with your competitors. Try to have a friendly, positive relationship with them rather than an adversarial one. It can not only make life and your business environment more pleasant, you will build relationships that will help all independent paralegals if the bar gets aggressive.*

Once all the IPs in your state are talking to each other, your next job is to establish a solid state-wide organization. There are a number of ways to do this, no one of which is the best in all circumstances. With this caution in mind, let me tell you some of the things Charles (Ed) Sherman and I did in the early 1970s as part of establishing California's pioneering Wave Project:

- Established a central office which, for a small fee, coordinated state-wide efforts of project members, and was available for counseling when the bar threatened any Wave Project member.

- Produced a quarterly newsletter to serve as a training vehicle and to give Wave Project members a forum in which to share good ideas and good gossip.

- Held regular meetings and training sessions. After an initial training course for new counselors, which lasted about four days, we periodically (three to four times a year) held follow-up two-day training sessions in different parts of the state. Incidentally, if you conduct this sort of training, keep things interesting by bringing in outside speakers who are expert in the area of the law you are working in. Also, leave plenty of time for your own political strategy sessions. Keep costs to a minimum, but be ready to chip in whatever it takes.

- Established the idea of centralized legal defense help for the 15-20 independent paralegals in the Wave Project. To accomplish this, the Wave Project assessed members a couple of dollars from every fee charged customers. The idea was to have each member independent paralegal know that he could get quick, effective legal help and counseling by picking up the phone. I strongly recommend that all paralegal organizations do this. If organized lawyerdom tries to put you in a small room with bars on the windows, it should go almost without saying that your ability to deal with your inevitable feelings of fear and paranoia will be greatly enhanced if you have set up a defense fund in advance.

One state that has a good organization is Oregon, where a membership group, Oregon Legal Technicians (OLT), represents many of the state's independent paralegals. The group meets fairly regularly, providing a great opportunity for members to communicate about common business and legal concerns. OLT also lobbies actively for legislation to break down the legal monopoly—including efforts to simplify legal forms—and is a sponsor of legislation to allow IPs to operate free of the fear of UPL prosecution. The organization also makes an effort to see that individual IPs follow honest business principles. Thus, if a new IP enters the field and engages in bait-and-switch advertising, or seems inadequately prepared, an OLT member is likely to offer counseling on how to improve his or her business. In California, the much larger California Association of Independent Paralegals (CAIP) plays a similar role.[2]

---

[2] CAIP, which is headquartered at 39120 Argonaut Way (Suite 114), Fremont, CA 94538, also offers out-of-state memberships, which are particularly attractive to IPs in states where there is as yet no statewide IP association.

In addition to forming an independent paralegal association in your state, it may also be to your advantage to join one or more existing traditional paralegal associations, especially those that are affiliated with a national organization such as the National Federation of Paralegal Associations (NFPA). These affiliations may make a number of benefits available to you, including the possibility of errors and omissions insurance. See Chapter 12 Section E for more on this type of insurance. As your independent paralegal association grows larger, it may be possible for it to join NFPA or another national association directly.

B. Independent Paralegals in California and Florida

Because Florida and California are the two states where the modern independent paralegal movement was born, and which currently have the most practicing independent paralegals, let's briefly look at the history and current political situation in each to illustrate the growth of the movement. Sorry, but it's simply beyond the scope of this book to do this for every state.

Florida

In the 1970s and early 1980s, Rosemary Furman, a former court clerk, began to help nonlawyers prepare legal paperwork. Along with the original Wave Project members, who did the same thing in California, Furman was an authentic pioneer. (See interview in the Appendix.) When the Florida bar mounted a campaign to close down her office in Jacksonville, Florida, culminating in a 30-day jail sentence from the Florida Supreme Court in 1984 (it was later commuted), Furman fought back. When she appeared on TV shows such as "60 Minutes," she did much to convince American consumers that the lawyer monopoly over legal services was so fraught with self-interest that it had to be broken.

In addition to Rosemary Furman's brave determination, the battle to allow IPs to operate in Florida was aided by several law suits prepared by the Washington-based consumer rights group, Public Citizen. Filed on behalf of Florida citizens who could not afford to hire lawyers, these suits argued that low-income people were being denied reasonable access to justice. Eventually, the activities of Furman and Public Citizen embarrassed the Florida courts into taking some first steps to provide better citizen access to the law. Specifically, the Florida Supreme Court approved a series of simplified legal forms designed to be used without a lawyer, including those necessary to obtain a divorce, collect child support, obtain a restraining order against domestic violence, as well as a number of landlord-tenant forms.[3] As this book goes to press, other forms are in the works.

Of great interest to Florida IPs is that, in adopting this simplified form approach, Florida has also changed its UPL rules as they concern the use of these forms. Specifically, the Supreme Court of Florida amended Chapter 10 of the Rules Regulating the Florida Bar to state:

> ...*For purposes of this chapter, it shall not constitute the unlicensed practice of law for nonlawyers to engage in limited oral communications to assist individuals in the completion of [approved] legal forms...Oral communications by nonlawyers are restricted to those communications reasonably necessary to elicit factual information to complete the form(s) and inform the individual how to file them...*

Also of interest is the fact that the Florida Bar has set up a legal technicians study committee to look at the feasibility of authorizing legal technicians to provide certain legal services directly to the public, and has recently stated that it's UPL for nonlawyers to prepare living trust forms. (See Chapter 2, Section C.)

California

The Golden State tends to be a trend setter. Certainly this is true when it comes to the independent paralegal movement. Thanks, in part, to the self-help law books published by Nolo Press and the organization of the Wave Project self-help divorce centers by Charles (Ed) Sherman and myself in 1972-73, California has always had more independent paralegals than any other state.

---

[3] These forms are available from the Florida Bar, 650 Apalachee Parkway, Tallahasse, Florida 32399.

In the mid-1980s, this rapidly growing new service industry was attacked by the Los Angeles County bar. It urged the California State bar to vigorously police the unauthorized practice of law, especially in the fields of domestic relations (divorce), bankruptcy, immigration and landlord/tenant law, all of which the Los Angeles attorney group claimed were rapidly being taken over by independent paralegals.

In response, the State bar appointed the Public Protection Committee to look into the L.A. bar's claims. The Committee was made up of a majority of lawyers and paralegals who worked for lawyers. In what is surely the most surprising event in recent California bar history, instead of proposing a crackdown on IPs, the Public Protection Committee unanimously recommended, in April 1988, that the California legislature completely abolish the state's UPL laws. It further concluded that independent paralegals should be allowed to provide all types of legal services as long as they are registered with a state agency and disclose their nonlawyer status to all customers.

Even though a sub-committee of Bar Governors largely supported the conclusions of the Public Protection Committee, its recommendations were rejected by the State bar in August 1989, after many local bar associations reacted in horror to the threatened loss of their traditional monopoly power. The California Bar then appointed a third group (The Commission on Legal Technicians) to restudy the issue. This Commission largely agreed with the conclusions of its predecessors and recommended that nonlawyers be authorized by the California Supreme Court to deliver legal services in several major areas (bankruptcy, family, immigration and landlord-tenant), under the terms of a licensing scheme that would be supervised by an independent state agency. However, after being repeatedly scaled back, the state Bar again refused to adopt their own committee's recommendations.[4] In the meantime, a much more ambitious proposal sponsored by a number of groups, including Nolo and HALT, the Washington, D.C.-based public interest organization that lobbies for better consumer access to the American legal system, has been introduced in the California legislature. Called the Affordable Legal Access bill, this legislation, which originally called for testing and regulating independent

---

[4] To obtain a copy of the Public Protection Committee's report (April 1988) or the Legal Technician Commission's report (July 1990), contact the California State Bar at 415-561-8200.

paralegals, stalled in 1992 in large part because of California's budgetary crisis, which all but precluded any new programs. In 1993 and again in 1994, the bill was reintroduced in a less ambitious form, which basically calls for registration of existing IPs and a study of whether or not more regulation is needed. UPL enforcement is left unaffected. As this book goes to press in the summer of 1994, this bill has been approved by key committees of both houses of the California Legislature and is thought to have a good chance of becoming law.

 See Section C, "Legislation to Legalize IPs," below, and the interview with former HALT Legislative Director Debbie Chalfie in the Appendix.

C. Legislation to Legalize IPs

In 1989-1990, Glen Nishimura and Debbie Chalfie, of HALT—An Organization of Americans for Legal Reform[5]—led an effort to draft model legislation to allow independent paralegals to render certain types of legal services directly to the public free of the fear of prosecution for unauthorized practice of law. The legislation, which was developed during a series of meetings between independent paralegals and consumer advocates, has served as a jumping off place for many pro-IP bills introduced in state legislatures.

The legislative purpose portion of the model bill states in part:

a. Indigent persons and persons of moderate income are generally unable to afford to hire lawyers to provide needed legal assistance. Studies have shown that roughly 80 percent of the legal needs of low-income Americans go unmet, and 130 million middle-income Americans are unable to get help with civil legal problems when they need it, because they cannot afford it. This has resulted in a two-tiered system of justice, with only the very rich able to afford legal services and the vast majority being shut out of the legal system.

b. The factors chiefly to blame for the high cost of legal services are the high cost involved in becoming a lawyer and the profession's monopoly over delivery of services. The time and money necessary to enter the [legal] field [college, law school, bar exam passage] involve high costs which,

---

[5] See Section F below for information on how to join HALT.

unless mitigated by a presence of competition, are inevitably passed on to the consumer.

c. New and innovative approaches to meet this overwhelming need are required because traditional solutions, such as government-funded legal aid and voluntary efforts by the bar to provide free legal services, even when obtained optimally, can accommodate only a very small fraction of that need. Permitting nonlawyer "legal technicians" to provide services directly to the public for out-of-court legal matters is just such an approach, and its advocates include consumer representatives, bar groups and legal scholars.

In brief outline here is what HALT's Legal Technician (Independent Paralegal) bill proposes:

- Legal technicians prepare paperwork and supply information in a long list of areas, including, but not limited to, the following:
  - (A) Immigration
  - (B) Family law
  - (C) Housing law
  - (D) Public benefit law
  - (E) Litigation support law
  - (F) Conservatorship and guardianship law
  - (G) Real estate law
  - (H) Liability law
  - (I) Estate administration law
  - (J) Consumer law
  - (K) Corporate/business law
  - (L) Intellectual property law
  - (M) Estate planning law
  - (N) Bankruptcy law
  - (O) Employment law
- Legal Technicians would operate under the general supervision and control of a Board of Legal Technicians, which would be under the general jurisdiction not of the state bar or Supreme Court but a public agency such as the Department of Consumer Affairs.
- People who run legal typing services limited to preparing legal paperwork following a customer's instructions would not be covered by the bill, so would not have to register with the Legal Technicians Board or meet any licensing requirements.

- All legal technicians would have to register with the Legal Technician Board and disclose to the public that they were not lawyers.
- Legal technicians who prepare certain types of forms must be licensed. It's up to the Board to decide which areas require licensure and which require registration only. In making this determination, "The Board shall balance consumer's interest in affordable costs with consumer's interest in receiving competent services...The Board shall require licensure only for those substantive areas or tasks in which it finds there is a substantial likelihood of irreparable harm to consumers, the ability of consumers to evaluate the quality of legal technicians' work is low, and mistakes cannot be easily corrected or remedied."
- In areas where legal technicians must be licensed, a license shall be granted upon completion of a "practice-oriented examination" on the law and procedures of the relevant specialty areas of no more than four hours.
- The bill also proposes a comprehensive system to handle consumer complaints, including quick investigation of claimed problems, and efforts to conciliate consumer claims. If this fails, the dispute would be promptly arbitrated. A compensation fund, paid for by legal technician registration fees, shall be available to compensate consumers who win arbitration awards against insolvent legal technicians.

In fairness, however, it should be noted that the approach taken by the HALT legislation, which essentially proposes a system of paralegal registration and, for some legal tasks, licensure in exchange for the right to operate, isn't universally favored. Some independent paralegals and many paralegals who work for lawyers are reluctant to let go of the present freedom to operate in an unregulated environment. After all, some independent paralegals argue, if much of the problem with the delivery of legal services can be traced to the monopoly power of a legal profession that depends on licensing to suppress competition, why should we go the same route? In addition, many people are concerned that regulation will be unfairly extended to typing services that do little but prepare legal forms under direct supervision of customers and do not provide legal information or advice.

I believe that IPs who type legal forms under the direct supervision of nonlawyer customers should not be regulated. However, IPs who wish to provide legal information and expertise should be willing to accept a reasonable level of state supervision if it is demonstrated that this is in the public interest. Regulation might appropriately include registration, skills testing and a recourse system to help customers who have received inadequate services. Why? Because the main argument that lawyers have always used when they attempt to suppress independent paralegals is that they are not competent and, therefore, allowing them to operate constitutes a serious risk to the public. An IP's having passed a test on the specific skills needed to prepare legal paperwork in the field in which the IP operates is an excellent way to refute this argument.

D. Introducing Legislation as a Technique to Build Political Support

Introducing legislation, such as has occurred in California, Oregon, Hawaii, Washington, Wisconsin and several other states, gives IPs a wonderful opportunity to build public support. Assuming the bill's sponsor is reasonably energetic in pushing it, hearings will be held. This will not only give IPs a chance to organize people to testify, and get sympathetic political interest groups to take a supportive stand, it will provide them with a legitimate opportunity to approach the media.

Before arranging for a sympathetic legislator to introduce legislation, try to get all the independent paralegals within your state to chip in and hire a part-time lobbyist to represent your group's interests in the state capitol. Obviously, if you already have a state-wide association (which, incidentally, should be organized as a nonprofit corporation), this is the appropriate entity to use to do the hiring. Fortunately, working with a lobbyist need not be prohibitively expensive. Many consumer-oriented lobbyists represent a number of small consumer, environmental, and other groups supporting themselves with a modest annual fee from each. Here again, HALT should be a source of good advice. (See Section F below for information on how to join HALT.)

Why do you need a part-time lobbyist? Both to teach you the legislative ropes and be your knowledgeable friend when it comes to advising you on how to deal with the governor and the legislature. You will want to lobby and testify on your own, too, but you will benefit greatly from someone who knows what it takes to get a bill passed.

E. Dangers of Licensing IPs

So far, I have primarily focused on the advantages of licensing independent paralegals. There are also some dangers. One that IPs who introduce legislation should be prepared to deal with is that the IP regulation they propose may be amended by lawyer interests in the legislature. If this is done, it will most likely be to give lawyers control of the IP regulatory body to try and burden IPs with bonding requirements or other harassing rules designed to put them out of business. In short, you can bet that lawyers will try to use their power to frustrate the growth of the independent paralegal movement. To prevent this, it's essential that independent paralegals do their homework before legislation is introduced so they know they have enough votes to insure that pro-IP legislation won't be hijacked by lawyer interests.

In addition to the threat that lawyers will control any IP licensing effort, there is another danger inherent in any independent paralegal licensing effort. This is that licensing will be used primarily to create a monopoly for those who have the licenses, but will not really guarantee the public good and honest paralegal service. To see how this occurs and a negative public image results, you need look no further than the legal profession, where lawyers need only take one very general examination (and in most states are not subject to any ongoing skills testing) in exchange for their lifetime right to practice.[6]

So, the question becomes how can IPs create an honest licensing system that is not controlled by lawyers and isn't so self-serving that it's sure to backfire on them in the long run? In "The Case Against Credentialism" (*The Atlantic,* December 1985), James Fallows points out that at least one American groups of workers has managed to develop a system of competence certification that really works. These are airline pilots who, according to Fallows, have a system that operates like this:

> *The pilot licensing system was built on the premise that competence was divisible: people can be good at one thing without being good at others, and they should be allowed to do only what they have mastered. As opposed to*

---

[6] Indeed, precisely because many consumers now understand that license to practice law means little when it comes to guaranteeing that a particular practitioner is competent, they are more likely to consider a paralegal or other self-help alternative.

receiving a blanket license, the way members of other professions do, pilots must work their way up through four certificate levels, from student to air-transport pilot, and be specifically qualified on each kind of aircraft they want to fly. What's more, a pilot must demonstrate at regular intervals that he is still competent. To keep his license, a pilot must take a review flight with an instructor every two years, and the pilots for commercial airlines must pass a battery of requalification tests every six months. "A small but regular percentage is washed out each time," John Mazor, of the Air Line Pilots Association, says. It is reassuring to know they are gone, but what about their tenured counterparts in the other professions? The results of this licensing scheme are a high level of proficiency and a profession more open socially than the rest.

What can IPs learn from this? First, that the public respects a licensing system in which the person licensed has really mastered the particular job. Thus an IP who wants to type divorce and bankruptcy forms should be separately licensed and tested in each field. Second, that licensing is of little value to the public (and therefore worthy of little respect) unless the licensees are regularly retested to be sure their skills are still sharp.

At this point, it's also necessary to remind you that most paralegals in the United States do not work independently but are employed by lawyers. Traditionally, these employed paralegals oppose licensure and certification, arguing that since they do not deal with the public directly, it isn't necessary. Some also oppose it because they are insecure about their own legal training and fear that they might have to go back to school to qualify or because they fear that any board established to regulate paralegals would be controlled by lawyers. I mention this not to deal with these arguments in detail, but to point out that because independent paralegals and lawyer-employed paralegals will not always agree on the licensure issue, it is essential that lines of communication be opened between the two groups so that they can hash out their differences.

One advantage of communicating with paralegals who work for lawyers is, of course, to present a united front to the bar. Another is to take advantage of the organizational skills employed paralegals have developed. There is a paralegal association in every good-sized city. In California, there are separate groups to represent the interests of paralegals who are employed by lawyers and those who work as freelancers. Most have regular meetings, newsletters, and sponsor training sessions. And while the long-term interests of employed, freelance and independent paralegals aren't the same, they do overlap to a considerable degree.

F. Lawsuits as a Paralegal Organizing Device

Another way to focus paralegal organizing efforts is around litigation. This happened to some extent in California in the 1970s, when the State Bar of California tried to pull the law licenses of Wave Project pioneers Charles (Ed) Sherman and Phyllis Eliasberg. In the early 1980s, the Florida Bar's efforts to persecute nonlawyer Rosemary Furman through a lawyer-controlled kangaroo court civil contempt proceeding resulted in national publicity and helped convince the public that the legal profession often abused its monopoly power over the legal system. More recently, the prosecution of Louisiana bankruptcy IP, Jerome Papania was widely reported, including being the centerpiece of an

ABC "20-20" show focusing on how the average American is denied access to the legal system.

One alternative to waiting for the bar to prosecute independent paralegals one-by-one is for IPs to get together and sue them. This can be done based upon any one of a number of legal theories, all of which come down to the fact that the bar is improperly using its monopoly power to prevent public access to the courts. This approach has been tried in Federal Court in Florida (*Dunn v. Florida Bar*), where Alan Morrison and David Vladeck of the Ralph Nader-affiliated Public Citizen Litigation Group in Washington D.C., argued a number of legal theories, including the fact that the bar's monopolistic practices deny citizens the right to access to the courts. Although this suit did not result in a court victory, it was, as noted in Section B, above, an important factor in the Florida Supreme Court's decision to require easy-to-use court forms and allow independent paralegals to prepare them without fear of being charged with unauthorized practice.

If you are interested in filing suit against the bar, however, be sure you know what's going on in this legal area in other parts of the country. Test case litigation is best coordinated so that the right case is fought on the right legal theories in the right court. In this context, HALT (again, at 1319 F Street, NW, Suite 300, Washington, DC 20004, 202/347-9600), is an excellent source of up-to-date information for its members.[7] Several HALT staffers work full-time in this area, and they produce a high quality quarterly publication entitled "Legal Reformer," which regularly carries helpful material on pending court cases which raise significant UPL issues.

And, as I mention in the Introduction, HALT's report, "Fixing the Lawyer Monopoly—The Right of Citizens to Employ Independent Paralegals When Handling Their Legal Affairs," is a must-read for anyone interested in becoming an IP. It's available to HALT members for $10.00.

Another nonprofit group that does excellent work in this area is the National Congress for Legal Reform (4427-A Wisconsin Ave., NW, Suite 200, Washington, D.C. 20016; 202/895-2805). Membership, which costs $19.00, includes a newsletter, which often deals with IP issues.

---

[7] HALT's membership fee of $15.00 is very reasonable. Be sure you join before you call and ask for information or help.

Appendix

Interviews

This book was first written in the mid-1980s and has been updated and revised a number of times. As part of doing this, new interviews have been added, some old interviews have been updated and a few interviews have been dropped because the person is no longer in the IP business and his or her remarks are now dated. The interview with Rosemary Furman, one of the true pioneers of the IP movement, appears just as it first did in 1986—some things are just too good to change.

Lois Isenberg Interview

Lois Isenberg has been a very successful paralegal for more than 20 years. She is currently President of the California Association of Independent Paralegals (CAIP). In addition, she teaches courses and workshops on how to start and operate an IP business.

Ralph Warner (RW): *Take me back a few years and tell me how you got started as an independent paralegal.*

Lois Isenberg (LI): My work background is in advertising, public relations and film production. In about 1973, I was producing educational films when I got a call for help from a friend who had started a WAVE Project do-it-yourself divorce office.

RW: *What sort of help?*

LI: She had no customers and she obviously needed some in a hurry if she was going to survive. I was on a two-week break between films and agreed to do what I could. I helped her define her market and we designed flyers. After a few days she literally got up from her desk, walked to the door of her office and, as she was exiting the door, said over her shoulder, "I don't want this business, it's yours."

RW: *She gave it to you?*

LI: Yes, but, of course, since there were no customers, she didn't give me much.

RW: *What did you do?*

LI: Got in touch with the WAVE Project people—you and Ed Sherman, among others—and got trained in how to fill out divorce forms. Then I moved the business to my house, where it stayed until 1979. During that time I bought the Hollywood WAVE Project office and moved it into my home also. Eventually, I opened an office on Wilshire Blvd. in Los Angeles.

RW: *Was the business supporting you decently by that time?*

LI: Yes and no. I was still doing other things and wasn't really focused on it. Then around 1980 I met a helpful lawyer, Anne Lober, who was actively involved in promoting mediation for divorcing couples. She encouraged and helped me to learn how to do other types of family law paperwork, including restraining orders and child support and custody modifications. After that I was able to find other helpful attorneys who taught me to do step-parent adoptions, guardianships and paternity.

RW: *Did this put you over the hump financially?*

LI: It was really ten years after I began that I had a viable business. But again, part of what took me so long was being serious about it. My business grew substantially when I moved it from my home to an office. Visibility is a very important part of a business's success and even though divorce is not exactly an impulse buy, when people see your sign day after day they will remember you when the need arises.

RW: *After a while, I'm sure you got lots of referrals from satisfied customers.*

LI: Definitely, referrals are about 50% of my business. But, obviously, it takes time to build a referral base. In the meantime, you must develop referral sources. In my case, one of these was working closely with the divorce mediation community—lawyers and others who understood that contested court actions were a terrible way to settle domestic disputes and encouraged people to arrive at their own solutions.

RW: *Do you work alone?*

LI: No. I have a full time assistant as well as a part-time receptionist-clerk.

RW: *Today, you are the President of the California Association of Independent Paralegals (CAIP). I'll ask you more about CAIP in a minute. Now I want to know when it dawned on you that lawyers didn't approve of what you were doing and that if the independent paralegal movement was going to survive you would have to be politically active and organized.*

LI: Well, it was obvious from day one that low-cost competition was going to annoy lawyers. I can't tell you how many times I was verbally attacked by an attorney in a social situation when I mentioned my work. And, of course, the fact that lawyers were maniacally opposed to what we were doing was a reason why the IP business was semi-underground for many years.

RW: *They couldn't swat you if they couldn't find you.*

LI: Precisely. Most of the early independent paralegals worked from their houses and, at least as far as lawyers were concerned, pretended not to exist. This strategy worked up to a point, but it also prevented us from finding each other and, worse, the public finding us.

RW: *Why did you stick your head above ground?*

LI: To see if I cast a shadow?

RW: *C'mon—seriously.*

LI: I am serious. Sooner or later, IPs have to climb out of their holes and fight for their right to exist. Here in California, in about 1986, ten or fifteen of us, led by Glynda Mathewson, who worked in Oakland, began meeting alternately in Northern and Southern California. We adopted the name California Association of Independent Paralegals and decided that CAIP would work towards improving the professionalism of the legal form preparation business.

RW: *How?*

LI: Continuing education for ourselves, establishing ethical standards for business and lobbying the state legislature in Sacramento to pass decent laws defining our occupation.

RW: *I know CAIP has close to 200 members these days, some from other states, but I know it hasn't been easy.*

LI: No. At first, getting members was tough. Many people who are attracted to the idea of being an independent paralegal are not joiners. We attract the legal visionary as well as the entrepreneur. The visionary is often focused on the cause of "legal access for all," while oftentimes the entrepreneur is looking for a quick success. What CAIP is trying to do is have all these individuals join together to create a viable force. We need to be able to have legislation passed that will elevate the position of the independent paralegal and provide protection against frivolous lawsuits.

CAIP not only wants to encourage a level of excellence among the independent paralegals, but also provide protection for the consumer as well.

RW: *What does CAIP do these days?*

LI: We have come a long way. We have a newsletter called ACCESS, an annual convention, training sessions, and we are extremely active in Sacramento, lobbying to try and open up the lawyer monopoly to recognize that independent paralegals are a viable legal option.

RW: *In addition, you have your own consulting business.*

LI: If running seminars on form preparation skills and business operations is a consulting business, the answer is yes. My major in college was education, but I never actively taught. In doing these seminars, not only do I get a chance to teach, which incidentally I really enjoy, but I also get to teach something I actually know about.

RW: *People fly in from all over, I understand.*

LI: I hope so.

RW: *How does a reader find out more?*

LI: Call me at 213/655-6141.

Jolene Jacobs Interview

Jolene Jacobs, a long-time friend, is one of the first successful, modern independent paralegals. She operated a divorce form typing business from 1973 until early 1994, when she sold her business. This interview was done in 1992.

Ralph Warner (RW): *How did you first become involved in paralegal work?*

Jolene Jacobs(JJ): In 1972, when I was just finishing my undergraduate degree, I was interested in doing some kind of consumer advocacy or public service work. I admired Ralph Nader and his Raiders and other individuals who battled large corporations for consumer rights and protection. In December of 1972, I met you and Ed Sherman. I heard about the Wave Project from a family friend who told me you were looking for people to train to type divorces based on the information in Ed's book, *How To Do Your Own Divorce in California*. I remember coming over to your old, brown-shingle house in Berkeley with several other recruits. You had samples of divorce forms taped to the dining room walls and we all sat around while you showed us how to fill them out, process them through the clerk's office and talked about how people could best represent themselves in court. What attracted me to the Wave Project was that although the divorce book worked well for lots of people, many others obviously needed more personal help than any book could provide—both of a secretarial nature and personal support. I signed on, along with a dozen or so others, to train as divorce counselors.

RW: *Come on, you must have been somewhat scared embarking on an illegal business fresh out of college.*

JJ: You warned us that there would be problems, possibly serious problems, with the bar, and that we might even face criminal charges. Oddly, I wasn't scared at that point. I believed the bar's monopoly control over access to legal information and legal assistance was a bad thing. My perspective on the work was that it was a consumer advocacy project rather than a career as a "paralegal." I was so excited that I didn't really worry about it. The prospect of helping people with very little money, and sometimes without much education, put their own decisions on paper, file their papers at court and represent themselves before a judge was truly exciting. While people may not have been happy about the outcome of their marriage, they could at least feel good about having done their own divorce.

RW: *When the Wave Project training was over, where did you start working?*

JJ: I opened an office in San Jose in 1973. I stayed there until 1978 and then moved to San Francisco, where I have been since.

RW: *Was it hard to get your business going?*

JJ: It was both simple and hard. I had never been self-employed and had no family history of self-employment as a model. I had just graduated from college with no debts, no responsibilities and a lot of enthusiasm, but not much else. Of course, I needed very little money to get by at that point. Incidentally, now I might not take that economic risk, so it was good that the chance to do something new crossed my path then.

I ended up in San Jose because you and Ed suggested that San Jose was a good place to start because there were no other Wave Project counselors in that area. It was somewhat difficult to move to a new town, look for a place to live and start a business in an area where I didn't know a soul.

The mechanics to set up an office weren't hard: get an office, telephone, typewriter, etc. The furniture and office equipment were particularly simple. I started with two wooden apple boxes and a typewriter. One apple box was for the customer to sit on and the other was for the typewriter. If I only had a picture!

It was harder to learn how to get the word out that this new self-help service was available. In addition to the fact that I knew nothing about marketing, I faced an old California law, passed in the 1890s but still on the books, which made it illegal to "aid or encourage birth control, abortion or divorce." These were all legal activities, yet, at least according to California law, it was illegal to give out information about them. This prevented me from advertising, so I took brochures around to public agencies such as social services and legal aid and to a local newspaper, which wrote a story about my service. Now and then, I was able to get a classified ad into the paper, but then a lawyer or the DA would see it and call the paper and get them to take it out, based on the 1890 law. Of course, I believed this law was unconstitutional, but it was upheld a few years later, I believe, in a case in Southern California. I think it is still on the books, but was forgotten as soon as lawyers wanted to advertise their own divorce services. At any rate, this old law and the determination of lawyers to enforce it was a serious obstacle to the growth of my business.

RW: *What about the local bar association? What was their position on your typing service?*

JJ: The bar association claimed at every opportunity that the Wave Project was a "fly by night" business, a rip-off, "here today and gone tomorrow," etc. It was difficult for me as an individual, and the Wave Project as a small group, to combat this. While people didn't particularly trust or like the bar association even then, they had no idea who we were and what our credentials or intentions were. In other words, typing divorce forms was a new field and there was no positive history of such a service to make people feel confident. So, if the bar said it was bad, some people, at least, were hesitant to take a risk. In fairness, I should say, however, that there were individual lawyers who supported me.

To face the bar alone would have been impossible for me. Being a part of a group backed up by you and Ed made me feel more confident, and help was just a phone call away. Later, the Wave Project counselors began a legal defense fund that we contributed to monthly. This made most of us feel more secure that we could weather a prosecution financially by pooling our money. And we did use money in the fund several times. But the risk of being put out of business, or being arrested, was always there.

RW: *How long were you in business before the bar figured out what you were doing?*

JJ: They noticed me almost immediately. The bar association had already criticized Nolo Press in general, and *How To Do Your Own Divorce in California* specifically, so they were watching everything you and Ed did, especially the Wave Project. Also, remember, there was an article about my new business in the newspaper and classified ads I placed, so my business wasn't a secret. I can think of five instances when I was investigated that I know about. There may have been others.

RW: *Can you tell me a little about the five?*

JJ: One involved an investigation by the district attorney. The Wave Project responded by hiring one of the best constitutional lawyers in the state. The DA was so impressed with the quality of the lawyer's work, and the apparent seriousness of the Wave Project in fighting prosecution, that the case was dropped "for the time being." The DA did successfully prosecute another paralegal who worked in the area, however. This person worked independently and had no support.

    Another time an investigation/prosecution was nipped in the bud because my roommate happened to be a law school classmate of a staff member in the DA's office who was supposed to write a memorandum recommending prosecution. Both my roommate and the classmate had actually done their own divorces using Ed Sherman's divorce book. This meant I had a friend to argue to the DA that while she had no trouble with a total self-help approach because she had the benefit of a legal education, the average consumer needed, and should be able to get, reasonably priced help preparing their papers.

RW: *That was a lucky coincidence, your roommate knowing the person who was to investigate you.*

JJ: Yes, but maybe it wasn't as important as I thought at the time, because a little later there was another investigation by the DA's office. This one I didn't know about until it was over. The investigator who recommended that I not be prosecuted called up to say how impressed he was with the quality of my work. Later, when he left the DA's office, he called and asked for a job at the Wave Project.

    The next incident was scarier. A judge who usually worked in criminal court, but was hearing domestic cases and was unfamiliar with the new trend of petitioners appearing in pro per—that is, representing themselves—told one of my customers that he would have me arrested if I didn't appear in his courtroom the next morning. I wasn't sure that he could legally pull off this King of England routine, but I went over. My customer was also ordered to be there. She was terrified. It didn't help that she had a heart problem.

    The clerk read me my rights, the stenographer took down every word, and so on. The judge assured me I would be prosecuted for all sorts of heinous, but not very specific, crimes if I didn't shut down my business. Afterwards, I raced back to my office and called a criminal lawyer, who called the judge. Also, again by coincidence, I knew the judge's former clerk. This person also happened to have worked as a divorce consultant. So, I called the former clerk, who also called the judge on my behalf. After talking to these two people, the judge decided to "put it on the back burner." I think he still would have pursued the matter with the DA to get me prosecuted, but he died suddenly.

RW: *Your experience really underlines the fact that the legal establishment isn't monolithic. At almost every level, from lawyer to law clerk, you found allies when you needed them. But don't let me interrupt a great story. What happened next?*

JJ: Several times a number of divorce typing offices in the Bay Area were investigated on the phone, with no resulting action. We never knew who was doing the investigating, but it was easy to tell something was going on, because the callers kept asking questions that required legal opinions. You can spot this technique because the questions are usually inappropriate—not what most people ask. I think somehow related to these calls was an incident where an undercover investigator posing as a customer walked in and asked some questions, which I answered. Since my responses were not the incriminating answers she expected, or hoped for, she left the office somewhat curtly.

There may have been investigations other than these. I expect there have been. Sometimes the investigator stands out like a sore thumb, or more like a pain in the neck. But there may have been times when I wasn't able to detect them. The point is, of course, to try to be careful all of the time.

RW: *Do you have any other advice for people just starting out about how to avoid unauthorized practice of law charges?*

JJ: I think the more friends and contacts someone has in the local legal world, the easier it is to find out what is going on, and to deal with problems that come up. Also, I would say it is important to have a good lawyer lined up in advance. This is one context in which lawyers have really done a good job for me. I wouldn't have expected it, but it's true. It's ironic, of course, that I need lawyers to save me from lawyers, but that's the American legal system in a nutshell. Also, you need to have friends in the media who will go to bat for you should things get rough. I certainly would have been prosecuted were it not for the realization that if lawyers go after paralegals who do good work and have access to the press, the public will see the lawyers as trying to unfairly suppress a person who is offering a reasonable alternative to their over-priced monopoly. In other words, you need to know how to play David to the bar's Goliath. This isn't hard, because the legal profession can't really deny that they are a monopoly, that their services are expensive and many people can't pay their fees. They claim that the public does not get competent help when they use paralegals, but this is increasingly being recognized as a diversion from the truth that lawyers go after paralegals because they don't want competition. The public has really come to understand as a result of the many recent revelations that lawyers don't regulate their own profession very well, and that hiring a lawyer is no guarantee of competent legal care.

RW: *Do you still fear bar harassment by the bar?*

JJ: Sure, remember, I have only related my personal experience. I have friends in the business who have been arrested and had their offices closed down and their livelihood lost. Certain areas of California seem to be safer than others to work in. But still, this is one job where a little paranoia is healthy. Even to be the subject of an investigation is no fun. A long prosecution is horrible. I admire the steadfastness and courage of Rosemary Furman of Florida in standing up to the bar. Because she was so vocal in her anger and her belief in the importance of what she was doing, the bar association came down very hard on her. It would have been so much easier to give up. We have all gained something from her fight and from the national publicity her case received. She went through a great deal, and I think that paralegals around the country should have provided more emotional and financial support—myself included.

RW: *Let's leave the unauthorized practice issue for a bit and come back to some of the practical problems of being an independent paralegal. What price did you first charge for a divorce? What do you charge now? Can you make a good living?*

JJ: Our first price was $55 for typing an uncontested divorce. This covered overhead and provided a small income. It wasn't really adequate, so we raised the price to $65, then $75. In California there are now two forms of divorce; my office charges $80 for the very simple variety and $180 for the more complicated standard form (and up to $210 if support is involved). Other paralegal offices charge slightly different fees for divorce. I think the two primary factors that affect price are the cost of office overhead and the price charged by competition. Initially, I think our services were underpriced. I know I was so into consumerism that I felt uncomfortable about charging very much at all. I had never had the experience of setting a fair market value on my own labor. In addition, I had no idea how much it cost just to run an office. Of course, now I am much more sympathetic to people who are self-employed and who have substantial overhead. I know it is certainly not all profit. The idea of charging a fair fee to cover good work and support oneself decently is comfortable to me now.

RW: *Can you make a good living now as an independent paralegal?*

JJ: My income is good, but my work is stressful and it doesn't always seem enough for the number of years of experience I have, or for the volume of work required and the level of stress that accompanies helping people do divorces. It goes beyond typing forms (that's the first layer). I end up being a social worker, family counselor, helping people find jobs and providing emotional support. Also, with the unresolved status of independent paralegals, the job never feels secure.

RW: *Why did you move to San Francisco from San Jose?*

JJ: I was in San Jose from 1973 until 1978. At that time, my friends who ran the San Francisco office of what by this time had changed in name from the Wave Project to Divorce Center, were completing law school and wanted to sell their office. I was ready for a change and I missed the central Bay Area (San Jose is 50 miles south), so I decided to sell my San Jose office and buy the San Francisco office.

      As it turned out, though, working in suburban San Jose was much easier than working in urban S.F. In San Jose, people were much more easygoing and trusting that I would do my best job for them. In San Francisco, people were fearful of being ripped off, more hostile, more angry, more demanding—all of the things I myself have started to become since I moved back to San Francisco. Also, in San Francisco I work with people from a number of countries, who speak many languages. The language barrier slows things down and makes the work harder. But I have learned so much about other cultures and have enjoyed these relationships to such a degree that I find this to be one of the most rewarding aspects of working in San Francisco.

RW: *Tell me a little about how your current office works.*

JJ: There are two rooms; one is a reception and secretarial area and the second is the area I work in. Sometimes the secretary and I share the same room, depending on the configuration of the office. Over the years, the office has moved several times within the same large building.

We try to get everyone to call before coming in or to make an appointment. I do all of the initial interviews, pre-hearing interviews, preparation of certain sets of papers. The secretary-receptionist types the other sets of forms and mails them out. The office is bilingual in Spanish.

Normally people come in between one and five times, depending on the complexity and how much people want to visit. For the simple form of divorce, some people come in once to give us all necessary information, pay the fee and ask that all papers be mailed.

We review all files at least three times a year and send out notes to customers we have not heard from in some time to make sure there hasn't been some misunderstanding about the status of the divorce. But we only send out one note. We want to let them know that their divorce is not final, but we don't want to push them into completing a divorce that they would just as well drop or delay.

The office is open five days a week, 9-6, with later, or earlier appointments possible. The customer who qualifies for the basic $80 divorce usually pays the entire fee at the first visit. For the more expensive divorces, we accept the fee paid in two payments. I've had some problem with bad checks. In addition to our fee, the customer will also have to pay a filing fee to the court, unless they are low income.

Often people need to get a consultation with an attorney about some unresolved legal issue, such as dividing an expensive asset, like a house or pension plan. Sometimes, the spouse is hiding assets, or the person who wants to file is so emotionally drained that they need someone to do all the work for them. I have a list of attorneys available to refer customers to who want or need to see someone.

Sometimes it's hard to get people to go to a lawyer, even when they should. They fear it. As a society, we're trained to go to the dentist and doctor, but we're not told that probably sometime in our lives we will need to see a lawyer. People feel very insecure in relating to lawyers. They don't know what the parameters of the relationship are, and what rights they have, that they are hiring the lawyer to do work for them. They fear, often with good reason, that once they get involved with a lawyer they will lose all control of their case and will end up with a $10,000 bill. In fact, I have had a number of customers who started with lawyers, spent thousands of dollars, and then felt the lawyer would not respect their decisions. As a result, these people fired the lawyer and decided to do it themselves.

RW: *What happens when you interview a customer?*

JJ: Usually only one person comes in, but sometimes they come with the spouse they are getting divorced from, which I prefer. Occasionally, of course, they come with children, friends or family. Sometimes, the parent wants to leave the child unattended in the waiting room, which I will not allow. (There is a window with a five-story drop.) I have toys for the children. Friends, of course, are no problem. In fact, sometimes they will speak up and offer information that the customer may not have brought up, and they will give a lot of support to the customer. My least favorite situation is where the parent comes in with the married daughter or son, and it is the parent who does all of the talking. Occasionally, there will be the married couple and representatives of both sides of the family. So, a good rule for any divorce typing office is to have plenty of chairs.

In most instances, it has been determined on the telephone which type of divorce they need, and they have been told what information they will need to bring. I give them a copy of the book *How To Do Your Own Divorce in California* and review the basic information it contains. I then have them sign a disclaimer which states that I am not a lawyer and they are responsible for all of their decisions. If they don't have any further questions, they can begin filling out the worksheets. If they want to think about it, they can take the book and the worksheets home and make another appointment. If the worksheets are completed right then, I immediately prepare the first set of papers. The customer then reviews the papers, signs and dates them, and they are ready to be filed by the customer. The customer is also responsible for serving the divorce papers on the spouse. In the simple form of divorce, called the "Summary Dissolution," there is no formal service of papers, since both the wife and husband sign the first set of forms.

The first interview can take anywhere from one to two hours, although two hours is unusual. The visits after that are shorter, maybe one-half hour.

I feel strongly that in addition to processing enormous amounts of paperwork, the job entails providing a lot of emotional support, information, and often referrals. People who are going through a divorce are usually going through changes in other parts of their lives as well. They may be changing jobs, looking for child care, having trouble finding affordable housing, having credit problems, car hassles, etc. They may not have family in the area, or even in this country, and sometimes don't even have friends they feel comfortable sharing this part of their lives with, so they really need to find an appropriate support group or get emotional help from another source. The point is that often people need more than just getting their papers typed.

RW: *What about marketing your services? How do people know how to find you?*

JJ: Primarily from referrals from previous customers. Positive recommendation by satisfied customers is a very powerful marketing device. I also get a lot of agency referrals. I also get referrals from the court clerk's office, even sometimes from lawyers and other unexpected sources. Advertising in the phone book and other lists where people look for information is also important. I don't do too much new marketing because I'm operating at maximum capacity—that's 60 to 70 new cases per month. I've given some thought to expanding my business, but haven't figured out how to do it in a high quality way.

RW: *What do you do if a customer says you did a poor job?*

JJ: Out of thousands of divorces, I only remember one time when I didn't do something correctly. This occurred in the first few months; the judge pointed out the problem and I was able to fix it. Generally, my high success rate is because I was carefully trained and give every customer a copy of *How To Do Your Own Divorce in California,* which we go through carefully. I encourage people to see an attorney if they have any questions that are not answered in the book, or if they need more information. The customers make all of the decisions about their divorces.

However, I can think of a few instances where I provided good service but the customer thought I did a poor job. For example, I typed the papers as directed in the divorce book, but a particular court clerk or judge would want them done a slightly different way and a nervous customer might wonder if I initially did them correctly or not. Of course, whenever there is any problem, I redo the papers at no extra cost. It is also the case (and anyone who serves the public will know this) that even though you try to provide excellent service to every single person, there are going to be a few who will find some problem, no matter how hard you try. Remember, for most people, going to a nonlawyer for help with a divorce is a new experience, and a number are unsure. But generally I have had very little trouble with this. By the end of almost every divorce I've typed, people feel that they have had excellent help, and usually refer their friends. Lawyers, of course, make a hue and cry about the "terrible" and "incompetent" work done by divorce consultants/ independent paralegals like myself, but I know of hundreds of thousands of divorces typed by IPs and I know of very few problems. Compare this to the number of complaints and lawsuits filed against lawyers!

RW: *How do you relate to lawyers in an organized sense?*

JJ: Not well. I see the California Bar Association, indeed, all bar associations, as monoliths with basically conservative memberships antagonistic to change that might erode their traditional paternalistic role and monopoly control. They represent an enormous concentration of power, money and legislative influence, and almost always use it to block constructive change.

I don't see individual lawyers as necessarily being part of the monolith, but put them in three general groupings. First, lawyers who may feel the adversarial system is not the best way to solve family problems and who support the development of a reasonable alternative for the delivery of legal services. In other words, they are at least somewhat critical of the legal monopoly the bar association is trying to protect.

Second, lawyers who are honestly opposed to "divorce consultants," as we are currently called in California, as not being in the public interest because there are no standards for training, licensing and we are not monitored in any way. Third, I would guess the majority of lawyers, who constantly and cynically cry "consumer protection" as an excuse to suppress alternatives and maintain their control.

Remember, divorce and family law used to be considered the "bread and butter" of law, and the most common reason the average person sought out a lawyer. Now, close to 60% of California divorces are done without lawyers, which is a loss of many millions of dollars of lawyers' income. And remember, this has all happened since 1971. Wouldn't you be threatened if you lost almost half of your business?

RW: *Do you think some lawyers who want to put you out of business are honestly motivated?*

JJ: Sure, I think that some lawyers actually believe that people want and need lawyers to make decisions for them. I once went to a bar association luncheon in Palo Alto, California, an upper-middle to upper-class area. At the luncheon, a lawyer told me that he thought people were "too stupid to make their own decisions" and that they needed lawyers' "firm guidance." Well, fortunately, a lot of people aren't too stupid to see this sort of arrogance for what it is.

I am also appalled at lawyers' lack of concern about the unavailability of legal services to poor and low-income people who can't pay lawyers' fees. This sort of attitude makes me think of all the people I have worked with who had very little money, and what a severe hardship it would have been for some of them to come up with the money to pay a lawyer. In fact, many of them couldn't come up with the money and weren't able to file for a divorce until they heard about the Wave Project/Divorce Center. So, I feel angry when I have any contact with lawyers who think like that. They live in a different world than I do.

RW: *Do you think there is any validity to the attorney charge that many independent paralegals are not sufficiently trained, and therefore may not be competent?*

JJ: Since lawyers have fought all legislation supporting training and licensure of independent paralegals, I question their right to make that charge. How can they work to keep us ignorant and then attack us for being ignorant? I support reasonable requirements for licensing and training and some kind of regulation done by an independent state agency— absolutely not by bar.

RW: *Do you think lawyers will eventually accept the presence of paralegals?*

JJ: They already have when it suits their convenience. They hire paralegals instead of lawyers and assign them the same type of work I do. So the consumer should have that same right. The way it is now, consumers have to pay lawyers' rates for paralegal work, which of course is the idea, from the lawyers' point of view. I think the future for IPs is bright because the public wants alternatives to lawyers. And, hopefully, through some evolutionary process, lawyers will learn to accept the right of the public to use independent paralegals. They may even find a way to work cooperatively with independent paralegals as they realize that IPs take the pressure off them to provide services to millions of low- and moderate-income people.

RW: *What would be your advice to someone starting out?*

JJ: Do you want me to give you a few bits of general advice, or a laundry list of helpful suggestions?

RW: *How about the whole list.*

JJ: You asked for it. I'd say the following:
- Read books, or attend workshops on starting a small business, but don't let them scare you off.
- Have adequate savings to carry you for a while.
- Get good initial training and periodic updates.
- Be willing to take a risk or start part-time and keep the security you have until you see if your paralegal business is going to fly or not. It's hard to tell. Sometimes it seems best to get your feet wet a toe at a time, and sometimes a new business will only work if you make a full-time commitment.
- Have lawyers quickly available to ask questions, and be happy to pay for the help.
- It is not necessary to spend a lot of money furnishing the office at least to start. Save your money for more important things.

- Select a convenient location, with easy access to public transportation. And, hopefully, an area without much competition.
- Cultivate the attitude that what is best for the customer will be best for your business.
- Give financial breaks to the deserving.
- You do not have to accept every customer. Screen out those not appropriate for a fill-in-the boxes clinic approach.
- Develop a fair refund policy.
- Build a network of supportive lawyers to refer your customers to.
- Build good relationships with the landlord, printer and other business people you deal with.
- Get known in your community. Dozens of groups will refer customers to you if they know about your service.
- Keep good records—every case in its own file, every disclaimer signed, every worksheet saved, etc.
- If you don't know a bookkeeping system, find a bookkeeper or accountant that specializes in small businesses and have them set up a simple system for you.
- Develop, if possible, good relationships with your competitors. Try to have a friendly, positive relationship with them rather than a cutthroat one. It can make life, and your business environment, more pleasant. You can help each other. In our group, we have shared advertising, even in cases where we were sharing the same area.
- Consider sharing office space, possibly with someone whose business or service complements yours, like a tax preparer.
- Be willing to spend money to improve your service. One way to do this is by using a small computer.
- Get insurance—liability and theft—if you have anything of value.
- Look for safety hazards in your office, especially if there will be children. For example, coffee pots with cords hanging down where the child can pull the pot over.
- Watch for changes or trends in your field by reading a local legal newspaper as well as specialized legal materials relevant to your work.
- Diversify beyond divorce and bankruptcy.

RW: *What's about the future? What are your plans?*

JJ: I have an interest in organizing paralegals and I do work to help make more types of paralegal assistance available to the public. There is a lot to be done to establish paralegal work as a "safe occupation." I have organized some community workshops and volunteer work around the subject of people doing their own divorce. I think I have a lot to teach others. And of course, I need to learn new things, too. I have taken some courses that I felt would improve my service: Spanish, business applications of computers, a one-year legal secretarial course and so on. I've also had to update my legal skills.

After 18 years of this work, I have considered a career change, but I think I am faced with the same thoughts that many who are considering trying to be an independent paralegal face: What should I do? Will I make more money? Do I need to be retrained? How much in debt do I want to go to be retrained? Do I want to move? Should I expand this business? Will I like my new career more, as much as, or less than the career I am leaving? Can I successfully work for someone else, or do I want to only consider careers that will allow me to continue to be self-employed?

Basically I feel that I have invested a great deal of energy in the work I am now doing, and find that hard to give up. So, I have turned a lot of my thinking to considering how the independent paralegal field will develop in the next few years and how to best facilitate and participate in that growth and change.

Robert Mission Interview

Robert Mission has been an independent paralegal for well over 20 years. One of the true pioneers in this business, Bob currently coordinates the Superior California Legal Clinic in Sacramento, California.

Ralph Warner (RW): *Bob, tell me about your background. How did you get into the independent paralegal business?*

Robert Mission (RM): In the late 1960s, I was a process server. I did gofer work for a lawyer and also worked with a private detective.

RW: *What does the "creep and peep" business have to do with helping non-lawyers prepare legal forms?*

RM: Well, in about 1971, I developed a package of divorce forms complete with simple instructions. I called it "Divorce Economically," and sold the packets for $35. I also helped people type the forms if they needed it. Then, in 1973, I ran into Charlie Bloodgood, a University of California law student who was running a divorce typing service in Sacramento that was affiliated with the Wave Project. As you know, the Wave Project system was based on Ed Sherman's book *How To Do Your Own Divorce in California,* published by Nolo Press. I immediately recognized that the Wave Project, which had training sessions, continuing education meetings, as well as the divorce book, embodied a more sophisticated approach than mine, so I got in touch with Charlie, met Ed and you, and joined up.

RW: *How did you and Charlie do?*

RM: Great, at least for awhile. We made contact with all sorts of community organizations, listed our service in the classifieds, and the people rolled in. After all, at about $75 to type a divorce, the price was right.

RW: *And then?*

RM: We had heard rumbles that the bar association was very unhappy about the so-called "do it yourself" movement, and was investigating our project. However, nothing direct was ever said until one afternoon in 1974, when a Sacramento County Deputy DA swooped into my office, identified himself, read me my rights and handcuffed me in front of a client.

RW: *Were you scared?*

RM: I didn't have time to figure out how I felt, I was so busy demanding to make a phone call. They finally let me call my attorney, the man I had worked for for years as a gofer. I was confident he would help me, but was told by his secretary that he had just had a heart attack and was in intensive care.

RW: *Oops!*

RM: Oops, nothing! I was so upset I demanded to talk to him—tubes and all.

RW: *What happened?*

RM: By the time I got downtown, my attorney's secretary had made some calls and I was released on my own recognizance, charged with the crime of unauthorized practice. My next step was to call Phyllis Eliasberg, a Southern California consumer advocate and lawyer who had taken over the Wave Project from you and Ed when you guys decided to concentrate on Nolo Press. Phyllis eventually referred me to a Sacramento County attorney, Jim Reed, to defend me.

RW: *Tell me a little about the defense.*

RM: It was based mostly on constitutional grounds, utilizing Ed Sherman's book and the Wave Project method. I maintained that I was only a typing service offering scrivener services, using as my guidelines *How To Do Your Own Divorce in California*. I pointed out that all my clients received a copy of the book, read it carefully, and made their own decisions. I argued that I clearly had a First Amendment right to refer my clients to Ed's book generally and, if they had a specific question, to the particular chapter that dealt with that procedure.

RW: *Did this defense work?*

RM: Beautifully! When the bar counsel took my deposition, he asked me questions related to complicated matters of contested divorce procedure. I replied, "I'm sorry, I can't answer that question." The bar counsel would ask me, "Why can't you answer?" I replied, "Because that information is not covered in *How To Do Your Own Divorce in California* and so to do so would constitute my giving legal advice."

RW: *What did you say when they asked you something that was covered in Ed's book?*

RM: Since I had directed clients to all the key passages so many times, I didn't even have to open the book. I just quoted the relevant passages verbatim.

RW: *What happened in court?*

RM: The criminal procedures simply stopped. Instead, the bar attorneys suggested to my attorney that we enter a broad stipulation as to how I could and couldn't operate. Their proposal was so strict that it would have effectively stopped our operation. I refused to go along, on my attorney, Jim Reed's, advice. Fortunately the judge agreed with Jim that what the bar wanted to force us to do was unconstitutional. I personally feel that in making this decision the judge was heavily influenced by the fact that I received referrals from dozens of public and private agencies, especially those designed to help low-income persons.

RW: *Could you give me several examples?*

RM: Well, agencies such as the State Department of Justice, County Welfare, McGeorge Law School, the Battered Women's Shelter, various community service organizations and, believe it or not, even the DA's office. In fact, the funniest thing about the whole thing was that the day the deputy DA arrested me, someone in the DA's office had referred me a client.

RW: *Was that the end of your troubles with the bar?*

RM: Not exactly. To the best of my remembrance, the judge suggested that the guidelines proposed by the bar be amended to allow me to still operate as a scrivener. Since these guidelines were basically the same as the Wave Project rules, I accepted them. I could see that to survive in Sacramento in the long run, I had to go along with some of what the bar wanted.

RW: *How did your new guidelines work out?*

RM: Well, in a sense I never used them as part of my service because by this time my partner, Charlie Bloodgood, had been threatened with reprisals by McGeorge Law School if he didn't quit the independent paralegal business. Incidentally, Charlie is now a prominent lawyer in the area, who recently ran for judge.

RW: *What did you do?*

RM: My attorney and I worked out a new way of operating. I bought out the Wave Project and reorganized operations completely, utilizing secretaries, independent paralegals and attorneys working together. We call it Superior California Legal Clinics, Inc. Charlie Bloodgood was president of our organization until 1984, supervising the operation of the clinic.

RW: *Who owns Superior California Legal Clinic?*

RM: It's a nonprofit corporation with a Board of Directors. Our mandate is to help low- and moderate-income people educate themselves to deal with the legal system.

RW: *Then, legally, you work for the nonprofit corporation?*

RM: Right. I'm an officer, on the Board of Directors and an employee.

RW: *Let me change the subject a little and ask what you really do, day by day.*

RM: In 19 years, I've personally (with secretarial assistance, of course) assisted in preparing about 15,000 uncontested divorces. In addition, I've counseled a great many individuals and couples who were going through changes in their lives. I also schedule the attorneys on their appointments for the actions that the Clinic doesn't do on a paralegal basis. In addition, I supervise the many procedures necessary to provide these services as reasonably and effectively as possible, following the prescribed guidelines of the Clinic.

RW: *Have you figured out what your average charge for typing a divorce has been over the years?*

RM: Well, it's gone from $35 in the beginning to close to $150 today for a fairly basic divorce. I guess the average would be about $90, with the exception of a simple Summary Dissolution, which has gone from $40 to $75 today.

RW: *What do you think the same people would have had to pay if they went to an individual attorney or legal clinic and both were represented?*

RM: On the average, with children and little property, probably about $1,000 using a heavily advertised clinic and a minimum of $1,500 for the same thing using a conventional private attorney.

RW: *So, even figuring that some people might have represented themselves or simply gotten along without a divorce, you saved people several million dollars over a period of 14 years.*

RM: Yes, in the divorce area, but Superior does lots of other things now, still at a very economical rate, using a sliding scale, so that all of our low-income clients receive service very economically.

RW: *Give me an example of the work you do.*

RM: We specialize in family law matters, including uncontested divorces, wills, bankruptcies, child support modifications, nonmarried custody actions, name changes and the like, but we also handle guardianships, paternity actions, adoptions, restraining orders and, by use of our attorney-referral procedure, some criminal and personal injury cases.

RW: *How does the Clinic work?*

RM: We use a paralegal approach on divorces, separations, annulments, etc. On the others, we refer to one of five attorneys who work with us, according to our sliding-fee schedule, which we make clear to everyone in advance.

RW: *What are your charges?*

RM: We have set charges for many actions. For example, a bankruptcy is currently $125-$150, a name change is $100, and so on. If a particular problem doesn't fit into a predictable category, we charge by the hour on a sliding scale based on our clients' income. This is basically $40 for low-income and $60 for middle-income people.

RW: *How does this compare to local attorney rates?*

RM: The going rate in Sacramento is $125 to $175 dollars per hour. The heavily-advertised legal clinics charge at least $150 per hour.

RW: *When you changed your method of operating to include attorneys, did the bar's attitude change?*

RM: It was a whole new ballgame from the moment we changed the name and included lawyers. I guess you could say it allowed me to become almost respectable.

RW: *But when it comes down to typing divorces, you are doing pretty much the same thing you always did?*

RM: Right, my approach is identical, only under supervision.

RW: *Does that make you smile?*

RM: Chuckle, somewhat, might be a better way to describe it.

RW: *In 19 years, you must have seen a lot of big changes. What's the biggest?*

RM: Attitude. These days the courts, the district attorney, social services and law schools all refer cases to us. That would have been unheard of 10 years ago. Now, when a person picks up a divorce form package at the court clerk's office, they get an information sheet with our name on it. And that's not only happening in Sacramento. We prepare forms for people in 26 counties, and in most of them, one or another county agency sends us referrals.

RW: *How do you prepare paperwork for people at a distance?*

RM: They call us and we do a little initial screening. If our service is appropriate for the customer, we send out an information package. The customer fills it out and sends in a money order. If we have more questions, we handle them by phone. Otherwise, we type the paper to send them out.

RW: *What do you think about the future of the independent paralegal business?*

RM: The surface hasn't even been scratched. There are certain to be more clinics with paralegals and attorneys working together on a more-or-less equal footing, because the economics of delivering legal services to low- and middle-income people don't allow for anything else. How can a person who makes $8 to $10 an hour afford to pay a lawyer $150 or more per hour? It doesn't make sense. There have been a lot of changes in our legal system over the past 19 years, and you know what?

RW: *I'll bite.*

RM: The changes in how legal services are delivered to people, whether by phone, computer, lawyer or independent paralegal, in the next 20 years are going to make what we have accomplished so far look small.

Virginia Simons Interview

Virginia Simons is an independent paralegal in Bakersfield, California. With over thirteen years in the business, she has much valuable experience in how to cope with bar association attacks, work with other paralegals and develop a paralegal business.

Ralph Warner (RW): *Let's start with your personal history as an independent paralegal.*

Virginia Simons(VS): I've been in the business since 1981. In the beginning, I only typed divorces and bankruptcies. Now I also do restraining orders in domestic violence situations, family law restraining orders, harassment orders, child support and custody orders, responses, guardianships, terminations of guardianship, stepparent adoptions, paternity orders, name changes and joinders on pension plans.

RW: *When did you first run into trouble with the local bar?*

VS: Not until 1988, when two other local typing service owners and I were sued by a bankruptcy court trustee.

RW: *I'm interested in why it took the bar eight years to go after you. In a metropolitan area with a population of about 360,000, your business can't have been a secret. Do you know why it took them so long?*

VS: I'm not sure. I tried to keep a very low profile at first. I figured that if I was a good little girl, no one would bother me.

RW: *But in 1988, they did sue you. Had you done something to be perceived as a bad little girl?*

VS: I wasn't doing anything different. It may have been that over the years, as there were more IPs in Bakersfield, lawyers felt they were losing so much business that they decided to crack down. Remember, I wasn't the only target—Marilyn Marvin and Bobbe Powers were also charged with unauthorized practice of law for bankruptcy form preparation.

RW: *What were your feelings when you learned of the suit?*

VS: I panicked. I really thought I would end up in jail. If you had heard the horrible stories about Kern County Jail that I have, you would have some idea of how scared I felt.

RW: *What did you do?*

VS: The hardest part was telling my husband. When I did, his first reaction was to tell me to quit the business and get a job.

RW: *Obviously, you didn't do that. What did you say to your husband to change his mind?*

VS: I said, "You've never backed away from a fight that you couldn't avoid with dignity. You've always told me there are times when you have to stand up and be ready to fight back."

RW: *What was his response?*

VS: He thought about what I said and replied, "Go for it. I'll back you, even if it means losing our house and savings"; and then he said, "You're right."

RW: *Once you had your domestic ducks in a row, what did you, Bobbe and Marilyn do?*

VS: First, we needed legal help. We had been sued in federal court and we had to respond. The first lawyer we approached turned us down flat. He refused to go against the local legal establishment.

RW: *Whoa. You mean this was so political, a local criminal lawyer who represents all sorts of unpopular people was afraid to take your money?*

VS: Yes. We finally got an attorney who made no bones about the fact that he thought we were guilty of UPL, but said that he was such a good lawyer he could get us off. I'm sorry I can't mention his name, but we had to promise that we wouldn't publicly associate his name with ours.

RW: *Was this because he feared the reaction of his lawyer colleagues?*

VS: Yes. At this point, local lawyers were determined to do away with our competition. Anyone who represented us was in danger of being seen as a traitor by their colleagues.

RW: *What next?*

VS: Even with a lawyer, we felt terribly lonely and isolated. Finally, we called Steve Elias, who is an author and editor with Nolo Press. Steve doesn't normally provide individual advice, but he got interested in the details of our case and came to Bakersfield. He really gave us the strength to go on. Catherine Jermany and Glynda Mathewson of the California Association of Independent Paralegals (CAIP) also helped spread the word about our plight and rallied crucial support. But it was really Steve who turned us around when he looked right at us and said "You have a basic personal choice to make. Either stop crying and moaning and enjoy the fight, or quit right now." We decided to put fear behind us and take the offensive.

RW: *What did you do?*

VS: Lots of things. We told each of our customers that we had been sued by a bankruptcy trustee in federal court in an effort to put us out of business, and got them to sign petitions on our behalf. We went to the bankruptcy court once a month when it was in session and took notes as to any unequal treatment given to nonlawyers representing themselves. We testified at public hearings at the state level, where the subject of whether IPs should be certified or licensed was being considered. In short, we started to have fun.

RW: *What happened at the trial?*

VS: The best thing was that 25 people came from all over California to be there to support us. Then, all of a sudden, it was over and we won. Patrick Kavanaugh, the bankruptcy trustee who sued us, thought it was a violation of UPL to simply type bankruptcy forms and didn't present any evidence as to how we were guilty of UPL. The judge, who would have loved to convict us, had to disagree, based on other court decisions that held that simply typing forms wasn't unauthorized practice. In short, he demanded that Kavanaugh produce evidence that we had given customers legal information. Since he wasn't prepared to do that, the judge reluctantly dismissed the case.

RW: *Great, you won. How did you celebrate?*

VS: We organized a public forum at a conference room at the Red Lion Inn on the subject of whether typing services should exist. A couple of lawyers showed up to speak on our side of the issue and several more who opposed us. The press covered it and began to get interested in our story.

RW: *Was this a continuation of your offensive?*

VS: Yes, we had decided to affirmatively contact and engage our opponents. We wanted to convince individual lawyers that many people who couldn't afford lawyer fees really needed our services. In addition, we wanted our adversaries to know that, personally, we weren't monsters. For example, we contacted each of the lawyers who spoke against typing services at the Red Lion Inn.

RW: *Did you apply the same strategy to Patrick Kavanaugh and Gary O'Neil, the two lawyers who had been your principal adversaries?*

VS: Yes, we did, but first we contacted the Kern County DA, because we heard he was thinking of filing criminal UPL charges against us. We asked for an appointment and discussed all the issues. In fact, there was no plan to go after us, but it was good to clear the air. We also contacted a local judge who was rumored to believe that we were keeping filing fees customers paid to us when we filed fee waivers based on the customer's poverty. Interestingly, the judge wasn't worried about that, but did say that, in his opinion, we were practicing law. He then added that given the difficulty in defining UPL, we were okay as long as we stuck to the types of form preparation we were doing.

RW: *In short, the judge presented you with a sort of horseback deal—you can violate the law a little bit, but don't go too far.*

VS: Something like that. But to get back to Kavanaugh and O'Neil, we tried to open up lines of communication. Initially, this happened at public meetings. For example, Kavanaugh and I were both on a bankruptcy subcommittee of the State Bar's committee looking into the possibility of licensing typing services. Of the two trustees and one bankruptcy judge on this subcommittee, Kavanaugh was the only one who provided unbiased opinions on how typing services could operate within the bankruptcy field. At a seminar where Gary O'Neil and I both sat on the panel, he claimed Kern County was unique because they had "all those sleaze-bag typing services." When it was my turn to speak, I introduced myself by saying I was one of the "sleaze-bags," and invited Gary to come to one of our local CAIP (California Association of Independent Paralegals) chapter meetings.

RW: *Did he come?*

VS: Yes, he did. First we invited him to lunch with the five of us who ran the main typing services in town. (Incidentally, to show solidarity, we always went together to meetings with the bar, judges or lawyers.) We worked out a plan for him to speak at our meeting and he invited us, in turn, to speak to a bar association lunch on the issue of whether legal typing services should be licensed.

RW: *Sounds great. Did the communication lead to anything positive?*

VS: Very much so. We had said to Gary that if he thought we were doing a bad job, why didn't he teach us to do better?

RW: *Did you learn anything?*

VS: Yes. It was extremely valuable,.

RW: *Why do you think you were suddenly beginning to be accepted?*

VS: It's complicated, of course, but I think, at bottom, lawyers are beginning to realize that the independent paralegal licensing issue isn't going away. The fact that IPs are organized at the state and local level, that legislation to legalize IPs has been introduced in Sacramento and that even state bar committees have made some positive recommendations all helps us. Why, we have even been invited to attend bar lunches.

RW: *Hey, that's a big change. Are paralegals who work for lawyers also invited?*

VS: Yes, and I guess you could say we are being included in a somewhat similar way.

RW: *Are there other signs that IPs are now considered to be part of the system?*

VS: You remember a few years ago we were afraid to be identified by some judges? Well now the courts ask us to type the names of our businesses on the top of all legal paperwork we prepare so we can be contacted if need be.

RW: *Just like lawyers do.*

VS: Precisely. And I'll tell you a positive recent development. The Kern County Domestic Violence Advisory Committee, which is made up of a number of public and private agencies interested in the subject, puts out several brochures aimed at battered women which are distributed at lots of places, including women's centers, social services agencies and so on. Anyway, the great thing is that IPs are officially listed as a place to get restraining order applications prepared.

RW: *Terrific! But tell me, is the District Attorney's Office a member of the Advisory Committee?*

VS: They sure are.

RW: *What about your competitors? The fact that you and many other typing services in town have worked so closely together tells me that you value cooperation.*

VS: Very much so. Solidarity in this business is essential. The bar is really impressed by the fact that we stick together and can't be picked off one by one.

RW: *Does this strategy extend to new typing services? After all, they are your competitors, much as you compete with lawyers.*

VS: Our strategy is to train the new people to do a good job. Sure I have mixed emotions at times, but by and large I think we all will prosper if the legal form typing business expands. Also, it just feels good to cooperate. It brings me lots of friends. Also, because I can get help from another knowledgeable IP if I need it, I can serve my customers better. And if I don't do a particular type of legal form typing, I can refer the customers to someone who does, either locally or elsewhere in the state.

RW: *Do you see any major changes in the IP business generally?*

VS: There is more competition in our area for basic form preparation for divorces. To prosper, IPs need to learn new skills. For example, a big part of my business these days is helping people prepare guardianships.

Many of my customers are grandparents who, due to the disintegration of their children's families must raise their grandkids and need legal authority to do so. Paternity is another fast-growing area that I've begun to develop.

Glynda Mathewson Interview

Glynda Mathewson is an independent paralegal based in Oakland, California. For many years she typed a number of family law forms, including divorce, guardianship, name change, child support modifications, probates, stepparent adoptions and wills as part of the business she began in 1984. She is a past president of the California Association of Independent Paralegals and a volunteer arbitrator with Oakland Better Business Bureau. In 1994 she sold her family law typing business and began a new venture helping people appeal from the denial of Social Security disability benefits.

Ralph Warner (RW): *How did you start in the independent paralegal business?*

Glynda Mathewson (GM): I prefer the term "public paralegal" or "legal technician," but to answer your question, my training is as a career counselor. In 1984, I became my own client in that I was looking for a career change for myself. A person I knew told me she was getting a divorce with the help of a nonlawyer divorce typing service in Oakland. I was fascinated that this occupation existed. To make a long story short, I investigated and learned that the divorce typing office was run by Sandra Edwards, who also had another, larger office in Walnut Creek, California. I also learned that Sandra followed a system originally taught by you and Ed Sherman as part of the Wave Project. It allows nonlawyers to prepare routine legal forms with little risk that they will be accused of practicing law without a license. I worked for Sandra for months—typing divorce forms as sort of a paid apprentice, and then I bought the Oakland office.

RW: *What other training did you have?*

GM: I read all the Nolo divorce materials many times, which, by this time, had been used by thousands of people to do their own divorces without help from lawyers. Also, remember, I was typing divorce forms every day under the supervision of a person who had been doing it for years. Under her training, I learned the appropriate work standards and ethical behavior that later helped build my reputation as a reliable service. In addition, I checked out lots of divorce files at the county clerk's office. Court files are public records, so I just checked dozens of random divorces and studied them. I do this with any new procedure I want to learn.

RW: *Where did you operate your first office?*

GM: On a neighborhood shopping street in a middle-class area, about a half-mile from Oakland's downtown area. At that point I was cautious and didn't want to be too close to the downtown legal establishment.

RW: *How did you build up your business?*

GM: It was slow at first. I didn't have much money for promotion, and any-way, I was worried that advertising might bring me trouble with the bar or the district attorney. As a result, I concentrated on building a personal referral network. I contacted the personnel offices of big businesses, social services agencies, child and family counselors, and even some lawyers, to tell them who I was and what I did.

RW: *Weren't you afraid of lawyers?*

GM: As I said, I was afraid of the bar association and the district attorney, but not necessarily of individual lawyers. I concentrated on lawyers I knew, or friends knew, and yes, some of them did refer me customers.

RW: *What advertising did you do?*

GM: I tried a few small classified ads in weekly shoppers and penny saver type papers. That didn't produce much, so finally I tried the big city paper, the *Oakland Tribune,* under the "legal services" classifieds heading. It didn't bring in much business at first, but I kept it in, and before long, the phone began ringing. It taught me a valuable lesson. In this business, you need to have an ad in the same place very day. When you do, lots of people eventually figure out it's there and tell others.

RW: *Okay, you started in 1984, how would you describe your business two years later.*

GM: I was having fun, but the business was in poor economic shape. I took in about $45,000 dollars that year and spent almost all of it on overhead and promotion.

RW: *How did you survive?*

GM: Fortunately, my former husband didn't own a business—he has a "regular" job with a "regular" paycheck—otherwise, I would not have been able to stick with it.

RW: *What did you do to improve things?*

GM: I got frustrated enough to see that I needed help on how to run a good small business and found an excellent small business consultant, Roger Pritchard, in Berkeley. He helped me focus on improving my business in a number of ways. The most important was making a marketing plan to produce more customers and sticking to it.

RW: *Can you give me some specifics?*

GM: For the first time, I kept track of where my customers came from. Once I knew that, I concentrated my marketing efforts on the best referral sources. Before I developed a plan, I was often spending as much time on promotional activities that produced 5% of my business as I was on those that produced 25%.

RW: *What else did Pritchard help you with?*

GM: He talked me out of borrowing money to expand the business. He got me to see that the additional money would be wasted until I had a better plan, and better day-to-day control. I was so frustrated, I cried, but he was right. Lack of money wasn't my problem; it was a symptom of running my business.

RW: *Insights are cheap. What did you do to change things?*

GM: As I said, I focused my marketing money and energy where it would do the most good. In addition, I began to offer more services, including typing name changes, child support modifications and guardianships. I also made an effort to stay in touch with former customers and others I had worked with to encourage word-of-mouth referrals. Suddenly, after three years or so, people began to see me as established and trustworthy. Individual lawyers, employees at the public law library, people at court offices dealing with child support, even the local bar's legal help service, began sending me people who couldn't afford a lawyer and weren't eligible for legal aid.

RW: *So you found your market niche?*

GM: Exactly. Whether or not they always want to admit it, in the high-cost Bay Area, lawyers can't afford to provide services to working people who have a family income of $50,000 or less. At the same time, they hate to admit that the American legal system is closed to the average person, so they refer these people to me.

RW: *Okay, your business improved; what next?*

GM: I got excited about running an excellent small business and began to see ways to improve it more. My biggest step was to move to an older professional building in downtown Oakland. Now I was near the courts, county offices, such as social services, and the DA's child support collection offices. I was also in the same neighborhood as the majority of Oakland's law firms.

RW: *Were you worried about becoming more visible to the legal establishment?*

GM: Not in the least. I had been threatened by a few lawyers and was investigated by the DA for unauthorized practice when I first started, but I was confident that I knew how to type forms without giving legal information. In short, I felt my business could stand scrutiny and there was no need to hide it. Also, by now, most of the people who might investigate me were sending me customers. I believed that if someone in the legal establishment tried to close me down, a number of conscientious lawyers who respected and trusted my work and knew I didn't practice law would stand up for me.

RW: *How did the move work out?*

GM: Business increased substantially right away. I began to get referrals from lawyers in my building, and when the feedback was good, from others in the downtown area.

RW: *Which leads me to ask whether lawyers, who have been enemies of the Independent Paralegal movement, are turning out to be friends.*

GM: Surprisingly, to some extent, some are. It's like a dual reality. At the state level, bar association types want to put IPs out of business, or to so limit what they can do that it amounts to the same thing. But at the local, day-to-day level, dozens of individual public and private lawyers, and even establishment legal agencies, which I won't name so as to not embarrass them, absolutely depend on the fact that legal typing services such as the one I ran exist. They know something bar associations don't know or won't admit; despite all the hoopla about providing legal access to ordinary Americans, the legal profession is economically completely unable to do it. In the S.F. Bay Area, lawyers claim they need a minimum of $150 an hour or more to get by; how in the world can they get that from people who make $10 an hour?

RW: *Are you pussyfooting around, saying that you have had referrals from court clerks, judges, the local bar associations and even the district attorney's office?*

GM: I'd better not comment.

RW: *Okay, let me change gears a little. Rose Palmer, who runs a service in Pittsburgh, Pennsylvania, to help women with divorces and child support, has reported that while the organized bar has been hostile to her organization's efforts to help women deal with issues of divorce, support, custody and domestic violence, she has gotten support from some judges, who see clearly that many of the people who need help can't afford lawyers. Have you had encouragement from the bench?*

GM: Yes, to a limited but very welcome degree. Some judges never grow up—they keep their narrow lawyer attitudes forever. But it's a mistake to see the judiciary as a monolith. A few judges helped me refine my paperwork technologies and generally supported my efforts. Also, after I became established, several court clerks became very supportive.

RW: *Have you done anything to encourage or institutionalize your relationship with judges or the courthouse personnel generally?*

GM: I made a habit of filing papers in person so that I could speak to the clerks, and I would drop by the law library often. Our local Independent Paralegal Association invited one of our area's most prominent family law judges to give us a training session. He did, and has generally let it be known that he supports IPs who do top quality form preparation and stay away from complicated areas of the law, where they don't have expertise. When he told me "Glynda, I recognize your paperwork because it's of such high quality," it made my month—or, more so, it made my year!

RW: *You raised the issue of how careful you are to avoid practicing law. Let me follow up on that. What did you do when people asked a question that requires legal expertise?*

GM: I didn't answer it. All my customers signed a statement saying they know I am not a lawyer and I don't give legal advice, so I am very clear on this point from the start. In addition, there was a prominent sign in my office that said, "We are not attorneys. We do not give legal advice."

RW: *Sure, but that didn't stop them from asking.*

GM: First, you must realize that most questions on the preprinted forms I typed aren't legal—it's the same sort of name, address and age type of information that any other government form requests. When questions on a form depend on a customer having some legal knowledge, it was typically fairly routine and accessible. For example, someone might ask if a certain type of property is community property and therefore owned by both spouses 50-50. I simply referred them to the relevant discussion in *California Marriage and Divorce Law,* or *How To Do Your Own Divorce in California,* both of which are available on my desk or in any bookstore in the state. If the answers weren't there, the person probably needs more in-depth information. An example might be a divorce where one person has a job which will provide a pension, or there's a lot of property involved and the couple is unclear about how to divide it.

RW: *So what did you do then?*

GM: Most legal information or help my customers needed could be efficiently provided by one of three sources. The first were lawyers who knew me and were willing to see a customer for a modest fee, provide the necessary information and perhaps do a property agreement before sending the customer back so I could finish typing the divorce. In many cases, though, the lawyer didn't really need to do any form preparation. There is a sample property settlement agreement in *How To Do Your Own*

Divorce, which I could prepare under the customer's supervision once they have the legal information they need.

The second is mediation. Suppose spouses haven't decided important issues, such as property division; in that case, I recommended mediation. Usually, after two or three mediation sessions, which might cost $200, the couple worked out their own compromise and the mediator wrote it down in a form that I then included with the papers I typed and submitted to the court. You might be surprised, but people are more savvy and knowledgeable than most lawyers want to admit, and given the sort of positive framework mediation offers, they will usually work out a mutually satisfactory and reasonably fair solution, whether it involves property division, custody, visitation or whatever.

Finally, there is a Divorce Helpline in Santa Cruz, California. This is a phone-in service where lawyers provide legal advice about self-help divorce for a reasonable fee. They even provide a service to compute the value of pensions, which can be complicated, especially if the person covered by the pension hasn't retired yet. Assuming the customer talks to the lawyers at Divorce Helpline for 15 or 20 minutes, they can get the legal help they need for $30 or $40, and I could finish typing their paperwork.

RW: *Sounds good. But you sold your family law form preparation business and moved on to something new. Can you tell me about it?*

GM: Yes. I'm now working with people to help prepare disability appeals—both SSI (that's welfare) and Social Security. Basically, I help people whose disability claims have been denied appeal.

RW: *What's that involve?*

GM: I help develop and prepare the case, including trying to get favorable medical reports. Then I help present the case to an administrative law judge.

RW: *Nonlawyers are allowed to do this by Federal law?*

GM: Yes—a provision of the Administrative Procedure Act authorizes nonlawyer representation.

RW: *Do lawyers handle these cases?*

GM: In the Bay Area, only a relative few do, so there is plenty of room for IPs.

RW: *How do you get paid?*

GM: You don't collect your fees up front. You get a percentage of the eventual disability award if there is one. But you can collect fees for medical reports and other expenses in advance.

RW: *Why the change in your business?*

GM: I got burned out doing divorces. Also, there is so much competitiveness in the self-help divorce business that it was hard to charge what I felt my services were worth. So I decided to develop a new professional life—something where I could really have fun helping people. But obviously I'm not alone in doing this—these days IPs have to be more imaginative as regards the types of businesses they develop.

Rosemary Furman Interview

Rosemary Furman began typing legal forms for low-income residents of Jacksonville, Florida in the early 1970s. Her inspired one-woman fight against the monopolistic practices of the Florida bar took her to the threshold of a Florida jail cell.

Ralph Warner (RW): *Lots of people know at least a little bit about what's happened to you in the last few years, including the fact that the Florida Bar Association tried to jail you for providing high quality, low-cost legal help to nonlawyers, so I'd like to start a little earlier. I'm curious—how did a respectable middle-aged woman, and mother of three, with no credentials as a radical, get to become Public Enemy Number One to American lawyerdom? What's your background? Were you born feisty, or is it something you just grew into?*

Rosemary Furman (RF): I was born in Alexandria, Virginia, where my grandmother owned a bakery and made a little bootleg beer in the back room. I spoke German as my first language until I was eight. I went to public school, first in Virginia and later in New York State, south of Albany, after being orphaned.

RW: *How did you get involved in the legal system?*

RF: Court reporting. I took classes to become a court reporter. It seemed like a very good income for the hours expended.

RW: *You mean you learned how to key punch one of those little transcribing machines?*

RF: Never! I learned Gregg shorthand, a far more accurate system, and one I keep up with today.

RW: *Where did you work as a court reporter?*

RF: Where didn't I work? I married a military man, and when he was transferred, I packed up the kids and went along. When I'd get to a new city I would put my name on the court reporter list and eventually I'd have a job. At one time or another, I worked in Trenton, New Jersey, Nassau County, Long Island, Boston, Washington, D.C., and Jacksonville, Florida.

RW: *So, it was as a court reporter that you first started seeing the legal system as being flawed?*

RF: If that's a polite way to say that I began to see lawyers as barracudas, preying on the public, you're right. You see, a court reporter quickly becomes part of the furniture, and lawyers and judges would often carry on their self-serving schemes in front of me, almost as if I weren't there. I mean, it isn't hard to understand what's going on if you literally see the money changing hands. How many times can you sit in a judge's office and watch the lawyers and judges bargain and sell clients for the highest fee and then go out into the public courtroom and put on a charade for the benefit of the public before you realize that our American justice system is run by a bunch of self-interested charlatans who call themselves officers of the court?

RW: *You just made some pretty strong statements. How about some specifics to back it up.*

RF: Okay, sure, but first, let me just say I'm an old-fashioned constitutionalist. I really believe in fundamental American values like the Bill of Rights, the right of every man and woman to vote, a court system where the average taxpaying citizen can get a fair shake and so on. You want an example of what turned me off? I could give you dozens, hundreds, but first let me say that any of the bailiffs, marshals, clerks and other personnel who work at the courthouse could tell you the same sort of thing. What goes on in the so-called halls of justice is closer to a Persian market, with the buying and selling of cases among lawyers, bargaining for probated sentences, cooling down clients whose conviction is a foregone conclusion to avoid violence in the...

RW: *Sorry to interrupt, but how about the example?*

RF: I was a court reporter in Jacksonville, Florida. I was sitting in the judge's office one morning listening to the local lawyers back door the judge when one lawyer said he represented Alfredo Fernandez (that's not the real name) and wanted to know how the judge was planning to handle Alfredo's case. The judge checked the file and determined that Alfredo was barely 18 and had been charged with possession of a controlled substance. I can't remember if it was speed or marijuana or what. As it was the kid's first offense, his parents were solid working people in the community and so on, the judge said he would sentence Alfredo to six months in jail, and then, when the parents were done fainting, suspend the sentence and send him home. Then he would withhold adjudication and if after six months Alfredo didn't get into more trouble, he would expunge the record upon Alfredo's petition.

RW: *That doesn't sound so bad.*

RF: Let me finish, please. The lawyer thanked the judge and walked over to the bookcase and selected the book containing the code section that applied to Alfredo. As it happened, the lawbooks were my responsibility as a chambers clerk, so I followed the lawyer into the court room, which was full of people waiting for the law and motion calendar. To make a long story short, the lawyer opened the book to the relevant page, put on a long face, and told the Fernandez parents that it looked like five years—the maximum penalty under the law in question—unless they could come up with $5,000 that morning, in which case he was almost sure he could get Alfredo off. The stunned parents left the courtroom, and the lawyer said "not ready" every time the case was called. An hour later the parents came back with an envelope full of money. The lawyer counted it quickly, answered "ready" when the case was called, and made a brief argument about what a good kid Alfredo was. The judge then gave Alfredo the six-month suspended sentence that he had planned to all along.

RW: *You have convinced me that there was one dishonest lawyer, but not that the judge knew about what was going on.*

RF: Come on. I saw a version of this same story no less than three times a week. Whenever lawyers spot a worried parent in the courtroom or the hall, they move in for the kill. And as to the judge knowing about it, who do you think judges are but lawyers in black dresses? In many states, you have to pay two-years' salary to the local politicos to get to be a judge. Where do you think the money comes from? To be specific, I can't tell you how many times I've seen lawyers (the DA and the defense lawyer) work out what was going to happen to a defendant with the judge in his office and then have the defense lawyer say that since he had gotten a good fee he had to put on a bit of a performance when they got into the courtroom. The other DA and the judge would laugh and someone would say, "Great, but don't go on so long we miss our starting time."

RW: *You're saying that lawyers and judges are buying and selling justice for their own ends?*

RF: You're damn right, I am. The lawyers that make their phony speeches to try and justify those big fees turn right around and make hefty contributions to the judge's next election campaign. Who do you think finances most judicial election campaigns? The lawyers who appear before those very judges, that's who. And the judges know darn well who contributes. And I might add, the recent scandals in Chicago, New York and Tampa involving judges taking bribes are just the tip of the iceberg. Ninety-nine percent of all judicial offenders go merrily on their way, playing the system for all it's worth.

RW: *Okay, let's get back to you. How did you break free of working at the courthouse and set up your own business?*

RF: Well, in 1972, I was involved in setting up a shelter for battered women in Jacksonville, Florida. On at least four occasions frustrated, battering husbands set fire to the shelter in an attempt to get at their wives. When we sought police protection, we learned that it was a crime to deny a man access to his wife in Florida. What to do? We concluded the only way we could get police protection was for the woman to file for divorce, so they would no longer be treated as some man's property. The problem was that most of the women who came to us had low incomes and couldn't afford a lawyer, and legal aid had a two-year backlog of divorce cases. If you're getting beaten all the time, two years can be a death sentence.

RW: *What happened?*

RF: As you can probably guess, since I had worked at the courthouse, I was elected to type the divorces. From there, one thing led to another and before long, I was doing a thriving legal typing business, which I called the Northside Secretarial Service.

RW: *What sorts of papers did you prepare?*

RF: Divorces, name changes, adoptions, bankruptcies, etc. I did the typing and my customers made their own decisions which, before lawyers captured the legal system and called it a crime, was an American tradition. Of course, everyone who came into my office signed a disclaimer stating that they knew I wasn't a lawyer.

RW: *Tell me about a couple of them.*

RF: Well, the ones I cared most about were situations in which people's lives were being negatively affected by the fact that they couldn't afford to hire a lawyer. For example, I helped grandparents prepare simple adoption papers to adopt their grandchild so that they could qualify for Navy benefits to repair the child's serious spinal problem. Local lawyers wanted $650, which the grandparents (he was retired) didn't have. Another time, I helped a high school graduate from a very poor family change his name officially to the name he had used all his life and which appeared on his school records. The name on his birth certificate was different, which confused things when it came to his getting a scholarship, loans and grants.

RW: *How did the bar close you down?*

RF: It's a long story, but part of it involved their hiring a former FBI agent to track down my clients. They found over 100. And even though none would testify against me and there was no proof that I did bad work, I was hauled into court on contempt of court charges for giving people legal advice. As far as the bar was concerned, if I told a person how to find the courthouse that constituted giving legal advice, so you can see the charge was a sick joke.

RW: *You mean, you weren't charged with a crime? I thought you ended up with a jail sentence.*

RF: Both are true. When you challenge lawyers, you have to be prepared for anything. They have usurped the power to simply lock you up, even though there is absolutely no legal justification for their action.

RW: *You're exaggerating.*

RF: The bar association complained about me. I was hauled before a contempt of court proceeding—a sort of kangaroo court where I had no right to a jury trial because I was charged with no crime. I was found guilty of competing with lawyers and sentenced to four months in jail by a judge, A.C. Soud, who said, and I am quoting him, "Only her imprisonment will provide the sting necessary to preserve the integrity of the court."

RW: *Are you serious?*

RF: Sure, and another judge, John Santora, chief circuit judge in Jacksonville, said publicly that people like me who ran public services as legal stenographers are "a cancer on society."

RW: *Did you go to jail?*

RF: I'm almost sixty years old, and the idea of doing hard time to appease a bunch of lawyers who were mad because I charged less than they did didn't appeal to me. I appealed and was eventually turned down by everyone, including the U.S. Supreme Court in the fall of 1984. Incidentally, in the whole process, everyone who passed on the question of my freedom was a lawyer. I was never charged with a crime, and never had a jury trial.

RW: *So, how come I'm not visiting you in jail right now?*

RF: A day before my sentence was to start, in November 1984, the Governor of Florida commuted my sentence in exchange for my promise not to run my business any longer.

RW: *What made him commute the sentence?*

RF: Tens of thousands of ordinary people wrote, called and telegraphed to support me. The interesting thing is that the governor, who as you can probably guess is also a lawyer, had no power to commute my sentence because I had never been charged with or found guilty of a crime. Remember, I was held in contempt of court, so only the original judge could have relieved me of the contempt citation.

RW: *Did the governor know he was acting illegally?*

RF: Sure, he went to Harvard Law School, but that isn't the point. When it comes to protecting their own, lawyers are perfectly willing to act illegally, and the public outcry produced by "60 Minutes" and other TV shows had made me a huge embarrassment to the Florida bar. In a way, it was funny. They became desperate to keep me out of the very jail they had conspired so hard to put me in.

RW: *What are you doing now?*

RF: Rabble rousing in what I consider to be the best tradition of men like Tom Paine, Tom Jefferson and Patrick Henry. I travel around the country talking to paralegal groups and others in the legal system who do the real work to tell them to challenge the bar by opening their own offices. I am particularly interested in pushing for a basic change in how our courthouses work. Instead of telling people they can't practice law, court clerks should actively help people prepare forms in most routine uncontested actions. After all, the public pays the salaries of these people. Why shouldn't they get help filling in the blanks on forms which are contained in the codes of civil procedure of the various states? We must break the monopoly of the lawyers over the delivery of legal services. The practice of law in the U.S. is a confidence game, nothing more.

When I'm home in Jacksonville, I train others to help the underserved Florida people of low and moderate incomes who have been abandoned by the bar association and who are suffering from economic hardship.

RW: *Do you expect the Florida bar to leave you in peace now?*

RF: Absolutely. They never dreamed that by attacking me they would bring the whole country down on themselves. But if they do come after me again, I'm ready to fight.

Robin Smith Interview

Robin Smith provides independent paralegal services at People's Paralegal, in Beaverton, Oregon. She has been involved in the consumer movement for over ten years and has been an independent paralegal since 1985.

Ralph Warner (RW): *Robin, why don't you start by telling me who works at People's Paralegal.*

Robin Smith (RS): We have a staff of three, counting me. Our receptionist screens new customers on the phone, makes appointments and when a customer comes in she helps them fill out our intake form. Our office manager helps customers complete the necessary substantive questionnaire based on the type of legal procedures they want. Incidentally, we used to ask customers to complete these questionnaires themselves, but doing so sometimes intimidated them, or they provided incorrect information which slowed things down.

RW: *Can you give me an example?*

RS: Sure. A divorce that involves minor children requires information about visitation. Seeing a question on a form that asks what type of visitation they want often confuses people. By contrast, in an interview setting, we can tell people that as long as both spouses agree, they can settle on any visitation terms they wish, or simply provide for reasonable and seasonable visitation under Oregon law. If they still have questions, we can then give them written information on the subject. For example, we often provide people with a copy of an Oregon court case in which the judge clearly explained the options and defines what reasonable and seasonable means.

RW: *Great. But let's get back to staffing. What do you handle?*

RS: Our office manager does most of the form preparation, which often involves inserting customers' information into a computerized form preparation system. Incidentally, our basic word processing program is Wordstar 5.0. We also use a document generation program called

OverDrive. A few forms still must be prepared using a typewriter. I handle interviews and form preparation in several areas, including living trust, incorporation and divorce modifications where the former spouses agree. I also handle the business side of our operation, which involves marketing, dealing with the media, supervising bookkeeping and so on.

RW: *What does your office look like?*

RS: People's Paralegal operates out of an upstairs, two-room office on a commercial street with older office buildings and store fronts. One room, which is very large, is divided by partitions into three spaces. One space functions as a reception-intake area with a play space for small children. It also houses our receptionist's desk and our computer. A second, more private space has two work tables where our office manager or I work with customers to fill out the questionnaires. My office, which serves as a file room as well, is just down the hall.

RW: *What sorts of legal actions do you handle?*

RS: Quite a range—divorce, bankruptcy, wills, living trusts, probate, stepparent adoption and small business incorporations make up most of it.

RW: *That's a lot. How do you get enough information to customers so they can sensibly tell you what to type?*

RS: In a remarkably high number of areas, people have a good grasp of what they want. For example, a customer might read about a probate-avoiding living trust and then go to a lawyer's "free" seminar at which the lawyer will provide a lot of basic information and then try to get a $1,500 fee. Similarly, a small businessperson who wants to incorporate is usually pretty savvy. In these situations, the customer doesn't need more information. Of course, in other types of form preparation, such as probate or adoption, they are more likely to. We give them procedural information, such as what forms are necessary to accomplish a particular task. Under Oregon law, we don't believe doing this is the unauthorized practice of law. When it comes to substantive questions, we have a whole library of information we've gathered from a number of sources, including Nolo Press publications, and we put the customers' hands on the information they need. Once they have educated themselves, we can go forward. For more complicated questions, we advise people to see a lawyer.

RW: *Have you been hassled by the bar around unauthorized practice issues?*

RS: We have been contacted several times, mostly based on our typing of probates. To do a probate, you need the original will. Sometimes this is in a lawyer's safe and that lawyer is hoping for a nice fat probate fee. When the executor asks the lawyer for the will and says she plans to handle the probate pro per with our help, the lawyer may complain to the bar, which then results in our being called.

RW: *How do you respond?*

RS: That we use the forms provided by the same legal printer that Oregon lawyers use, and that we type and file them in the order required by the court. All information is supplied by the executor, who often has a copy of the will. So far, that seems to satisfy the bar.

RW: *Do you make a good living?*

RS: Charging $175 for a divorce, $225 for a stepparent adoption and $225-$275 for a living trust (which includes transferring real estate deeds in the name of the trust) and so on, you don't get rich. But we make a decent living and, even though I work very hard, I love what I do. I really feel I provide services people need at a fair price.

RW: *What's your attitude about companies who advertise kits, training packages and franchises to get people started as IPs and charge huge fees?*

RS: It's often customer fraud, especially when people are conned into spending lots of money based on a promise of big dollar returns. In fact, many of these promoters act like they are selling a franchise but don't comply with state franchise laws. But even more basically, the IP business is not one where huge returns are possible. We are not mass-producing anything—if an office does lots of form preparation, they must hire people and buy equipment to do the intakes and process the forms. In short, the overhead increases with the growth of the business. At the prices we charge, there isn't a big profit margin and that isn't likely to change. If IPs try to raise prices too much, someone new will open an office and undercut them.

RW: *Let's shift gears a little. How do you do your marketing?*

RS: Our biggest source of customers is the positive recommendations from people we have worked with before. Every day we get calls from new customers who have heard about us from someone we worked with previously. To help this along, we keep a mailing list of all our customers and once a year send them a letter reminding them of our services and telling them about anything new we offer. We include a discount coupon that they can use or give a friend.

RW: *What about public agencies and community organizations? Do you market to them?*

RS: Definitely. It's our second largest source of referrals. We contact all sorts of agencies—from the military to battered women's shelters to sheriff's victims' rights office to senior organizations. We have a large list that we regularly update and add to. We make every effort to stay in touch with people who are in a position to refer others. For example, one of our referral sources is the Boys and Girls Aid Society, a prominent legal group that handles adoptions. We prepare the court petition and other documents necessary to adopt.

RW: *What else do you do?*

RS: Lots of community activities. For example, the Chamber of Commerce to which I belong has an event called "Good Neighbor Days," a sort of local fair to raise money for area nonprofits. It's fun—you know, baby races, pie throwing, chili cook off, crafts booths and so on. Along with a lot of other small business, we take a booth. We also do some advertising—our yellow pages ads under "divorce" and "paralegals" produces the most. We also have a classified ad in the big Portland daily and also in the local free classified paper called "The Nickel," and in a paper for seniors. In each, we target our message to our audience. For example, in the senior paper we list wills and trust.

RW: *Finally, if you were going to give someone contemplating going into the paralegal business some advice, what would it be?*

RS: To be successful as in Independent Paralegal, you must have a tough side. Or maybe a better way to put it is that you must be a little bit of a renegade, willing to be controversial and unafraid of the Bar Association. I am not suggesting belligerence, but if you are easily pushed around or intimidated, this isn't the business for you.

For example, suppose someone calls your from the state bar and says: "This is Investigator Smith from the Unauthorized Practice of Law Committee. We have received a complaint that you are practicing law without a license. Did you do Ms. Neededhelp's Probate?"

Your answer: "Yes, we typed the papers."

Investigator Smith: "Did you select the documents?"

Your answer: "We prepared the papers in the order in which the court requires."

Investigator Smith: "The committee will bring this up at our next meeting. Thank you for your time."

If having someone call and question you like this would be overwhelming, then this business is not for you, at least until the laws are changed and the legal system reformed to allow for licensing of this profession. I say this because every IP runs the daily risk of the next call or visit being from a prosecutor or bar official. It just goes with the territory of trying to stand up to a powerful self-interest monopoly. However, if you enjoy (or don't mind) controversy, and you like hard work, enjoy a challenge and can manage a business, being an IP is a great business to be in. Personally, I've always enjoyed controversy.

Rose Palmer Interview

Rose Palmer is Executive Director of Support, Inc., a Pittsburgh, Pennsylvania-based organization that informs, counsels and provides advocacy assistance for women on issues of child support, custody, visitation and domestic violence. This interview was done in 1992.

Ralph Warner (RW): *Rose, take me back a few years and explain how you got involved in helping women with support issues.*

Rose Palmer (RP): It all began in the late 1970s with my own personal struggles as a single parent. I was literally depriving my kids of necessities to pay lawyer fees to try and collect support I desperately needed. And to add insult to injury, I wasn't getting any results.

RW: *You were in the same situation as millions of others. What was the catalyst that led to your decision to make a career out of helping other women learn how to cope with the legal system?*

RP: At one point during my case, when we were in court, I saw that a legal mistake was being made. I interrupted and pointed it out. Even though I was correct and the error had the potential to jeopardize my rights, the Allegheny County hearing officer (in the role of a judge) told me to "shut up." She stated, "You have an attorney; he will speak for you. You do not talk unless I ask you to." Her attitude made me furious. It was as if I had no right to speak, even when the lawyers were messing up. It was a real turning point for me. I went home determined to learn how to do my own legal research and to take charge of my own legal destiny. Soon after, I got in touch with other women who were in the same situation, and Legal Advocacy for Women was born.

RW: *Where did you start your new work?*

RP: At the Pittsburgh YWCA. They gave us space in December of 1979. We stayed there for more than a year, but eventually left and ran our program out of a spare bedroom, because we were simply too controversial for the Y. They had a conservative board, and challenging the legal power structure worried them.

RW: *When did you come out of the bedroom and really get established in Pittsburgh?*

RP: October 1983, and like so many things in life, the story of how we got our first grant has an odd twist. The wife of a city councilman came to us for help with a long story of how she was being victimized by her husband. We were doing consciousness-raising activities at the time—marches, picketing and other events—to focus attention on how divorced, separated and single women with children were being discriminated against, and we saw her situation as a chance to further dramatize the issue.

RW: *So you took it public?*

RP: In a big way. And, of course, we got lots of publicity. There was only one problem. The heroine of our little drama was lying.

RW: *Oops. You mean the city councilman hadn't mistreated your client?*

RP: Nope. James O'Malley was a nice guy—such a good man, in fact, that despite our part in unfairly attacking him, he took an interest in what we were doing, applauded our goals and counseled us to form a formal nonprofit corporation. He then used his influence to get us our first grant.

RW: *What a wonderful story, but don't stop. What happened next?*

RP: With a real office and a few dollars to pay staff, we were much more visible. In fact, in 1985 we saw 700 clients in person and counseled another 2,000 by phone. There was only one problem—all of this activity got us in hot water with the county bar association.

RW: *How exactly did it occur?*

RP: We helped a woman with minor children involved in a divorce, whose husband was represented by a prominent local lawyer. Our client was awarded everything she asked for—child support, day care and medical care. The same day the judge made the award, the lawyer filed charges with the Unauthorized Practice of Law (UPL) Committee of the Allegheny County bar association, charging us with practicing law without a license.

RW: *So that started a brouhaha about what you could do and not infringe on lawyer turf?*

RP: You bet. They challenged everything, right down to our right to use our name, which at that time was Legal Advocacy for Women. They questioned our right to go into court with women and counsel them as part of court proceedings, as well as helping women prepare budget sheets and other court forms.

RW: *I know you are doing all these things and lots more today, so you must have prevailed.*

RP: We are, and you're right, we eventually did, but it was a real struggle. Fortunately, the media was very sympathetic. Lawyers, after all, do not and can not provide affordable legal services to the average person, so if we were put out of business, it was obvious that no one was going to help a lot of desperate mothers. Also, we had (and still do, I should add) some brave people on our board of directors. Several local lawyers, judges and other prominent people who spoke out on our behalf. The result was compromise in the form of a consent order. We agreed to change our name from "Legal Advocacy for Women" to "Support, Inc.," not to whisper to our clients in court and not to use or touch the counsel table when we sat next to our clients in court. We could talk to our clients in a normal voice in court and ask for a recess at any time to confer privately in the hall, all of which was fine with us and, of course, made whispering unnecessary.

RW: *No, you can't be serious! The lawyers actually claimed that someone using their tables made you guilty of unauthorized practice of law?*

RP: Funny isn't it? But they were so desperate to draw a bright line between us and them that they drew it along the edge of the table. Since our clients can sit at the table, we had to be able to be there too in order to provide counseling and support. But since it's called the counsel table, and lawyers see this as a synonym for lawyer, we can't touch it or put our papers or research materials on it.

RW: *Lawyers go to law school for three years to make distinctions like that.*

RP: Apparently.

RW: *But otherwise, you carried on the same services as before? You still taught women how to use the legal system and helped them prepare paperwork and accompanied them to court?*

RP: Yes. In a way, it was as if the bar backed down but declared victory.

RW: *Does the Gilbert & Sullivan aspect of this story continue?*

RP: You bet. The next year, Councilman O'Malley helped sponsor an art show/benefit at the main city-county building, with all proceeds going to our organization. The opening was great—fancy dress and so on. Even the mayor presided at the opening ceremonies. There was only one hitch: the invitation went out saying the benefit was for "Support, Inc. (Legal Advocacy for Women)." There was no AKA before Legal Advocacy for Women, or other explanation that this was our former name. Even though we had nothing to do with printing or paying for the invitations (the city did that), attorney James Victor Voss, the same person who had gone after us before, filed another UPL complaint. Fortunately, this one died quickly when we showed that we weren't really using the old name.

RW: *What's new? What are you are you doing now that you didn't used to do?*

RP: For one thing, we have grown. We now see over 1,000 people in person each year and help 4,000 more by phone. In addition, since there are now more types of pre-printed forms available for the confirmation of child custody, visitation and so on, it means we help clients with more paperwork. We also have worked with courts to set up a court-approved visitation room so fathers can visit their children during the time when allegations of violence that form the basis for temporary protective (restraining) orders are being investigated. Incidentally, this gives us status as a public service with the courts. Also, I should mention our clinical program. Working with the two local law schools, third-year students are assigned to work with us as part of a family law clinical program, for which the students get credit. Since they are bar-certified to appear in court and supervised by Lesley Grey, a practicing lawyer who works with our program, it's a real plus.

RW: *Has the bar caused further trouble?*

RP: We have been investigated more than once. You can often tell when you get an inappropriate telephone call or visit, but officially we have been left alone.

RW: *Perhaps you have convinced them that you are too determined an opponent.*

RP: I don't know, but we do have allies. The media, particularly, gives us fair treatment. We are well into our second decade of service, so we have built a reputation as being a trustworthy news source. When you are under attack, it's terribly important to have access to the media to get your story out. To achieve this, you must make yourselves available, tell the truth and be ready to substantiate your statements.

RW: *Support, Inc. has obviously grown in lots of ways. Personally, what have you been doing to stay excited and not get stale?*

RP: I have done general mediation training at the college level and then followed up with specific courses in family mediation. I also host a TV show on our local city cable station which allows me to teach large numbers of women how to deal with the support problem. In a sense, I do self-help law on TV. It's exciting. I've even had family court judges appear in mock courtroom scenes to teach women how to handle the court process.

RW: *Didn't I also hear that you ran for public office?*

RP: Yes, for the state legislature, against a prominent and very entrenched opponent who had heavy financial backing and had been in office 20 years. I had no chance, but I had a great time and got plenty of opportunity to talk about consumer justice issues. The fact that the average person has no access to law is beginning to be important to voters. People know that our present system—which provides access to our legal system only for those who can afford high lawyer fees—is unfair.

RW: *Let me ask you one final thing. What about fathers? Aren't they victimized by the legal system, too? Who helps them?*

RP: The answer to your first question is yes, absolutely. The legal system treats everyone shabbily. For example, if a father loses his job or suffers a loss of income and can't afford to pay as much child support, he needs to get his support order reduced. But most fathers don't know how to do this, and if they can't afford to pay their normal bills, including child support, how can they afford a lawyer? The result is that the father, who may be doing his best, becomes a statistic for violating his child support order. In fact, the real statistic should indicate that one more person was denied access to the law. In short, the father who couldn't afford to petition the court to reduce his support order because of changed circumstances now is likely to be prosecuted because the system made it impossible for him to take advantage of his legal rights. Although I don't always agree with the positions fathers' groups take, I certainly support their efforts to teach men how to use the legal system and develop better ways for fathers to get affordable legal access. For example, I often invite fathers' groups to participate in my TV show, and Support, Inc. has dealt with both genders on issues of child support since 1989. Men and women will only achieve real structural reform when they realize that law in America is administered primarily for the benefit of lawyers and victimizes both groups. Men and women must work together to achieve a more democratic justice system, as well as to cooperate to raise good kids.

Judy Lamb Interview

Judy Lamb is the Director of the Court Advocacy Program, a nonprofit service organization located in Weibern, New York, which provides legal information and emotional support to women dealing with domestic problems, including child custody and support, divorce, paternity and physical abuse.

Ralph Warner (RW): *Judy, tell me a little about what you do.*

Judy Lamb (JL): I'm the director of the Court Advocacy Program here in the Buffalo, N.Y. area. We provide information, referral and support to women concerned with being physically abused (battered) as well as those who need information about and/or assistance with divorce, custody, child support and paternity. Our services focus primarily on promoting personal growth, self-esteem and self-sufficiency. For the past four years, we have received approximately 6,000 phone calls and have provided a supportive presence in over 800 court appearances.

RW: *You operate as a nonprofit?*

JL: Yes, the Court Advocacy Program is a joint, state-funded program sponsored by the Western New York Coalition of Women for Child Support and Friendship House, a local umbrella organization which provides help for low-income citizens in a number of ways.

RW: *What do you do?*

JL: We distribute pamphlets about women's legal rights, hold occasional public information meetings and provide individual and group counseling designed to empower women to make their own decisions. Unlike lawyers, we never tell people what to do. It's a fundamental part of our approach that women, especially battered and abused women, have to decide for themselves to change their lives. If and when they do, we provide basic legal and practical information to assist them to do it.

RW: *Does this mean you go to court with women?*

JL: Often we do, if we're asked to. For example, a woman who has been battered might go to court to ask for a protective order, or a woman who has separated from her husband might request support. We would accompany them to court and sit in the back of the courtroom. The woman would present her own case if she didn't have a lawyer, or her lawyer would present it. We don't speak in court except in the very rare circumstances of being asked to participate by the referee or judge.

RW: *What if a woman is confused and wants your help in the middle of the proceeding?*

JL: It has happened, and we can provide counseling if the referee or judge temporarily delays the proceeding so we can confer. But remember, we only provide social work-type personal support and basic legal and practical information. We don't tell a woman what choice to make. Our job is to help people find the power to make their own choices. On the whole, judges and hearing examiners have been quite sensitive in allowing court advocates to support their clients. Unfortunately, on occasion, our clients did not receive that same sensitivity from lawyers.

RW: *All of this sounds pretty non-controversial.*

JL: That's what I thought, until I got a letter from the Erie County Bar Association asking me to appear before their Unlawful Practice Committee.

RW: *When was this?*

JL: Spring, 1989.

RW: *What reason did they give you?*

JL: That's it. The letter was quite vague, just stating that they wanted to discuss the activities of my program. It wasn't until the last sentence that I realized we were in trouble.

RW: *What was that sentence?*

JL: Well, the whole context of the letter appeared as if it was an invitation to a social function, but the last sentence said that when I appear before the Committee, I could be represented by a lawyer if I chose.

RW: *I see. The iron fist in the velvet glove approach. So what did you do?*

JL: I got on the phone to talk to the couple of local lawyers who were friendly to our program to find out what was going on.

RW: *And?*

JL: And it turned out that the bar was acting because they had received a letter of complaint about the program from a local lawyer who had recently lost a case. She represented the batterer and we provided support and information to the victim.

RW: *You mean a lawyer with a bad case of sour grapes wanted to put you out of business?*

JL: Essentially.

RW: *So what happened?*

JL: Even though the bar is, in my view, just a private trade group and shouldn't have the power to order me to do anything, I concluded that our program would be best served if I cooperated, so I went to the Unauthorized Practice Committee meeting. It consisted of ten lawyers (nine of them men) grilling me about everything Court Advocacy did.

RW: *Such as?*

JL: Oh, they objected to our use of the word "Advocacy" because only lawyers should be able to use that word. I pointed out that all of our materials say clearly that we are not lawyers and don't give legal advice, and that all sorts of groups advocate things, but they weren't convinced. They also wanted to know about the public education program we run to educate people about New York's new child support guidelines and the basic procedures of divorce. In fact, the public education program focused primarily on assertiveness in the legal system.

RW: *What was the objection?*

JL: To this day, I'm not really sure, but I think it came down to the fact that, in their view, lawyers own the law and have the right to sell it to the public. Anyone else who gets involved in public education about legal issues is trespassing on their turf. At the bar meeting, they were concerned about the fact that we charged a small fee for one of the pubic meetings. Their comment was I might be talking clients from attorneys. They were also concerned about my education. They claimed I wasn't qualified. They weren't interested in whether I knew and understood the new child support guidelines I had discussed at the meeting (in fact, I did, but many of them didn't). It was simple; if I wasn't an attorney, I wasn't qualified.

RW: *Even assuming, for purposes of argument, that lawyers are right when they claim they are the best qualified to provide legal information about physical abuse and child support, the next question is are lawyers doing this for low-income women.*

JL: That's it, they aren't. In fact, many laugh at the entire issue, believing that the problems of battered woman don't exist or are greatly exaggerated. Some even think our written materials telling woman their rights are hilarious. Just the same, some local lawyers do make a little money from representing desperate women who somehow scrape a legal fee together. They don't want to lose the business.

RW: *So, back to the story, what happened at the meeting?*

JL: Well, the funny thing is that so much of this sounds trivial when you explain it. One of their big objections had to do with the fact that the local Supreme (trial) Court clerk would occasionally notify me that a case had been dropped from the calender and reset for a different day.

RW: *What does that have to do with UPL?*

JL: What does any of this have to do with UPL? According to them, knowing in advance when a case would be heard was a lawyer privilege and, incidentally, one they often used to exert power over clients ("only I know when the court will proceed"). They just hated the fact that a nonlawyer had this information and could pass it on to their clients before they got around to it. I guess it is all part of their feeling that the legal system is set up for lawyers rather than the public.

RW: *What happened after the meeting?*

JL· Well, the funny thing is that even though there was a formal complaint against us, I never saw it or had a chance to directly respond. I heard via the grapevine that it was withdrawn. Part of the reason may have been that I did get the word out as to what was happening to our program. The UPL committee definitely knew that if they tried to close us down, we would fight back, including challenging their right to harass us on both anti-trust and constitutional grounds.

RW: *Could you explain that more?*

JL: Well, I was hardly being given a fair hearing, was I? My accusers were my judges. Also, where does the bar get the legal authority to establish a monopoly cartel and then claim the right to put competitors out of business? The whole thing smells bad.

RW: *Did the bar issue a formal statement?*

JL: No. I received some suspicious phone calls and visits from men posing as people needing help in child support matters, but that was it for eight months. Of course, despite our best efforts not to be intimidated, we all felt pressure. Finally, I received a call from the president of the UPL committee, who asked for a meeting and to review all of our material (handouts). At first, he wanted me to again appear before the UPL committee, but I refused. I let them know through my advising attorney that I would meet with the president of the committee alone, one-to-one, and that he could review materials but not copy them. After some fencing about time and location, I went to this office, but refused to allow him to make copies.

RW: *Weren't they widely available to the public?*

JL: Sure, but I wasn't going to submit them to an official inspection. I wasn't going to play willing victim to their kangaroo court approach.

RW: *So what happened at the meeting?*

JL: Essentially, the bar president kept politely trying to tell me that only lawyers could deal with legal affairs and I kept politely saying I didn't agree. I was obviously very angry about this continued intimidation process. He couldn't understand why. When I raised objections to the way I had been treated before the UPL Committee, he told me that lawyers and judges are brought in before committees all of the time. I replied that it wasn't quite the same—lawyers and judges were judged by their peers, but I wasn't. I suggested that my peers or the community should also judge my services through a public hearing. I went on to suggest the holding of a public hearing on the quality and availability of legal services to citizens of low and moderate incomes.

RW: *In short, the meeting was part of a continuing bar effort to put you in your place—intimidate you—and you politely tried to turn the tables, right?*

JL: Right—but I really believe what I said. The legal system must better serve the average citizen. The idea that lawyers own the law is absurd and produces bad results, especially in domestic disputes. It's appalling that our society countenances a system in which lawyers routinely fan the flames of domestic disputes because, by doing so, they profit.

RW: *Do they catch themselves playing such a negative role?*

JL: A good question. Normally I think they pretend that no conflict exists between their interests and those of their clients. But deep down, they must know there often is. I think trying to suppress this knowledge accounts for much of their anger when the conflicts are pointed out.

RW: *But since you are one of the people doing the pointing out, doesn't it mean you will probably stay on the hot spot?*

JL: Yes, but I see that as an opportunity. Our program really is based on a different model than lawyers—we don't tell people what to do. Or, to put it in lawyer terms, we don't give advice—either personal or legal. So again, in lawyer terms, we don't practice law.

RW: *I don't follow your point.*

JL: Well, if the practice of law consists of doing what lawyers do, or acting like a lawyer, we don't. We do something different and I think it needs to be better understood. We give people access to the law itself, and basic consumer information about the law.

RW: *It sounds a little bit like Alcoholics Anonymous approach. People can be given information about the problems concerning liquor, but whether to drink or not must be their own choice. If they want to die in the gutter—fine.*

JL: Well, that's the extreme, but in a way, yes. If a battered woman decides to stay in an abusive situation, that's her choice. We can only provide emotional support. However, if she wants to change her circumstances, we provide the information and referrals necessary for her to change her life.

RW: *What's next for your program? How would you like to grow and expand?*

JL: It is really unfortunate, but our court advocacy program right now is on hold. Our four-year grant ended in October 1990, and due to the devastating state budget cuts, public funding for non-residential domestic violence programs is nil. We hope to secure funding privately or through another public agency in Western New York. Our staff of three has always utilized student interns and volunteers, and hopefully we could increase this. Victims of either physical, emotional, verbal or economic abuse need help, and we plan to survive to provide it.

Catherine Jermany Interview

Catherine Jermany is the former Director of the National Association for Independent Paralegals, a nonprofit support and training group which provided help for independent paralegals for many years. For more than 20 years she has conducted paralegal training for a number of organizations, including the Legal Services Corporation, where she served as Director of Paralegal Training and Career Development, the National Paralegal Institute, as their training director, and the Children's Defense Fund, as their Community Legal Education Specialist.

Ralph Warner (RW): *How did you get involved in a legal career?*

Catherine Jermany (CJ): If I really go back to the roots of it, it's because of my grandmother Callie Jackson, who started her own legal-help service, The Listening Post, in 1929. She was a grand old lady who died at the age of 105 in 1978. She lived in the big house of a courtway and was the informal lawyer for everyone around. My memories date from my own childhood in the late 1940s and early 1950s. She ran her business from her home and handled leases, burial rights advocacy (black people even had trouble getting equal rights after they were dead in those days), employment claims, you name it. Remember, in those days few people had access to the formal legal system, except perhaps for the very few who had money. People like my grandmother filled in the void—serving as legal advocates to unserved people. Today we would call her a "paralegal," a term which, incidentally, she would have hated.

RW: *Why is that?*

CJ: Because she was a proud, effective person. She wasn't para-anything or sub-anything. It wasn't in her nature to kowtow to anyone.

RW: *Somehow your being around Callie as a child inspired you?*

CJ: It sure did. For example, she built a library full of notebooks about people's legal rights which she kept on a shelf beside the sugar bowl. I keep similar types of notebooks today, although in the last ten years, lots of my information has been transferred to computer disks.

The other big influence was my father, who absolutely insisted on perfection. If you didn't get something right the first time, you could just keep doing it over until you did.

RW: *When did you first get involved in law?*

CJ: When I was fourteen, it was obvious to me that some elderly friends who used to live down the street, and had subsequently gone into a nursing home, were being mistreated. This was before all the modern nursing home regulations, so there were no obvious legal handles to use to help them. To make a long story short, I succeeded in going before the L.A. County Board of Supervisors and getting my friends reinstated in another nursing home (they had been kicked out of the first one when we complained), and having the first home closed down. The whole experience taught me that there was a process to deal with everything. This was a powerful lesson—to get things done you simply had to learn the process and then go step by step.

RW: *How did you get involved with paralegals?*

CJ: I was involved with the Southern Christian Leadership Conference before Martin Luther King, Jr. was murdered. I organized in the South and West, and was also deeply involved in the Welfare Rights Movement. In 1968, there was a poor people's campaign in Washington D.C. I handled the parade permits, contracts, and even carried the money. In a sense, I was bag lady for the campaign.

RW: *Where does the paralegal work come in?*

CJ: In 1969, I was back in Los Angeles and I started an organization called the "Dependency Prevention Center," or DPC, to teach poor people how to stand on their own feet. We did welfare, health, housing, and education rights training. I was also still very involved with the local welfare rights organization. Both organizations were doing all sorts of things that were basically legal advocacy. In short, we were doing work that the Legal Aid Society of Los Angeles was unable to do because they didn't always understand the needs of the community. At any rate, a series of confrontations with Legal Service resulted in a number of community people who were trained by DPC being included on the Legal Services Board.

The next step, of course, was to get community people into the Legal Services offices themselves. We did this by doing welfare rights advocacy on a volunteer basis right at the Legal Aid office, throughout California and other states. Then, when openings for interviewers, receptionists and eventually case advocates happened, our people got the jobs. Of course, these new employees were short on traditional legal skills. They had plenty of fire to change things, but most had never worked in an office before. Through DPC, we provided the training.

RW: *What next?*

CJ: Because of all these activities, I ended up on the Board of Directors of the National Paralegal Institute in 1971 and I worked as a paralegal for the Children's Defense Fund.

RW: *You sure got around.*

CJ: I'm only telling you half of it.

RW: *What is the National Paralegal Institute and when did you start to work there?*

CJ: In 1973, the National Paralegal Institute, which is still in operation today, was founded to determine and define the role of paralegals. It conducted numerous studies and was the first to design and implement training for the nonlawyer staff of Legal Services Offices. Then, in 1976, when Legal Services brought all its training in-house, I did the same work for the federally funded Legal Services Corporation, as Director of Training.

RW: *What exactly did you do?*

CJ: Our job was to figure out what the various types of people who had stumbled into paralegal jobs in Legal Services offices needed to know to do their jobs better. For example, since lawyers don't like to interview people, or attend welfare or unemployment hearings, we taught laypeople how to do it. I trained people from Mississippi to Maine to Micronesia. Eventually we even trained lawyers how to run their offices better by the effective use of paralegals.

RW: *Looking back, how do you feel about the work you did in the early- and mid-1970s?*

CJ: On balance, great. We taught people lots of good things, but maybe in retrospect some not so good ones, too. For example, we trained paralegals to make lawyers more efficient. You know, things like tickler systems, efficient filing, doing their client interviews, etc.

RW: *And you see that as a mistake now?*

CJ: Well, in the sense that we taught paralegals to be somewhat dependent, yes. We supported the traditional lawyer-dominated system of delivering services that I now see is often a mistake. Let's get rid of the label "para" and call them legal specialists. Let's get specialists thinking and acting like entrepreneurs. The age of the deregulation of lawyers' monopoly is at hand. People need to be ready.

RW: *So you see paralegals escaping from lawyers?*

CJ: Sure, legal specialists should be able to work with or without lawyer supervisors as they choose. And they will be able to very soon now. The age of legal entrepreneurs providing routine legal services is already upon us because the public demands it. People are sick of our inefficient, over-priced, uncaring legal delivery system. It's got to change. And you know it's funny—in many ways people in low-income communities are open to change because they have had such minimal access to lawyers that their tradition of legal self-reliance is stronger.

RW: *And they have less to lose.*

CJ: That too.

RW: *If you wanted to open your own independent business to help nonlawyers deal with the legal system, would you go to a two- or three-year paralegal school?*

CJ: Personally, no. The reason is simple. Paralegal education is almost always general in nature. It's very weak on usable skills. Or, to say that another way, they don't teach you to do specific tasks independently.

RW: *What does an independent paralegal or legal specialist—someone who is working with nonlawyers around specific form filling-out tasks —need to know?*

CJ: Three things. First, they have to be able to deal with real people in the (often frustrating) course of real-life, legal problem solving. That is, they need to have good interviewing, counseling, data management and hand-holding skills. And don't underestimate the value of hand holding. People very often are unable to tell you what they really want or need— it's up to you to be able to help them find out not only what they need, but be able to guide them through the self-help law materials that are appropriate to their situation. Second, the independent paralegal must know how to do the mechanics of the particular task. Third, they must have enough general background or breadth in the particular subject area to be able to help the customer avoid the obvious pitfalls and get legal advice when needed.

RW: *How do people who have never done interviewing in a legal context, kept files or run an office learn to do this well?*

CJ: For starters, they need at least some structured interviewing, fact gathering, management and analysis training skills. There are definite techniques in conducting a customer visit and being able to assist the customer use the information properly.

RW: *You think about the independent paralegal movement every day. Tell me what's going on.*

CJ: The growth is unbelievable. There are now many thousands of IPs.

RW: *Where do all these people come from?*

CJ: All over the U.S. The largest concentration is in California, of course. You would expect that, since the IP movement was born here and it's also the most populous state.

RW: *What sorts of backgrounds do IPs have?*

CJ: A wide variety. Former teachers, business people, social workers, you name it. About one-third are graduates of a formal paralegal school who often work in law firms now or have done so until recently. The goal of many of these people is to combine freelancing for lawyers with working directly for the public.

RW: *What about the other two-thirds? You said they came from a wide variety of backgrounds. Can you be a little more specific?*

CJ: A large group are business people who already deal directly with the public, such as tax preparers, public stenographers, people who run telephone answering services and so on. They see learning legal form preparation skills as a way to expand the services they already offer to the public.

RW: *Give me an example.*

CJ: Take someone who runs a credit repair and counseling service—not the sleazy variety, but an honest business. It's not hard to learn how to type bankruptcy forms for those who can't realistically avoid bankruptcy. It's a great combination because credit counseling is generally recognized as a nonlawyer function. This means, in the credit context, nonlawyers can actually transfer legal information and expertise without falling victim to UPL charges. Then, if necessary, they can simply transfer over to the typing service model to prepare bankruptcy forms.

RW: *I gather bankruptcy form preparation is a fast-growing Independent Paralegal area. What are some others?*

CJ: Well, bankruptcy is the second, only after the demand for wills. With hard economic times, there is an unfulfilled need in virtually every community. Also living trusts, immigration form preparation, guardianships and support modifications are all rapidly growing areas.

RW: *What about the traditional bread and butter area—divorce?*

CJ: About 75% of all IPs already do divorces. In some states, such as California, Arizona and Oregon, the business is pretty well saturated. There are really not enough divorces to go around when you figure that there are lots of low-cost alternatives to IPs—for example, self-help law-books, battered woman's shelters and legal services for the poor all take chunks of the divorce business. And then, of course, lawyers have held on to most of the most affluent 25% of the market. In other states, where the IP movement is really just getting going, there is still plenty of opportunity to type divorces. But remember, as the U.S. population ages, divorce won't be the fast-growing field it was from the mid-1960s to the mid-1980s.

RW: *Let me pick one of the legal areas you mentioned—living trusts. Tell me what's going on.*

CJ: As you know, lots of lawyers have begun to advertise living trust seminars. These are typically designed to sell living trusts for $1,500-$2,500 each, a vastly inflated price given the amount of work involved. It didn't take IPs and financial planners long to see that they could make a good living doing the same thing for $250-$300.

RW: *Are you saying that IPs are engaging in guerrilla marketing by playing off the lawyers' seminar ads?*

CJ: Sure, many list their services in the same senior papers and newsletters that the lawyers advertise in. And some even stand right up and explain that they help people do much the same thing for much less money using a self-help typing approach.

RW: *Don't the lawyers have a cow?*

CJ: Well, a calf anyway, but there isn't much they can do. Remember it's a public meeting in a hotel conference room, so they can't call the cops. Often they try and retaliate in other ways. They might complain to the bar association or write a letter to a local newspaper attempting to put down nonlawyer services.

RW: *How do paralegals avoid UPL charges?*

CJ: They can give or sell customers Denis Clifford's *Make Your Own Living Trust,* which has sold over 150,000 copies direct to the public. As long as the customer has the book and the IP follows the customer's instructions, there is no UPL problem.

RW: *Isn't this approach hard for some consumers, especially those that aren't experienced in the use of a fairly sophisticated book?*

CJ: Not if the IP is trained properly to act as a coach or guide to help the person extract relevant information from the self-help resource. To go back to bankruptcy for a second, it's important for the customer to locate the exempt property information for the state where he or she lives. For the IP to simply tell the customer this information has been held to be unauthorized practice. This is a ridiculous, lawyer-centric, legal rule, of course, but for now we are stuck with it. At any rate, to circumvent it, a well-trained IP can simply direct the consumer to the part of the book where this information is clearly spelled out.

RW: *Do you see this typing service model in which the consumer is educated to make their own decisions primarily as a cover-your-behind device for the IP.*

CJ:. No. It's an affirmative way to do business. The concept of self-reliance is buried deep in the American psyche. When functioning properly, the IP acts as a helper to the self-helper. When you see it that way, it's an exciting business niche. And best of all, approached this way, the consumer doesn't see the IP as a second-class lawyer and feel cheated because he or she can't afford a "real" lawyer. Instead, customers see the IP as a positive adjunct to their own learning process.

RW: *If we make an analogy to adding on a deck to a house, would it be fair to say that the IP should play the role of a teacher to a self-help builder rather than that of a cheap unlicensed contractor?*

CJ: Yes, and the best part is that whether it's a deck or a divorce, once a person really learns to do the particular task, they are empowered to attack other, larger problems. In the legal area, it really builds better citizens.

RW: *How can a want-to-be independent paralegal learn the necessary skills?*

CJ: To actually fill out the forms, you would be better off starting with a good self-help book, such as Nolo's *How to File for Bankruptcy,* hanging around the bankruptcy court and then volunteering in an office where a lot of bankruptcies are typed, such as a consumer legal services office. Remember, rule number one of learning any skill is to carefully observe the correct practice of that skill and then to correctly practice the skill yourself. This can best be done by volunteering and finding a mentor.

RW: *What else?*

CJ: Take a good course. Any legal area can be broken down into a finite number of discrete variables. These variables are interrelated. Understanding the forest is not only knowing what the main variables are but how they relate to each other. To impart this type of information to independent paralegals necessarily requires the use of outlines, charts, lists of steps and some basic rules. Many paralegal organizations sponsor lectures and workshops on all sorts of legal tasks, including bankruptcy.

RW: *When you teach IPs, what is your approach?*

CJ: Basically, I've always used an extended and detailed hypothetical case that covers an entire range of variables in the field. In working through the hypothetical, I teach the three skills I mentioned earlier and emphasize the relationships between the various factors that will be present in each individual case.

RW: *Okay, can you tell me why it is so important to have a broad base of background information on a particular subject area. After all, don't most self-help typing services just type forms?*

CJ: If they do, they may find themselves in trouble in a hurry. For example, suppose someone gives you a set of facts and asks for a particular result. You need to know whether their fact situation entitles them to the remedy they want under current laws, and you also need to know whether the remedy they want is appropriate under the circumstances. What's more, you must know the self-help law material better than the customer in order to point out any mistakes they may have made and direct them to the part of the book or other resource that contains the correct information.

RW: *Can you be specific?*

CJ: Let's stick with bankruptcy. Suppose someone lists a whole bunch of bank credit card accounts and you see the dates involved indicate that the person was borrowing money from one bank, then opening another account, paying back the first and so on until they got a very high credit limit. They then borrow a lot of money and declare bankruptcy to avoid getting involved. In short, you need to know what an illegal credit and kiting scheme is so you can decline to type the papers in this sort of situation.

RW: *Is this sort of thing a big danger to an independent legal worker?*

CJ: In any field, 15% or 20% of the people who walk in will be asking for help you can't provide, or there will be some other reason why you should not handle their business, like avoiding the occasional crook. You absolutely need to know enough to spot all the issues that may affect the case. As I've said, you have to live the particular areas of the law you are working in before you open your business. Remember, as with any professional, you have to be extremely careful not to get in over your head.

RW: *I know you have worked with IPs all over the country who are trying to survive in an often hostile, lawyer-dominated legal environment. Tell me what you tell them.*

CJ: The key is to know your limitations. Everywhere throughout the U.S., the UPL laws are interpreted the same. Nonlawyers cannot do what lawyers do. This simply means that to minimize your risk of UPL, you must operate as a self-help law specialist, guiding your customers through published materials, without personally providing legal advice and preparing the paperwork under their direction. Secondly, to get a strong statewide organization in place to help IPs with organizing, training and fighting back against lawyer harassment. In many of the Western states, especially California, Oregon and Arizona, IP organizations already exist. In states where the movement is newer, a new IP may need to work to pull an organization together. It's really something IPs need to do, since a strong organization offers obvious protection against UPL charges. It's not hard to see that it's a lot easier for the bar to pick off an isolated IP than it is to go up against a well-organized group.

RW: *The main purpose of the state groups is to protect members from unauthorized practice charges?*

CJ: No, that's only one function. Once the group is in place, it can start training members in the right ways to do business—good skills development, good consumer recourse and other honest business practices. A consumer needs to know he or she will get good services from an IP. If they do, they will use more services, tell their friends and won't complain to the bar. It's a virtuous circle.

RW: *How many states currently have formal independent paralegal organizations?*

CJ: Sixteen have organizations that meet on a regular basis and do the things I just mentioned. In quite a few more, organizations are at a formative stage. In some areas—where population density is low, it will be necessary to take a regional approach.

RW: *What do you see for the legal movement in the years just ahead?*

CJ: Right now, the movement is consumer driven—consumers want and need better legal access at a reasonable cost. Unfortunately, some IPs don't see that—they believe they are prospering because of something they are doing as individuals. So the answer is that IPs will do well individually and as a group as long as they see that their continued success depends on their doing an excellent job to meet consumer needs. People are fed up with lawyers—not only because of ridiculous fees, but because lawyers deny them control over their own lives. As long as IPs deliver good services that empower people at a reasonable cost, all will be well. If they begin to act like junior lawyers, they will be in trouble.

Stephen Elias Interview

Stephen Elias is the author of a number of self-help law books and software, including *How To File for Bankruptcy, Legal Research: How to Find and Understand the Law* and *WillMaker*. As well as serving as Associate Publisher at Nolo Press, Steve is a member of the California State Bar Committee on the Delivery of Legal Services to Middle Income persons, and in that capacity is educating California lawyers about how to work with, rather than against, independent paralegals and their customers.

Ralph Warner (RW): *Twenty-five years ago non-lawyers who typed legal forms and helped people accomplish basic legal tasks barely existed. If you had a legal problem, you either went to a lawyer or ignored it. But now, in many parts of the U.S., there are loads of independent paralegals helping people accomplish all sorts of legal tasks. What happened?*

Stephen Elias (SE): Well, the larger trend is that more and more people are solving their own simple legal problems without lawyers. To do that they need information about the law, how to use courts and so on.

RW: *And somehow independent paralegals have become part of that.*

SE: Sure, because they figured out a basic rule of life—the first thing many people do when they need information is to ask someone who knows more than they do.

RW: *That person used to be a lawyer—at least for people who could afford it. But now, for some reason, many people are less anxious to ask lawyers for help.*

SE: Lawyers come with too much unattractive baggage. Not only do they cost a great deal, but there is also a basic trust issue—many people fear that they don't have their best interests at heart.

RW: *So independent paralegals have at least partially replaced lawyers as legal information providers.*

SE: Right, but remember, independent paralegals are only part of a larger trend towards self-help law solutions. People are getting legal information from literally dozens of places these days—self-help law books, software, law libraries and online data networks, to mention just a few. The point is that the more the demand for legal information increases, the greater the supply becomes.

RW: *But what's that got to do with independent paralegals, except that it's all part of the same trend towards more self-help in the legal system?*

SE: The easier it is to obtain legal information, the greater the need for informed people—we call them experts—to help the public deal with it. Small business people who call themselves independent paralegals have stepped in to fill this need. Again, it's demand calling forth supply.

RW: *But isn't there a risk that independent paralegals are a transitory phenomena? To take an example, as courthouses increasingly provide computer kiosks to help people file their own divorce paperwork, won't the role of the independent paralegal—which usually is to help people prepare these same documents—be eliminated?*

SE: Not really. Take the kiosk example. What the kiosk amounts to is a Versateller-like machine designed to help people complete simple legal paperwork. But to work well, the machine will need to provide the user with lots of back-up legal information in the form of help. And the basic program driving the kiosk will need lots of branches and twigs to take care of the hundreds of different personal and legal problems. At each one of these branches some people will want help or advice from a human being to augment what they are getting on the screen.

RW: *Which means human advisors won't be replaced.*

SE: Far from it. As more and more people do their own law—whether computers are involved or not—there will be more and more demand for human backup in the form of advice or coaching.

RW: *Give me an example of how someone with a particular legal problem 20 years from now will be able to find both rich legal information and human coaching to solve it.*

SE: Forget about 20 years from now. It's already happening. Say you are an inventor and you want to get a patent for a new type of golf tee you just created. You can get an easy-to-use, off-the-shelf computer program called *Patent It Yourself* which will take you through every step of the patent process as well as providing structured legal help to help you deal with dozens of patent-related tasks. And when you need to search to see if anyone else has already invented your golf tee, you can order the search via electronic mail from a patent search service. All of this is easy to do. It's a little like having an old-time patent lawyer at your elbow.

RW: *But not quite.*

SE: No. There is no direct human help, which is where the independent paralegal comes in. There are already people who sell affordable support services to self-help patent drafters. For example, whether you have a computer program to help or not, drafting a patent claim can be tricky, with lots of judgment calls. An inventor who only files the occasional patent will benefit from working with someone who is much further up the learning curve.

RW: *But I thought the computer version of* Patent It Yourself *broke the process of obtaining a patent down into a bunch of simple steps.*

SE: Yes, but unlike a Versateller transaction, which we talked about earlier, many areas of law—in this case patent law—are far trickier.

RW: *Which just means more steps, right? Can't you simplify almost anything into lots of little steps?*

SE: In theory, but in practice the complexity of the total task overwhelms the simplicity of the little steps and people bog down. Filing a tax return is a good example.

RW: *You mean there are loads of IRS booklets, self-help law books, do-it-yourself software and even online advice, but lots of people still turn to humans for help.*

SE: Absolutely. Tax preparers, enrolled agents, accountants and even tax lawyers have plenty of business and every year it grows. The same thing will happen in literally hundreds of legal areas as more people do it themselves and more information becomes available. Helpers—independent paralegals, if you want to use that term—will carve out loads of new small businesses.

RW: *But Steve, if independent paralegals really becomes human helpers in the broader sense, instead of just form preparers, aren't they going to be guilty of the unauthorized practice of law?*

SE: In the short term, there may be some risk of being nailed for UPL as paralegals expand into areas still occupied by lawyers. Of course, the approach that beats UPL now will still often work in these new areas.

RW: *You mean where the paralegal gives their customers basic information in a First Amendment protected format such as a book or a software program, and then helps the customers find the specific information they are looking for in those resources?*

SE: Yes. But I also think that very soon paralegals will be able to provide basic legal information directly without running much risk of a UPL prosecution. This is because the more common certain types of legal information become—for instance when information about divorce is available on a divorce kiosk at every courthouse—the more they stop being owned by lawyers and instead fall under the general rubric of "consumer information," which can be freely passed along by anyone.

RW: *So you see information escaping lawyer control in ever-increasing amounts?*

SE: It's a no-brainer since it's already happening. Take bankruptcy: Thirty years ago lawyers owned the information. Now all the basic facts—for example, how many years you have to wait to be able to file a second Chapter 7 bankruptcy, or laws regulating pushy bill collectors, or the definition of a secured loan—have become consumer information available to anyone.

RW: *Would you go so far as to predict that the very concept of UPL is doomed?*

SE: Probably not in the sense that only lawyers can represent others in the courts. But as legal information itself becomes freely available to the public in a variety of ways, lawyers will find it harder to enforce the UPL laws. Certainly UPL is doomed when it comes to providing legal information to people about the substance of the law and how to use the courts.

Debbie Chalfie Interview

Debbie Chalfie is the former Legislative Director of HALT—An Organization of Americans for Legal Reform. She is a leader in the effort to provide the average American better and fairer access to law and has spearheaded HALT's efforts to pass legislation allowing non-lawyers to deliver legal services to the public.

Ralph Warner (RW): *Debbie, can you begin by telling me a little about who you are and what you do.*

Debbie Chalfie (DC): I've been at HALT since 1985. Incidentally, for the uninitiated, HALT is the only national public interest group representing consumers of legal services—the average American who needs access to the legal system.

RW: *Before we get into what you do at HALT, fill me in on your background.*

DC: In college, in the mid-1970s I was actively involved in the women's movement and civil rights issues, mostly on anti-rape and anti-violence concerns. I graduated in 1979 and went on to law school.

RW: *You didn't come out a typical lawyer, or for that matter, even a typical public interest lawyer. Most lawyers, no matter what side of an issue they are on, look and sound, even smell like lawyers; you don't.*

DC: Thanks. I'm sure a little lawyer must have rubbed off, but I was protected to some extent by the fact that I didn't go to law school with the intention of becoming a practicing lawyer. I wanted to learn what lawyers knew, not to be one. I wanted the information and skills lawyers had to help me work on issues I believed in.

RW: *I have heard thousands of law students say much the same thing when they entered law school, but by the time they left, they looked exactly like lawyer clones.*

DC: Maybe the difference is that many of those people really wanted to be lawyers—lawyers for good causes, perhaps, but lawyers just the same. I really didn't want to be a lawyer, so I was never on the same track.

RW: *How did you end up working with HALT?*

DC: HALT was my second job out of law school. After graduating, my first job was at a public interest law firm, where I worked on civil rights and consumer protection issues. It was there that I began to see accountability of lawyers to clients as a key problem within our legal system.

RW: *Slow that down for me.*

DC: This public interest law firm was also a teaching clinic for law students. Each week, we conducted a seminar for the students on the practicalities of public interest law. One of those seminars was about the dilemma public interest lawyers face when their clients' needs and desires conflict with their own agenda and goals. I respected the dedication and work of public interest lawyers, but I was disturbed that very few of them wanted to face the fact that it was the lawyers, not the clients, who were calling the shots.

RW: *This connects pretty directly to issues HALT worries about, doesn't it—the American legal system primarily serves lawyers' interests, and the concerns of the average American have been forgotten?*

DC: Absolutely. Consumers of legal services have almost no rights. It's really the last frontier of consumer advocacy. Led by lawyers, consumers have won reforms in loads of areas, such as product safety, fair credit, the environment, even health care and the quality and availability of services provided by doctors. But lawyers have a huge blind spot when it comes to consumer rights—themselves. Even most public interest lawyers don't see that the American legal system is run in large measure to benefit the legal elite, not the public.

RW: *Let's get down to the bare bones; do you mean that ordinary citizens are denied reasonable access to the laws and legal procedures that affect their lives?*

DC: Sure. And that's why the work HALT does is so necessary. The legal system is structured in such a way that most people can't vindicate their rights. The legal system is expensive, slow, unduly antagonistic and often inequitable. This means most people are shut out and ill served. HALT seeks to make the legal system more affordable and accessible, and the legal profession more responsive and accountable, to the public. We educate the public about their options and we also lobby for legal reform.

RW: *Today you are in California, trying to get the California legislature to adopt HALT-sponsored legislation designed to cut back the lawyers' monopoly on providing legal services. Under the HALT bill, legal technicians (independent paralegals) could legally deliver services to the public.*

DC: Yes. Unauthorized practice of law statutes (UPL laws) are used by lawyers to kill competition. Doing away with them, or at last sharply curtailing them, is at the heart of HALT's agenda to provide consumers better legal access.

RW: *Can you explain why in a bit more detail?*

DC: UPL laws, which ensure lawyers a monopoly over the delivery of legal services, have the direct effect of keeping prices for legal services beyond the reach of millions. By being able to jail their competitors, lawyers are free to charge more. Since there is no place else to get legal information or help with filing legal paperwork, you either pay a lawyer or go without.

RW: *Without UPL laws, all sorts of people would be able to sell legal information and form-preparation assistance and advice, and consumers would be free to decide who to buy it from and how much to pay.*

DC: Exactly. They could choose to purchase services from a lawyer and pay a relatively high price or shop around for other providers. It's what we already do in hundreds of areas of our lives. For example, when we need to fix our car, we can go to a dealer, an independent garage that specializes in our particular make of car, or a corner gas station. It's up to us as consumers to make the choice—and for the most part, we make it well.

RW: *Bar associations, judges and other lawyer interest groups say that non-lawyers aren't competent to render legal services.*

DC: They may say that, but the facts don't back them up. Lawyers claim that only they, because of their training, are competent to perform divorces, bankruptcies, name changes and other routine legal tasks. Yet lawyers are not trained in law school or tested on bar examinations to deliver these basic consumer services. Also, all the studies show that consumers who've used paralegals have few complaints, while nearly 100,000 complaints are filed against lawyers every year. In short, the lawyers' monopoly is no guarantee of competence or consumer protection, and there is no intellectual basis to justify restricting competition by non-lawyers. But even if lawyers cleaned up their acts and delivered a better quality service to consumers, it would make no difference—what good is a monopoly, even a high quality one, which sets prices so high the vast majority of people can't afford their services? It's a question of balance. Sure, consumers want competent service, but they also want affordable access. A better setup would address both interests.

RW: *What specifically is HALT doing to cut back or eliminate UPL laws?*

DC: Ever since its founding in the late 1970s, HALT has been a strong proponent of busting the lawyer monopoly. For example, in the early 1980s, we supported Rosemary Furman, the Florida legal secretary who typed low-cost divorces and provided other legal paperwork services for very low fees, and, as a result, was hounded by the Florida bar. We organized the public awareness and letter-writing campaign that kept her from going to jail. We have also won legislation to allow court clerks to give consumers over-the-counter legal information and form-processing help.

RW: *Great, but what about legislation that will really change things?*

DC: In California, HALT is spearheading a bill to allow nonlawyer legal technicians (or Independent Paralegals—call them by whatever name you like) to provide legal services directly to the public without lawyer supervision.

RW: *In all areas?*

DC: For starters, in at least 16 areas of law—divorce, bankruptcy, real estate transactions, immigration, small business incorporation, probate, wills, consumer complaints and other everyday legal matters.

RW: *You mean the HALT bill would suspend UPL in these areas to let non-lawyers freely compete?*

DC: Yes, but they would have to meet some sensible requirements. For example, a legal tech would have to register with a state agency, be at least 18, have no prior convictions for consumer fraud and could not be a disbarred lawyer. In addition, for services where a consumer could be irreparably harmed if the services were not done right, paralegals would have to pass a practice-related test.

RW: *You mean these nonlawyers would have to take a mini-bar examination?*

DC: No, the exam they would take would be directly related to the particular task to be performed. Unlike the bar exam, it wouldn't test theoretical knowledge, but whether a provider knew the rules and procedures to competently do the work.

RW: *So someone working in the immigration area would not be tested about probate, right? But what exactly would they be tested on?*

DC: The details of each test would be up to a board under the jurisdiction of the Department of Consumer Affairs. But the point would be to test on one's actual competence to do the work. For example, in the immigration field, a candidate might be asked, "If a person with permanent resident status wanted to bring a family member to the U.S., what procedures are available and how should the necessary applications be completed?"

RW: *Once a person registered or passed this exam, they could open a street corner office on the order of an H & R Block tax preparation office?*

DC: Yes. And remember, the test would only be required in relatively complex areas, or where consumers need an up-front assurance of competence. If a legal tech wanted to do a basic uncontested divorce or probate, he or she would need to register with the state, but not pass an exam. And typing services wouldn't have to do anything, as long as they limit their services to just typing.

RW: *Don't nonlawyer legal services like you describe already exist in most California cities?*

DC: Yes, so in some ways the HALT-sponsored bill legislates the status quo.

RW: *If that's true, why do we need it?*

DC: Today, nonlawyer providers exist under a cloud of possible illegality. They're always open to selective prosecution, which usually happens when they get a complaint from a lawyer stung by the competition. The

HALT bill would remove this daily threat, allowing the existing ones to flourish and encourage many more people to enter the field. When this happens, consumers will have much better access to affordable legal help.

RW: *How would doing away with UPL change the way typing services work?*

DC: Today, many typing service operators are afraid to answer even the simplest legal question for fear of being charged with UPL. They have to refer all customers to other information sources, which can be cumbersome. In the 16 areas covered by our bill, this would no longer be necessary.

RW: *You mean the so-called model I talk about in this book of always referring a customer who asks for legal information to a protected source of legal information, such as books, videos or lawyers, could be bypassed?*

DC: Right, but remember the HALT bill wouldn't restrict or regulate self-help typing services in any way. No one would have to take an exam or register to be a public stenographer. The HALT bill would legalize everyone, but it would only regulate those who wanted to do more than type.

RW: *What about the rest of the country? So far, your bill has only been introduced in California?*

DC: It's also been introduced in Oregon, and we are in touch with legislators in other states who are interested in introducing it. We are excited about that, and expect that by the time these words are published, it will be introduced in at least two more states.

Index

Note: This index does not include the Appendix Interviews.

CATALOG

... more books & software from Nolo

Living Trust Maker
Version 2.0

Put your assets into a trust and save your heirs the headache, time and expense of probate with this easy-to-use software. Use it to set up an individual or shared marital trust, transfer property to the trust, and change or revoke the trust at any time. Its manual guides you through the process, and legal help screens and an on-line glossary explain key legal terms and concepts. Good in all states except Louisiana.

WINDOWS $79.95/LTWI2
MACINTOSH $79.95/LTM1

Nolo's Personal RecordKeeper
Version 3.0

Finally, a safe, accessible place for your important records. Over 200 categories and subcategories to organize and store your important financial, legal and personal information, compute your net worth and create inventories for insurance records. Export your net worth and home inventory data to Quicken®.

DOS $49.95/FRI3
MACINTOSH $49.95/FRM3

BUSINESS/WORKPLACE

The Legal Guide for Starting & Running a Small Business
Attorney Fred S. Steingold. Nat'l 1st ed.

An essential resource for every small business owner. Find out how to form a sole proprietorship, partnership or corporation, negotiate a favorable lease, hire and fire employees, write contracts and resolve disputes.

$22.95/RUNS

How to Write a Business Plan
Mike McKeever. Nat'l 4th ed.

Shows you how to write the business plan and loan package necessary to finance your business and make it work.

$21.95/SBS

Sexual Harassment on the Job: What it is and How To Stop it
Attorneys William Petrocelli & Barbara Kate Repa. Nat'l 2nd ed.

An invaluable resource for both employees experiencing harassment and employers interested in creating a policy against sexual harassment and a procedure for handling complaints.

$18.95/HARS

Marketing Without Advertising
Michael Phillips & Salli Rasberry. Nat'l 1st ed.

Practical steps for building and expanding a small business without spending a lot of money on advertising.

$14.00/MWAD

Your Rights in the Workplace
Attorney Barbara Kate Repa. Nat'l 2nd ed.

Comprehensive guide to workplace rights—from hiring to firing. Covers wages and overtime, parental leave, unemployment and disability insurance, worker's comp, job safety, discrimination and illegal firings and layoffs.

$15.95/YRW

The Partnership Book
Attorneys Denis Clifford & Ralph Warner. Nat'l 4th ed.

Shows you step-by-step how to write a solid partnership agreement that meets your needs. It covers initial contributions to the business, wages, profit-sharing, buy-outs, death or retirement of a partner and disputes.

$24.95/PART

The California Nonprofit Corporation Handbook
Attorney Anthony Mancuso. CA 6th ed.

Shows you step-by-step how to form and operate a nonprofit corporation in California. It includes the latest corporate and tax law changes, and the forms for the Articles, Bylaws and Minutes.

$29.95/NON

How to Form Your Own California Corporation
Attorney Anthony Mancuso. CA 8th ed.

This book contain the forms, instructions and tax information you need to incorporate a small business yourself and save hundreds of dollars in lawyers' fees.

$29.95/CCOR

The California Professional Corporation Handbook
Attorney Anthony Mancuso. CA 5th ed.

Health care professionals, lawyers, accountants and members of certain other professions must fulfill special requirements when forming a corporation in California. Contains up-to-date tax information plus all forms and instructions necessary.

$34.95/PROF

The Independent Paralegal's Handbook
Attorney Ralph Warner. Nat'l 3rd ed.

Provides legal and business guidelines for anyone who wants to go into business as an independent paralegal helping consumers with routine legal tasks.

$29.95 PARA

 books with disk

How to Form a Nonprofit Corporation
Attorney Anthony Mancuso. Nat'l 2nd ed.

Explains the legal formalities involved and provides detailed information on the differences in the law among all 50 states. It also contains forms for the Articles, Bylaws and Minutes you need, along with complete instructions for obtaining federal 501(c)(3) tax exemptions and qualifying for public charity status. Includes incorporation forms on disk.

DOS $39.95/NNP

How to Form Your Own California Corporation With Corporate Records Binder & Disk

Attorney Anthony Mancuso. CA 1st ed.

How to Form Your Own California Corporation is also available in a handy new format. It includes all the forms and instructions you need to form your own corporation, a corporate records binder, stock certificates and all incorporation forms on disk.

DOS $39.95/CACI

Taking Care of Your Corporation, Vol. 1: Director and Shareholder Meetings Made Easy

Attorney Anthony Mancuso. Nat'l 1st ed.

This book takes the drudgery out of the necessary task of holding meetings of the board of directors and shareholders. It shows how to comply with state laws for holding meetings, how to prepare minutes for annual and special meetings, take corporate action by written consent, hold real or paper meetings and handle corporate formalities using e-mail, computer bulletin boards, fax and telephone and video conferencing. Includes all corporate forms on disk.

DOS $26.95/CORK

Software Development
A Legal Guide

Attorney Stephen Fishman. Nat'l 1st ed.

Explains patent, copyright, trademark and trade secret protection and shows how to draft development contracts and employment agreements. Includes all contracts and agreements on disk.

DOS $44.95/SFT

The California Nonprofit Corporation Handbook

Attorney Anthony Mancuso. CA 2nd ed.

This book with disk package shows you step-by-step how to form and operate a nonprofit corporation in California. Included on disk are the forms for the Articles, Bylaws and Minutes.

DOS & MACINTOSH $39.95/NPI

software

California Incorporator

Version 1.0 (good only in CA)

Answer the questions on the screen and this software program will print out the 35-40 pages of documents you need to make your California corporation legal. A 200-page manual explains the incorporation process.

DOS $129.00/INCI

Nolo's Partnership Maker

Version 1.0

Prepares a legal partnership agreement for doing business in any state. Select and assemble the standard partnership clauses provided or create your own customized agreement. Includes on-line legal help screens, glossary and tutorial, and a manual that takes you through the process step-by-step.

DOS $129.95/PAGI1

audio cassette tapes

How to Start Your Own Business:
Small Business Law

Attorney Ralph Warner with Joanne Greene. Nat'l 1st ed. 60 minutes

This tape covers what every small business owner needs to know about organizing as a sole proprietorship, partnership or corporation, protecting the business name, renting space, hiring employees and paying taxes.

$14.95/TBUS

Getting Started as an Independent Paralegal

Attorney Ralph Warner. Nat'l 2nd ed. Two tapes, approx. 2 hrs.

Practical and legal advice on going into business as an independent paralegal from the author of *The Independent Paralegal's Handbook*.

$44.95/GSIP

GOING TO COURT

Represent Yourself in Court

Attorneys Paul Bergman & Sara Berman-Barrett. Nat'l 1st ed.

Handle your own civil court case from start to finish without a lawyer with the most thorough guide to contested court cases ever published for the non-lawyer. Covers all aspects of civil trials.

$29.95/RYC

Everybody's Guide to Small Claims Court

Attorney Ralph Warner. Nat'l 5th ed. CA 11th ed.

These books will help you decide if you should sue in Small Claims Court, show you how to file and serve papers, tell you what to bring to court and how to collect a judgment.

National $18.95/NSCC
California $18.95/CSCC

Everybody's Guide to Municipal Court

Judge Roderic Duncan. CA 1st ed.

Sue and defend cases for up to $25,000 in California Municipal Court. Gives step-by-step instructions for preparing and filing forms, gathering evidence and appearing in court.

$29.95/MUNI

Fight Your Ticket

Attorney David Brown. CA 5th ed.

Shows you how to fight an unfair traffic ticket—when you're stopped, at arraignment, at trial and on appeal.

$18.95/FYT

Collect Your Court Judgment

Gini Graham Scott, Attorney Stephen Elias & Lisa Goldoftas. CA 2nd ed.

Contains step-by-step instructions and all the forms you need to collect a court judgment from the debtor's bank accounts, wages, business receipts, real estate or other assets.

$19.95/JUDG

How to Change Your Name
Attorneys David Loeb & David Brown. CA 6th ed.
All the forms and instructions you need to change your name in California.
$24.95/NAME

The Criminal Records Book
Attorney Warren Siegel. CA 3rd ed.
Shows you step-by-step how to seal criminal records, dismiss convictions, destroy marijuana records and reduce felony convictions.
$19.95/CRIM

audio cassette tapes

Winning in Small Claims Court
Attorney Ralph Warner with Joanne Greene. Nat'l 1st ed. 60 minutes
Guides you through all the major issues involved in preparing and winning a small claims court case—deciding if there is a good case, assessing whether you can collect if you win, preparing your evidence, and arguing before the judge.
$14.95/TWIN

THE NEIGHBORHOOD

Neighbor Law:
Fences, Trees, Boundaries & Noise
Attorney Cora Jordan. Nat'l 2nd ed.
Answers common questions about the subjects that most often trigger disputes between neighbors. It explains how to find the law and resolve disputes without a nasty lawsuit.
$16.95/NEI

Dog Law
Attorney Mary Randolph. Nat'l 2nd ed.
A practical guide to the laws that affect dog owners and their neighbors. Answers common questions about biting, barking, veterinarians and more.
$12.95/DOG

Safe Homes, Safe Neighborhoods:
Stopping Crime Where You Live
Stephanie Mann with M.C. Blakeman. Nat'l 1st ed.
Learn how you and your neighbors can work together to protect yourselves, your families and property from crime. Explains how to form a neighborhood crime prevention group; avoid burglaries, car thefts, muggings and rapes; combat gangs and drug dealing; improve home security and make the neighborhood safer for children.
$14.95/SAFE

FAMILY MATTERS

Nolo's Pocket Guide to Family Law
Attorneys Robin Leonard & Stephen Elias. Nat'l 3rd ed.
Help for anyone who has a question or problem involving family law—marriage, divorce, adoption or living together.
$14.95/FLD

Divorce & Money
Violet Woodhouse & Victoria Felton-Collins with M.C. Blakeman. Nat'l 2nd ed.
Explains how to evaluate such major assets as family homes and businesses, investments, pensions, and how to arrive at a fair division of property.
$21.95/DIMO

Smart Ways to Save Money During and After Divorce
Victoria F. Collins & Ginita Wall. Nat'l 1st ed.
If you're going through a divorce, most likely you're faced with an overwhelming number of financial decisions. Here's a book packed with information on how to save money before, during and after divorce. It covers how to keep attorney's fees low, save on taxes, divide assets fairly, understand child support and alimony obligations and put aside money now for expenses later.
$14.95/SAVMO

The Living Together Kit
Attorneys Toni Ihara & Ralph Warner. Nat'l 7th ed.
A detailed guide designed to help the increasing number of unmarried couples living together understand the laws that affect them. Sample agreements and instructions are included.
$24.95/LTK

A Legal Guide for Lesbian and Gay Couples
Attorneys Hayden Curry, Denis Clifford & Robin Leonard. Nat'l 8th ed.
This book shows lesbian and gay couples how to write a living-together contract, plan for medical emergencies, understand the practical and legal aspects of having and raising children and plan their estates. Includes forms and sample agreements.
$24.95/LG

Divorce:
A New Yorker's Guide to Doing it Yourself
Bliss Alexandra. New York 1st ed.
Step-by-step instructions and all the forms you need to do your own divorce and save thousands of dollars in legal fees. Shows you how to divide property, arrange custody of the children, set child support and maintenance (alimony), draft a divorce agreement and fill out and file all forms.
$24.95/NYDIV

How to Raise or Lower Child Support in California
Judge Roderic Duncan & Attorney Warren Siegel. CA 2nd ed.
Appropriate for parents on either side of the support issue. All the forms and instructions necessary to raise or lower an existing child support order.
$17.95/CHLD

The Guardianship Book
Lisa Goldoftas & Attorney David Brown. CA 1st ed.
Step-by-step instructions and the forms needed to obtain a legal guardianship of a minor without a lawyer.
$19.95/GB

How to Adopt Your Stepchild in California

Frank Zagone & Attorney Mary Randolph. CA 4th ed.

Forms and step-by-step instructions for completing a simple uncontested step-parent adoption in California.
$22.95/ADOP

How to Do Your Own Divorce

Attorney Charles Sherman (Texas ed. by Sherman & Simons). CA 19th ed. & Texas 5th ed.

These books contain all the forms and instructions you need to do your own uncontested divorce without a lawyer.
California $21.95/CDIV
Texas $17.95/TDIV

California Marriage & Divorce Law

Attorneys Ralph Warner, Toni Ihara & Stephen Elias. CA 11th ed.

Explains community property, pre-nuptial contracts, foreign marriages, buying a house, getting a divorce, dividing property, and more. Pre-nuptial contracts included.
$19.95/MARR

Practical Divorce Solutions

Attorney Charles Sherman. Nat'l 1st ed.

Covers the emotional aspects of divorce and provides an overview of the legal and financial considerations.
$14.95/PDS

MONEY MATTERS

Money Troubles:
Legal Strategies to Cope With Your Debts

Attorney Robin Leonard. Nat'l 2nd ed.

Essential for anyone who has gotten behind on bills. It shows how to obtain a credit file, negotiate with persistent creditors, challenge wage attachments, contend with property repossessions and more.
$16.95/MT

Stand Up to the IRS

Attorney Fred Daily. Nat'l 2nd ed.

Gives detailed strategies on surviving an audit, appealing an audit decision, going to Tax Court and dealing with IRS collectors. It also discusses filing delinquent tax returns, tax crimes, concerns of small business people and getting help from the IRS ombudsman.
$21.95/SIRS

How to File for Bankruptcy

Attorneys Stephen Elias, Albin Renauer & Robin Leonard. Nat'l 4th ed.

Trying to decide whether or not filing for bankruptcy makes sense? This book contains an overview of the process and all the forms plus step-by-step instructions you need to file for Chapter 7 Bankruptcy.
$25.95/HFB

Simple Contracts for Personal Use

Attorney Stephen Elias & Marcia Stewart. Nat'l 2nd ed.

Contains clearly written legal form contracts to buy and sell property, borrow and lend money, store and lend personal property, release others from personal liability, or pay a contractor to do home repairs. Includes agreements to arrange child care and other household help.
$16.95/CONT

---

law form kits

Nolo's Law Forms Kit:
Rebuild Your Credit

Attorney Robin Leonard. Nat'l 1st ed.

Provides strategies for dealing with debts and rebuilding your credit. Shows you how to negotiate with creditors and collection agencies, clean up your credit file, devise a spending plan and get credit in your name.
$14.95/KCRD

Nolo's Law Form Kit:
Personal Bankruptcy

Attorneys Steve Elias, Albin Renauer & Robin Leonard and Lisa Goldoftas. Nat'l 1st ed.

All the forms and instructions you need to file for Chapter 7 bankruptcy.
$14.95/KBNK

Nolo's Law Form Kit:
Power of Attorney

Attorneys Denis Clifford & Mary Randolph and Lisa Goldoftas. Nat'l 1st ed.

Create a conventional power of attorney to assign someone you trust to take care of your finances, business, real estate or children when you are away or unavailable. Provides all the forms with step-by-step instructions.
$14.95/KPA

Nolo's Law Form Kit:
Loan Agreements

Attorney Stephen Elias, Marcia Stewart & Lisa Goldoftas. Nat'l 1st ed.

Provides all the forms and instructions necessary to create a legal and effective promissory note. Shows how to decide on an interest rate, set a payment schedule and keep track of payments.
$14.95/KLOAN

Nolo's Law Form Kit:
Buy and Sell Contracts

Attorney Stephen Elias, Marcia Stewart & Lisa Goldoftas. Nat'l 1st ed.

Step-by-step instructions and all the forms necessary for creating bills of sale for cars, boats, computers, electronic equipment, household appliances and other personal property.
$9.95/KCONT

PATENT, COPYRIGHT &TRADEMARK

Patent It Yourself

Attorney David Pressman. Nat'l 3rd ed.

From the patent search to the actual application, this book covers everything including the use and licensing of patents, successful marketing and how to deal with infringement.
$39.95/PAT

TO ORDER CALL 1-800-992-6656

Trademark: How to Name Your Business & Product

Attorneys Kate McGrath & Stephen Elias, with Trademark Attorney Sarah Shena. Nat'l 1st ed.

Learn how to choose a name or logo that others can't copy, conduct a trademark search, register a trademark with the U.S. Patent and Trademark Office and protect and maintain the trademark.

$29.95/TRD

The Inventor's Notebook

Fred Grissom & Attorney David Pressman. Nat'l 1st ed.

Helps you document the process of successful independent inventing by providing forms, instructions, references to relevant areas of patent law, a bibliography of legal and non-legal aids and more.

$19.95/INOT

The Copyright Handbook

Attorney Stephen Fishman. Nat'l 2nd ed.

Provides forms and step-by-step instructions for protecting all types of written expression under U.S. and international copyright law. Covers copyright infringement, fair use, works for hire and transfers of copyright ownership.

$24.95/COHA

software

Patent It Yourself Software

Version 1.0

Patent It Yourself is also available in software. With separate tracks for novice and expert users, it takes you through the process step-by-step. It shows how to evaluate patentability of your invention, how to prepare and file your patent application and how to generate all the forms you need to protect and exploit your invention.

Windows $229.95/PYW1

LANDLORDS & TENANTS

The Landlord's Law Book, Vol. 1:
Rights & Responsibilities

Attorneys David Brown & Ralph Warner. CA 4th ed.

Essential for every California landlord. Covers deposits, leases and rental agreements, inspections (tenants' privacy rights), habitability (rent withholding), ending a tenancy, liability and rent control. Forms included.

$32.95/LBRT

The Landlord's Law Book, Vol. 2:
Evictions

Attorney David Brown. CA 4th ed.

Shows step-by-step how to go to court and evict a tenant. Contains all the tear-out forms and necessary instructions.

$32.95/LBEV

Nolo's Law Form Kit:
Leases & Rental Agreements

Attorney Ralph Warner & Marcia Stewart. CA 1st ed.

With these easy-to-use forms and instructions, California landlords can prepare their own rental application, fixed term lease, month-to-month agreement and notice to pay rent or quit.

$14.95/KLEAS

Tenants' Rights

Attorneys Myron Moskovitz & Ralph Warner. CA 12th ed.

This practical guide to dealing with your landlord explains your rights under federal law, California law and rent control ordinances. Forms included.

$18.95/CTEN

HOMEOWNERS

How to Buy a House in California

Attorney Ralph Warner, Ira Serkes & George Devine. CA 3rd ed.

Effective strategies for finding a house, working with an agent, making an offer and negotiating intelligently. Includes information on all types of mortgages as well as private financing options.

$24.95/BHCA

For Sale By Owner

George Devine. CA 2nd ed.

Everything you need to know to sell your own house, from pricing and marketing, to writing a contract and going through escrow. Disclosure and contract forms included.

$24.95/FSBO

Homestead Your House

Attorneys Ralph Warner, Charles Sherman & Toni Ihara. CA 8th ed.

Shows you how to file a Declaration of Homestead and includes complete instructions and tear-out forms.

$9.95/HOME

The Deeds Book

Attorney Mary Randolph. CA 2rd ed.

Shows you how to fill out and file the right kind of deed when transferring property. Outlines the legal requirements of real property transfer.

$16.95/DEED

JUST FOR FUN

Devil's Advocates:
The Unnatural History of Lawyers

by Andrew & Jonathan Roth. Nat'l 1st ed.

A hilarious look at the history of the legal profession.

$12.95/DA

29 Reasons Not to Go to Law School

Attorneys Ralph Warner & Toni Ihara. Nat'l 4th ed.

Filled with humor, this book can save you three years, $150,000 and your sanity.

$9.95/29R

Poetic Justice: The Funniest, Meanest Things Ever Said About Lawyers

Edited by Jonathan & Andrew Roth. Nat'l 1st ed.

A great gift for anyone in the legal profession who has managed to maintain a sense of humor.

$9.95/PJ

Nolo's Favorite Lawyer Jokes on Disk

Over 200 jokes and hilariously nasty remarks about lawyers. 100% guaranteed to produce an evening of chuckles and drive every lawyer you know nuts.
IBM PC $9.95/JODI
MACINTOSH $9.95/JODM

OLDER AMERICANS

Beat the Nursing Home Trap:
A Consumer's Guide to Choosing and Financing Long-term Care

Attorney Joseph Matthews. Nat'l 1st ed.
Guides you in choosing and paying for long-term care, alerting you to practical concerns and explaining laws that may affect your decisions.
$18.95/ELD

Social Security, Medicare & Pensions

Attorney Joseph Matthews with Dorothy Matthews Berman. Nat'l 5th ed.
Offers invaluable guidance through the current maze of rights and benefits for those 55 and over, including Medicare, Medicaid and Social Security retirement and disability benefits, and age discrimination protections.
$18.95/SOA

CONSUMER/REFERENCE

Legal Research Made Easy:
A Roadmap Through the Law Library Maze

2-1/2 hr. videotape and 40-page manual.
Nolo Press/Legal Star Communications. Nat'l 1st ed.
Professor Bob Berring explains how to use all the basic legal research tools in your local law library with an easy-to-follow six-step research plan and a sense of humor.
$89.95/LRME

Legal Research:
How to Find and Understand the Law

Attorneys Stephen Elias & Susan Levinkind. Nat'l 3rd ed.
A valuable tool on its own or as a companion to just about every other Nolo book. Gives easy-to-use, step-by-step instructions on how to find legal information.
$19.95/LRES

Nolo's Pocket Guide to California Law

Attorney Lisa Guerin & Nolo Press Editors. CA 2nd ed.
Get quick clear answers to questions about child support, custody, consumer rights, employee rights, government benefits, divorce, bankruptcy, adoption, wills and much more.
$10.95/CLAW

Nolo's Pocket Guide to California Law on Disk

This handy resource is also availaable on disk. With this new format you can rapidly search through California law by topic and subtopic, or by using the key-word index. The program tracks and saves searches, and allows you to save text to a file for later use.
Windows $24.95/CLWIN
Macintosh $24.95/CLM

Nolo's Pocket Guide to Consumer Rights

Barbara Kaufman. CA 2nd ed.
Practical advice on hundreds of consumer topics. Shows Californians how and where to complain about everything from accountants, misleading advertisements and lost baggage to vacation scams and dishonored warranties.
$12.95/CAG

Nolo's Law Form Kit:
Hiring Child Care & Household Help

Attorney Stephen Elias. Nat'l 1st ed.
All the necessary forms and instructions for fulfilling your legal and tax responsibilities. Includes employment contracts, application forms and required IRS forms.
$14.95/KCHLD

How to Win Your Personal Injury Claim

Attorney Joseph Matthews. Nat'l 1st ed.
Armed with the right information anyone can handle a personal injury claim. This step-by-step guide shows you how to avoid insurance company runarounds, evaluate what your claim is worth, obtain a full and fair settlement and save for yourself what you would pay a lawyer.
$24.95/PICL

Fed Up with the Legal System:
What's Wrong and How to Fix It

Attorneys Ralph Warner & Stephen Elias. Nat'l 2nd ed.
Forty common-sense proposals to make our legal system fairer, faster, cheaper and more accessible.
$9.95/LEG

IMMIGRATION

How to Get a Green Card:
Legal Ways to Stay in the U.S.A.

Attorney Loida Nicolas Lewis with Len T. Madlanscay. Nat'l 1st ed.
By a former INS attorney, this book clearly explains the steps involved in getting a green card. It covers who can qualify, what documents to present, and how to fill out all the forms and have them processed. Tear-out forms included.
$22.95/GRN

Como Obtener La Tajeta Verde:
Maneras Legitimas de Permanacer en los EE.UU.

Attorney Loida Nicolas Lewis with Len T. Madlanscay. Nat'l 1st ed.
The Spanish edition of How to Get a Green Card.

ORDER FORM

Code	Quantity	Title	Unit Price	Total

Subtotal	
California residents add Sales Tax	
Shipping & Handling ($4 for 1st item; $1 each additional)	
2nd day UPS (additional $5; $8 in Alaska and Hawaii)	
TOTAL	

Name

Address

(UPS to street address, Priority Mail to P.O. boxes)

**FOR FASTER SERVICE, USE YOUR CREDIT CARD
AND OUR TOLL-FREE NUMBERS**

Monday-Friday, 7 a.m. to 6 p.m. Pacific Time

Order Line	1 (800) 992-6656 (in the 510 area code, call 549-4648)
General Information	1 (510) 549-1976
Fax your order	1 (800) 645-0895 (in the 510 area code, call 548-5902)

METHOD OF PAYMENT

☐ Check enclosed   ☐ VISA   ☐ Mastercard   ☐ Discover Card   ☐ American Express

Account #   Expiration Date

Authorizing Signature

Daytime Phone

**MAIL YOUR ORDER WITH A CHECK OR MONEY ORDER
MADE PAYABLE TO:
NOLO PRESS, 950 PARKER ST., BERKELEY, CA 94710**

Get 25% off
your next purchase

Recycle your out-of-date books

It's important to have the most current legal information. Because laws and legal procedures change often, we update our books regularly. To help keep you up-to-date we are extending this special offer. Cut out and mail the title portion of the cover of any old Nolo book with your next order and we'll give you a 25% discount off the retail price of ANY new Nolo book you purchase directly from us. For current prices and editions call us at 1-800-992-6656.

This offer is to individuals only.

VISIT OUR STORE

If you live in the Bay Area, be sure to visit the Nolo Press Bookstore on the corner of 9th & Parker Streets in west Berkeley. You'll find our complete line of books and software—all at a discount. CALL 1-510-704-2248 for hours.

ALLOW 2-3 WEEKS FOR DELIVERY.
PRICES SUBJECT TO CHANGE.

When you register, we'll send you our quarterly newspaper, the *Nolo News*, free for two years. (U.S. addresses only.) Here's what you'll get in every issue:

■ INFORMATIVE ARTICLES

Written by Nolo editors, articles provide practical legal information on issues you encounter in everyday life: family law, wills, debts, consumer rights, and much more.

■ UPDATE SERVICE

The *Nolo News* keeps you informed of legal changes that affect any Nolo book and software program.

■ BOOK AND SOFTWARE REVIEWS

We're always looking for good legal and consumer books and software from other publishers. When we find them, we review them and offer them in our mail order catalog.

■ ANSWERS TO YOUR LEGAL QUESTIONS

Our readers are always challenging us with good questions on a variety of legal issues. So in each issue, "Auntie Nolo" gives sage advice and sound information.

■ COMPLETE NOLO PRESS CATALOG

The *Nolo News* contains an up-to-the-minute catalog of all Nolo books and software, which you can order using our "800" toll-free order line. And you can see at a glance if you're using an out-of-date version of a Nolo product.

■ LAWYER JOKES

Nolo's famous lawyer joke column continually gets the goat of the legal establishment. If we print a joke you send in, you'll get a $20 Nolo gift certificate.

We promise *never* to give your name and address to any other organization.

COMPLETE AND MAIL TODAY

THE INDEPENDENT PARALEGAL'S HANDBOOK   Registration Card

We'd like to know what you think! Please take a moment to fill out and return this postage paid card for a free two year subscription to the *Nolo News*. If you already receive the *Nolo News*, we'll extend your subscription.

Name _____ Ph.(   ) _____

Address _____

City _____ State _____ Zip _____

Where did you hear about this book? _____

For what purpose did you use this book? _____

Did you consult a lawyer?	Yes	No		Not Applicable		
Was it easy for you to use this book?	(very easy) 5	4	3	2	1	(very difficult)
Did you find this book helpful?	(very) 5	4	3	2	1	(not at all)

Comments _____

_____

_____

_____

_____

_____

THANK YOU   PARA 3.0

[Nolo books are]..."written in plain language, free of legal mumbo jumbo, and spiced with witty personal observations."

—ASSOCIATED PRESS

"Well-produced and slickly written, the [Nolo] books are designed to take the mystery out of seemingly involved procedures, carefully avoiding legalese and leading the reader step-by-step through such everyday legal problems as filling out forms, making up contracts, and even how to behave in court."

—SAN FRANCISCO EXAMINER

"...Nolo publications...guide people simply through the how, when, where and why of law."

—WASHINGTON POST

"Increasingly, people who are not lawyers are performing tasks usually regarded as legal work... And consumers, using books like Nolo's, do routine legal work themselves."

—NEW YORK TIMES

"...All of [Nolo's] books are easy-to-understand, are updated regularly, provide pull-out forms...and are often quite moving in their sense of compassion for the struggles of the lay reader."

—SAN FRANCISCO CHRONICLE